The Regency Miss's Survival Guide to Bath

Sarah J. Waldock

ISBN-13 9781688066793

Dedication

To Barb Seebaldt for making it possible to visit Bath
To Anne and Michelle for letting me drag you around Bath
To the ladies of the Georgette Heyer Appreciation Group for your input;
And to Simon my lovely husband for reading out six-point print from Mr. Carey's 'Roads'
To William, who rescued Anne and me from the exigencies of travel at Paddington Station.
To Elizabeth, Heather, Laura, Helen and Gina who said it was worth while to continue with this when I was in a blue funk about it.

Other books by Sarah Waldock

Sarah writes predominantly Regency Romances:

The Brandon Scandals Series

The Hasty Proposal
The Reprobate's Redemption
The Advertised Bride
The Wandering Widow
The Braithwate letters
Heiress in Hiding

The Charity School Series

Elinor's Endowment
Ophelia's Opportunity
Abigail's Adventure
Marianne's Misanthrope
Emma's Education/Grace's Gift
Anne's Achievement
Daisy's Destiny
Libby's Luck

Spinoffs:
The Moorwick Tales
Fantasia on a House Party

Rookwood Series

The Unwilling Viscount
The Enterprising Emigrée

One off Regencies

Vanities and Vexations [Jane Austen sequel]
Cousin Prudence [Jane Austen sequel]
Friends and Fortunes
None so Blind
The Unwilling Viscount
Belles and Bucks [short stories]

The Seven Stepsisters series

Elizabeth
Diana [WIP]
Minerva[WIP]
Flora [WIP]
Catherine [WIP]
Jane [WIP]
Anne [WIP]

The Georgian Gambles series

The Valiant Viscount [formerly The Pugilist Peer]
Ace of Schemes

Other

William Price

William Price and the 'Thrush', naval adventure and Jane Austen tribute

William Price Sails North

100 years of Cat Days: 365 anecdotes

Sarah also writes historical mysteries

Regency period 'Jane, Bow Street Consultant 'series, a Jane Austen tribute

Death of a Fop
Jane and the Bow Street Runner [3 novellas]
Jane and the Opera Dancer
Jane and the Christmas Masquerades [2 novellas]
Jane and the Hidden Hoard
Jane and the Burning Question [short stories]
Jane and the Sins of Society
Jane and the Actresses
Jane and the Careless Corpse

'Felicia and Robin' series set in the Renaissance

Poison for a Poison Tongue
The Mary Rose Mystery
Died True Blue
Frauds, Fools and Fairies
The Bishop of Brangling
The Hazard Chase
Heretics, Hatreds and Histories
The Midsummer Mysteries
The Colour of Murder
Falsehood most Foul
The Monkshithe Mysteries
Toll the Dead Man's bells
Wells, Wool and Wickedness
The Missing Hostage

Children's stories

Tabitha Tabs the Farm kitten

A School for Ordinary Princesses [sequel to Frances Hodgson Burnett's 'A Little Princess.]

The Royal Draxiers series

Bess and the Dragons
Bess and the Queen
Bess and the Succession
Bess and the Paying Scholars
Bess and the Gunpowder Plot [wip]
Bess and the Necromancer [wip]

Non-Fiction

Writing Regency Romances by dice

Fantasy

Falconburg Divided [book 1 of the Falconburg brothers series]
Falconburg Rising [book 2 of the Falconburg brothers series]
Falconburg Ascendant [book 3 of the Falconburg brothers series, WIP]

Scarlet Pimpernel spinoffs

The Redemption of Chauvelin
Chauvelin and the League

Other Baroness Orczy spinoffs

Lady Molly – Married

Sarah Waldock grew up in Suffolk and still resides there, in charge of a husband, and under the ownership of sundry cats. All Sarah's cats are rescue cats and many of them have special needs. They like to help her write and may be found engaging in such helpful pastimes as turning the screen display upside-down, or typing random messages in kittycode into her computer.

Sarah claims to be an artist who writes. Her degree is in art, and she got her best marks writing essays for it. She writes largely historical novels, in order to retain some hold on sanity in an increasingly insane world. There are some writers who claim to write because they have some control over their fictional worlds, but Sarah admits to being thoroughly bullied by her characters who do their own thing and often refuse to comply with her ideas. It makes life more interesting, and she enjoys the surprises they spring on her. Her characters' surprises are usually less messy [and much less noisy] than the surprises her cats spring.

Sarah has tried most of the crafts and avocations which she mentions in her books, on the principle that it is easier to write about what you know. She does not ride horses, since the Good Lord in his mercy saw fit to invent Gottleib Daimler to save her from that experience; and she has not tried blacksmithing. She would like to wave cheerily at anyone in any security services who wonder about middle aged women who read up about gunpowder and poisonous plants.

Sarah would like to note that any typos remaining in the text after several betas, an editor and proofreader have been over it are caused by the well-known phenomenon of *cat-induced editing syndrome* from the help engendered by busy little bottoms on the keyboard.

This is her excuse and you are stuck with it.

And yes, there are two more cat bums on the edge of the picture as well as the 4 on her lap/chest

You may find out more about Sarah at her blog site, at:

http://sarahs-history-place.blogspot.co.uk/

Or on Facebook for advance news of writing

https://www.facebook.com/pages/Sarah-J-Waldock-Author/520919511296291

Contents

Forward and Explanation of Money

This guide has been taken from primary sources as far as possible, utilising extant newspaper reports and period guide books to give as authentic a flavour as possible. I have left in many of the rather individualistic spellings in order to give a close feel of the period.

I have used the measurements of the time, but have converted furlongs into decimal fractions of a mile for the convenience of the reader. A mile is approximately a kilometre and a half. A foot is about 30cm. A yard is a little under a metre.

Money

Until the Great Recoinage of 1816, the monetary system was, frankly, a mess, but I do not intend going too deeply into this for a brief explanation.
The guinea was used for most large transactions in the period and although the guinea stopped being legal tender as a coin in 1817, being replaced by the sovereign, it was still used as a measure in the purchasing of horses even though the coin no longer existed.
1 guinea, [1g] equalled one pound and one shilling, [£1/1/-]. The sovereign was one pound only.
Auctions have been held in guineas until decimalisation in 1972, and a professional, eg a doctor, would also charge in guineas.

12 pennies = 1 shilling
20 shillings = 1 pound.
240 pennies = 1 pound.

£ = pounds, s = shillings d = pence

I have used the convention £X/Y/Zd to signify X pounds, Y shillings and Z pence. The pound sign is a stylised 'L' for 'livre', the 'd' stands for 'denarius', 'shilling' is an Anglo-Saxon word. A dash denotes zero eg £1/-/6d is one pound, no shillings and 6d: 5/- denotes five shillings, no pence. The pound column is left off when only shillings and pence are used, equally 6d is six pence, and the pounds and shillings positions not used.

Othcr Money terms.

Sovereign – a pound. Gold. The obverse showed St George inadequately dressed for horse riding, killing a rather weedy dragon.

Silver coins
The *crown* was 5/- [five shillings]
Half a crown was 2/6d [two shillings and sixpence].
There were not many crowns in circulation as they were unwieldy coins, being 1oz [one ounce] of silver, but like the guinea, the amount was used as a measure. The half-crown was more common.
A *groat* was 4d [four pence] It was a silver coin
A *thruppenny*[three pennies] piece was silver. These were, by the time, only issued as Maundy Money [largesse from the Crown to the disabled] and were less in general circulation. There were a number of designs of the obverse.
A *sixpenny* piece was a silver coin
The *shilling* was silver, one of a number of designs on the obverse showing the arms of the countries of the union arranged in a cross.

Copper Coins
A *farthing*, [from fourthing] was ¼ of a penny. It was a copper coin. They were all old coins as none were minted after the 1770s
A *penny* was copper, and had Britannia on the obverse. Nicknamed cartwheels for the size of them – they were about 2" across and thick. Old pennies, from before 1796, were silver. Some were still in circulation until the Great Recoinage of 1816.
A *ha'penny* was also copper and had Britannia like the penny on the obverse.
There were also many private tokens of copper issued by towns, guilds and some workplaces; there are comments at various of the entertainments in Bath that no tokesns except those of the city of Bath would be taken. In 1817, as part of a monetary overhaul. The great re-coinage of 1816, l, these were no longer legal tender at all. Also, many copper coins were actually forgeries until the Great Recoinage!

There was also paper money, which ran from one pound up. These were issued by individual banks.

Maps of Bath and surrounding area

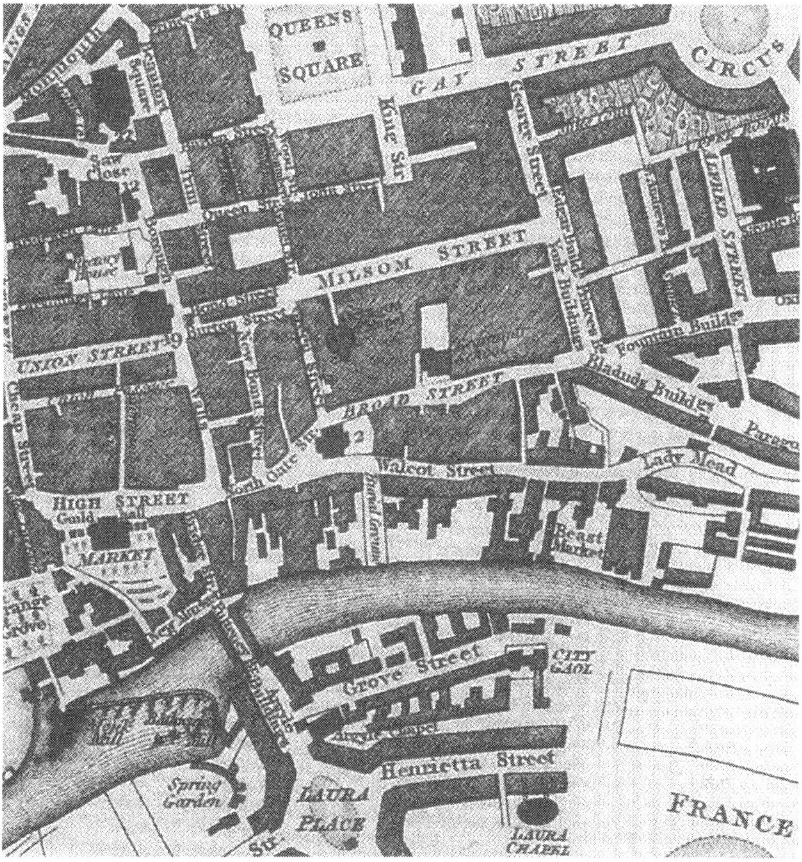

City Centre from 1818 map

It is strongly advised that the maps presented here are used in conjunction with modern maps or Google Maps to compare with a higher resolution than I can give in this little book as regards the street plan – modern Bath has a slightly different layout of the Southern end of Milsom Street for example.

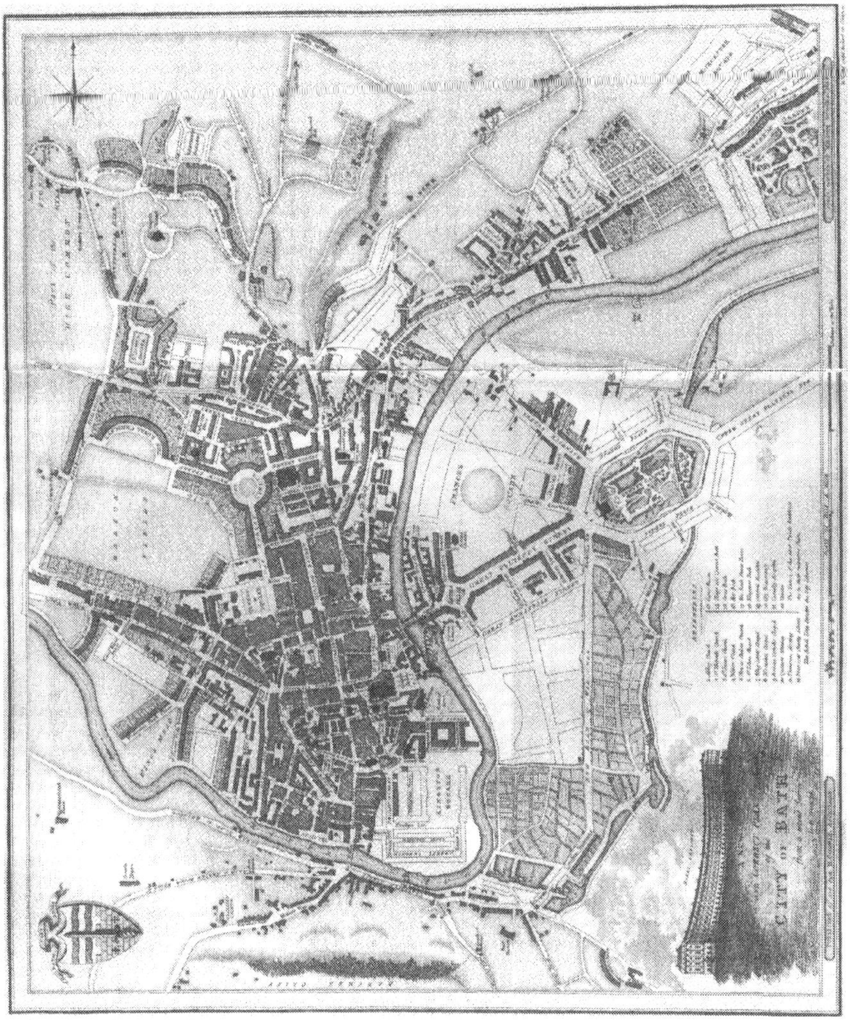

The 1818 map

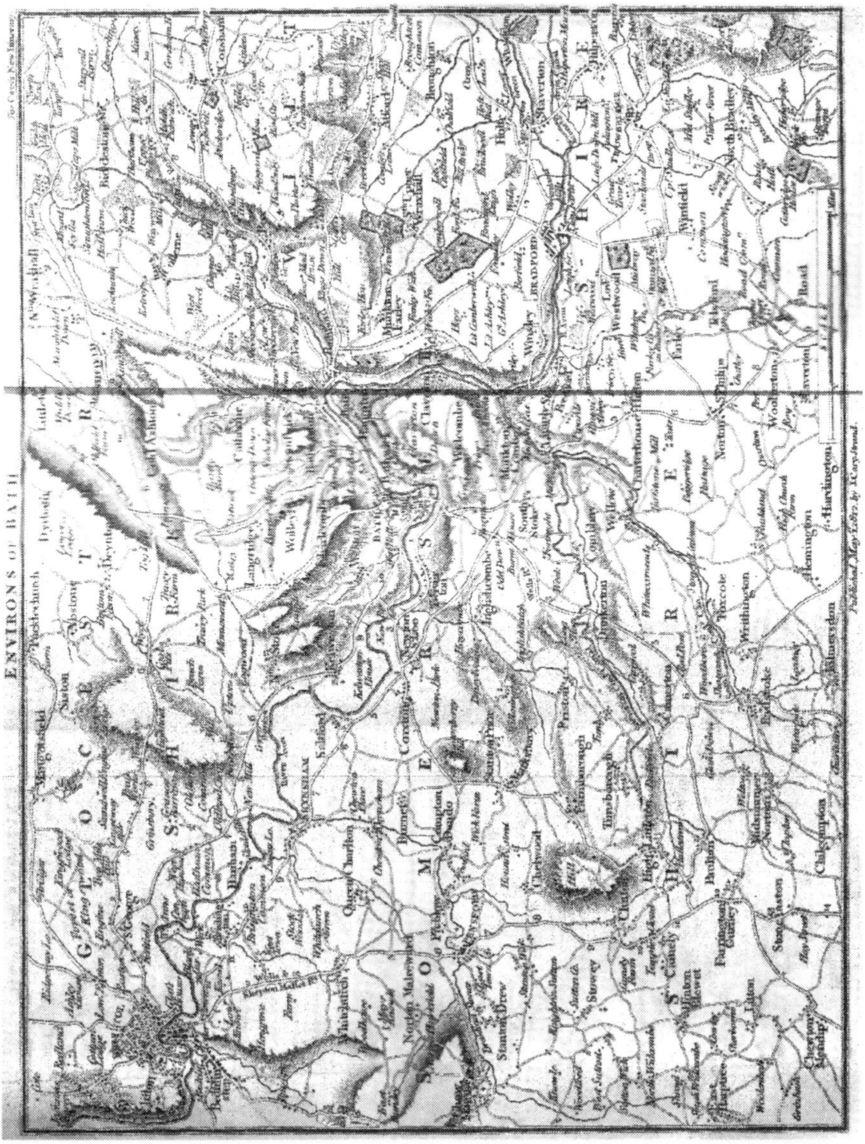

Bath and Environs, from Cary's Itinerary

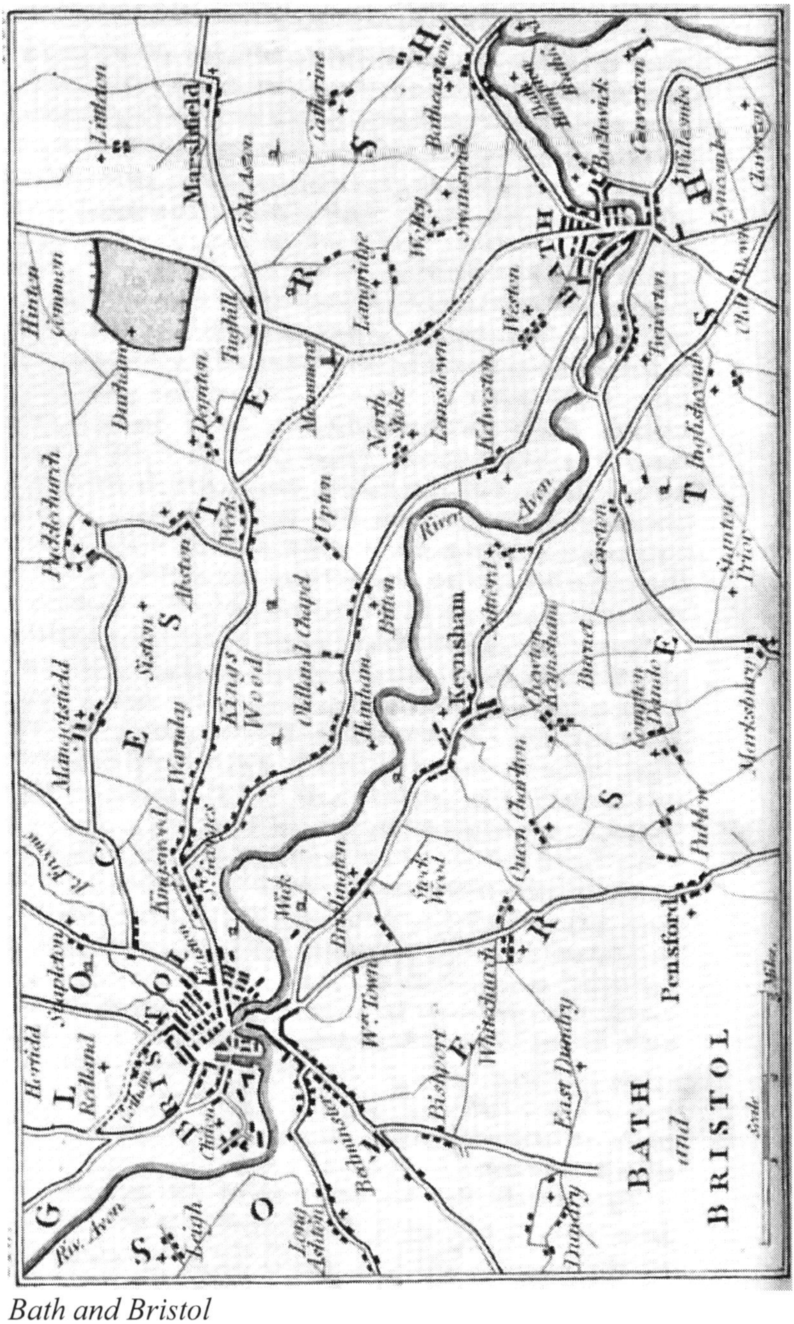

Bath and Bristol

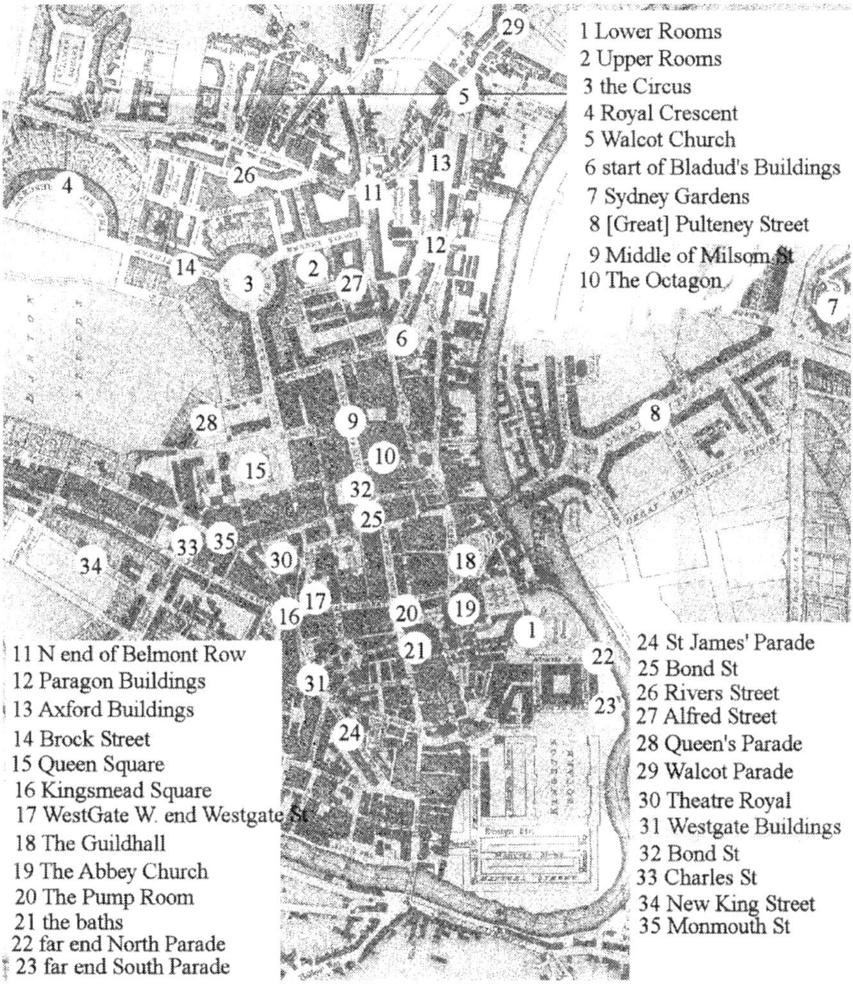

This shows all the locations measured to and from in the section on chair prices and distances, which are also locations which may be considered desirable for a visit.

Maps of Bath and surrounding area

Chapter One: Travelling to Bath

In order to travel to Bath from London, one has several options, depending largely on one's own means and the urgency of the trip.

One might go with one's own carriage, if owned, hiring horses perhaps at each stage, or going slowly to rest one's own. It is not desirable to travel at more than 6mph average if not changing horses, which may be covered by taking one day in four as a total rest day for the nags. One might go on the Mail for a faster journey and lower cost, though it is most unconvivial and not genteel. The speed of a post chaise, or 'yellow bounder' might be attractive, or hiring a chaise and four; or one might use the stage coach. Whichever method one uses, the route on the Bath road is the same as the one travelled by the stage coach, and that is what I have presented.

Bath from London.

There are two routes to Bath from London, one which goes via Chippenham, the other via Devizes. The routes diverge at Beckhampton Inn. The coach routes list the places where they stop to drop or take on passengers.
After 1776 there was a £5 stamp duty on all coaches, so they had to pay their taxes and charge accordingly. In addition, from 1783 a further 1/2d per mile was levied, meaning that packing them full meant the company lost less.
I have no specific prices but using an average cost, 21/- inside or 12/- riding on the roof seem reasonable estimates as the average. Fare to stages in proportion. Perhaps it might cost more to travel in the carriage specialising in taking families and invalids, or for the speed of any coach which can do the journey in but 14 hours!

The mail coach is another alternative. In 1794 it stopped to change horses every 7-10 miles and the trip cost 4d a mile. That would be 412d, or £1/14/4d.
In 1800 it was 2-3d per mile, and the trip to Bath was £1/5/-, or outside on the roof 12/6d, or half price.

To hire a post chaise would cost £1 a mile – which included the hire of the Postillion. This when a large comfortable carriage would cost as much as the hire of a carriage 103 miles to Bath. [but of course, horses, stabling, a groom etc added more; at least £80 each per horse and the cost of around £80 per year per horse for stabling, feed, groom and other essentials]

Remember to tip the head Porter well at every coaching inn. He will make sure you are not fed on left-overs from the previous coach, reheated, and might not charge as much as for candles in your room – up to 5/- extra!

Is it hot and dusty when you travel? You need not fear the dust of the road. The great Beau Nash, whose memory still lives, arranged to have pumps placed at two mile intervals along the road from London to Bath, and employed roadmen to water the road and lay the dust.

Bath via Chippenham [continues to Exeter]

Distance in miles [fractions are eights as given originally in furlongs] from Hyde Park Corner
CITIES and MARKET TOWNS in capitals, city marked C, Borough town B, Post offices/receiving office P; Post Office PO; Market House MH; Toll Gate TG; ***TG*** major tollgates pay up to next major gate. On l = on left, on r = on right. R. = river, arr. = arrive, dep. = depart
The building to which distance is measured noted in brackets
All data is taken from the Post Office survey 1812
Note: the mail mentioned is that carried between the start and end destinations, not all the mail coaches passing through some hubs; arr[ive] signifies 'from London' and dep[arts] signifies 'to London' – not the same mailcoach!
Where place names have changed, I have tried to put both, but if I have not succeeded, then I have stuck with the extant designation.

	Distance in miles	Observations
Kensington, [church]	1.625	
Hammersmith [Windsor Castle inn]	3.5	
Turnham Green [The Old Packhorse inn]	5	
London Stile	6	Old Staging post
The Star and Garter	6.125	On l., road to Kew and Richmond
BRENTFORD MH	7.125	237 houses, 1,443 inhabitants. Mail arr 9.20pm dep 5.45 am. On l., road to Hampton Court
[two bridges]		Cross Grand Junction Canal and R. Brent
Smallbury Green tollgate	8.25	**TG**
HOUNSLOW P [the George inn] First stage out of London, horses changed Handled 300 coaches a day, 2000 horses stabled at the 3 inns, the *George*, the *Red Lion* and the *Rose and Crown*.	9.375	Mail arr 9.40 pm dep 5.30am On l. great trunk road to Landsend 7 other mails passed through Hounslow
Hounslow Heath		Known for its fogs and mud up to 2" deep; haunt of highwaymen.
Cranford Bridge the *White Hart* inn	12.25	On l. 0.5 miles Cranford Park, seat of Earl Berkeley
Sipson Green *Magpies Inn* popular with coaches	13.375	

Longford *King's Head* famous coaching inn *Punchbowl Inn* just after small bridge	15	Crosses old road and new road to Bushey Park. On l. Stanwell and Stanwell Place
[several bridges] these divide Colnebrook between Middlesex and Buckinghamshire		Crossing 2 branches of R. Colne and recross the Colne King John's Hospital
Entering Buckinghamshire		A watersplash which can be bumpy
COLNEBROOK P MH *Old George*, the *Red Lion* and the *Ostrich* 3rd oldest inn in England, current building c 1400. The *Crown* inn.	16.625 Mail from London 2 hours	Mail arr 10.35pm dep 4.45 am. On r. Richings, Richings Park
Langley Broom	18.25	On l. Ditton Park, on r., Lanley Park
Tetsworth Water	19.25	
SLOUGH PO The *Rose and Crown*	20.5	Mail arr 11.50pm dep 4.15am. On l. road to Windsor On l. is Dr. Herschel's reflecting telescope, and on r. 2 miles away seat of Earl of Sefton, Stoke. A fine inn, The Crown
[on road from Slough and at Salt Hill] the Motem Mound where Eton boys in fancy dress waylaid travellers for 'salt' [money] which went to pay the senior boy's way at King's Cambridge.	Motem now Montem	Can see Windsor Castle and Eton College and St Leonard's Hill, Earl Harcourt's seat
Salt Hill	21.25	On l. a red house.

[Maidenhead Bridge] The *Orkney Arms* on Bucks side.	25.25 TG for bridge	Crosses R. Thames. On r. white house, on top of hill big house; on r., ruins of Cleifden
Entering Berkshire		
MAIDENHEAD P Stage change. Inns: The *Bear*, with lifesize bear carving; The *Greyhound* also the *Sun*, the *Red Lion* and the *Crown*	26	Mail arr 11.45 pm dep 3.30 am. MH, 160 houses, 949 inhabitants. On r., road to Great Marlow, on l., Ives House, on r., Hall Place and Bisham Abbey [Geo. Van Sittart esq]
	26.5 TG	Visible the spire of Bray church, whence the notorious vicar of the song, Simon Aleyn
The Folly The *Fleece*	26.75	On r., road to Henley and Oxford
Maidenhead Thicket, a source of highwaymen after the tollgate on both sides of road, 368 acres of scrub and woodland.	28	On l, can see spire of Shottesbrook Church
In the coming region, a brickmaking area, Berkshire clays produce fine bricks of various colours and a local speciality is a vitrified brick called 'Reading Grey' or 'grizzel' from the French 'grisaille', a painting in grey. Produced by throwing salt over the sand coating before firing, giving a fine glassy surface with silver-grey tones over the colour like the bloom on a peach.		
Littlewick Green with the *Seven Stars* inn and Knowl Hill's *The Bird in Hand* are not mentioned in Cary's Itinerary.		
Kiln Green	31	
Hare Hatch The *Horse and Groom*	32	

Entering Wiltshire		
Twyford P The *Bell*, the *Bull* the *Waggon and Horses*	33.75	Almshouses on l; silk mill. Red brick and grizzel buildings.
[bridge]		Cross R. Loddon and admire Sutton's Seed Trial Ground on the way downhill, founded 1806
Re-enter Berkshire		
[turnoff]	37.75	On l., road to Oakingham
[bridge]	38.75	Over R. Kennet, a tributary to the R. Thames
On the road		Said to walk here, two ghosts, Henry VIII in Lincoln Green, and the Abbot of Reading
READING B P Stage change The *Turk's Head* a coaching in from 1567; the *Crown*; the *George* also 16th century. Major coaching inn to east of town. The *Bear*, the *Seven Bridges House* of Simonds brewery est. 1785 [building 1790]; the *Sun Inn*.	38.875	1,783 houses, 7,942 inhabitants. Mail arr 1.25am dep 1.55 am. On r., road to Henley on l., road to Basingstoke. Assizes held here. On l., Early Court, on r., Caversham House. Ruins of the Abbey.
Castle Hill out of town	39. 375 TG	Coley Park on l., of road
	40. 375	on r., Prospect hill
Calcot Green	41.5	On r, Calcott House, home of the Berkshire Lady who fought a duel to win a husband in 1712, Frances Kendrick.

Theal[e] The *Old Angel* Inn, the *Crown*, the *Bull and Lamb*, and the *Falcon*	43.625	
	44.625	On l., road to Wallingford
Puntfield The *Three Kings and Jack's Booth*	45	To r of road is Englefield Ho. Beenham ho. on hill
Aldermaston The *Hare and Hounds* and *Rising Sun*	48	On l., road to Basingstoke. Wharf on the canal.
Woolhampton PO *The Angel Inn* with a curious sign, and *Falmouth arms*	49.125	Paper mill from 1805
	50.125	On r., Woolhampton House, on l.m Waring Place
	52	On r., Midgham House
Thatcham *The King's Head*, some coaches stopped and allowed half an hour to eat. Good food. Also the *White Hart.*	52.75	Perpendicular chapel, 1707; Blue Coat School 1304, rich mouldings about door and windows.
Speenhamland *George and Pelican* excellent food but high cost at the Pelican. The *Bacon Arms* and next door the *Chequers* ? Stage change	55.75	Essentially a suburb of Newbury with inns and posting houses. The theatre is just up from the Bacon Arms.
NEWBURY P The main road passes through the north end, Speenhamland. not through the town proper.	55.75	965 houses, 4,275 inhabitants. Mails arr 3.45am dep 11.35pm On r., road to Oxford.

<table>
<tr><td colspan="3">From Newbury to Bath, the road is remarkable for its hills, necessitating much skidding and unskidding, and renowned for accidents.
Upward slopes had an automatic failsafe called a drag-shaft, hinged onto the rear axle-tree which dug in if the coach rolled backwards. It could be raised to go backwards deliberately. Going downhill, the coachman had to stop to fit a shoe, or skid-pan. This looked like a shovel, chained to the side of the coach. It put a drag on one wheel's motion, slowing the coach considerably. If it was not in the right place, or broke, there could be a nasty accident, with the coach pursuing the horses, who tended to run away to avoid this.</td></tr>
<tr><td>Speen Hill
The Castle Inn opposite the column is the stopping place of the mail.</td><td>56.125</td><td>On r., Donnington Castle House and an 18' column with a metal ball on top, commemorating a cavalier defence</td></tr>
<tr><td>Speen
The hare and hounds
1765</td><td>56.75</td><td></td></tr>
<tr><td>Benham Park</td><td>57.675</td><td></td></tr>
<tr><td>Halfway
Halfway inn</td><td>59.675
TG</td><td>Cross the R. Kennet
Denford Lodge on r.</td></tr>
<tr><td></td><td>64</td><td>Re-Cross the River Kennet famous for trout and crayfish.</td></tr>
<tr><td>HUNGERFORD P
The Black Bear inn.</td><td>64.125
Mailcoach 1 hr Newbury - Hungerford</td><td>393 houses 1,987 inhabitants. Mail arr. 4.40 am, dep 10.40 pm. On r., road to Oxford.</td></tr>
<tr><td>The Downs</td><td>64. 675</td><td>On r., Littlecot Park and Littlecot Hall</td></tr>
<tr><td colspan="3">This region said to be haunted by a baby burned to death by 'Wild' [Wm] Darrell as soon as it was delivered. The Downs are haunted by Darrell and his hounds fleeing the vengeful infant. Having been haunted to death and falling from his horse at the stile.</td></tr>
<tr><td></td><td>66.675</td><td>Ramsbury Manor Ho.</td></tr>
</table>

Cross to Wiltshire		
Froxfield Stage change for some companies	66.875	On r., almshouse for clergyman's widows founded Duchess Somerset, 1694
	Approx 70	Cross R. Kennet
Marlborough Forest [start] AKA Savernake Forest	71.125	On l., Savernake Lodge
Marlborough Forest [end]	72.625 **TG**	
Driving down Forest Hill is hazardous. Often the horses have to be given their own sweet time to make it. There are often gypsy encampments on either side of the hill who will help get coaches to London back up the hill by pushing, or climbing on and 'walking' the spokes; often the coachmen would let them sell wild strawberries and tell fortunes to the passengers. On outskirts of Marlborough a thatched house with 3 straw birds on roof indicating a thatcher. Cross R. Kennet		
MARLBOROUGH B P MH Stage change after Froxfield On l, *Castle Inn*, a very fine inn. Built 1700-20 for Duke of Somerset. Later an inn. Also the *Hart* Inn and *Ailsbury Arms; the Castle and Ball* 16th century timber frame behind colonnaded front. Escaped fires of 1653 which led to banning thatch in the town, but up until 1764 known as the *Antelope*. The *Royal Oak* has bow windows and colonnades and fishscale tiling. Pepys liked it.	74.125	464 houses, 1,367 inhabitants. Mail arr 6am dep 9.30pm On l., road to Swindon, on r., road to Andover. . Original castle was 11th century, known locally as The Mound. Marlborough was built new after a fire in 1653. White horse on hill cut in 1804 by boys of Mr. Greazley's Academy. Small and large Mop Fairs or hiring fairs held on the Saturdays each side of Michaelmas.
Manton	75.5	

Fifield [Fyfield]	76.75	Grey Wethers sarsen stones n. of road and s. at Lockeridge Dene
Overton	77.875	On l. Lockridge House. Roman road leaves Bath road and runs over down to W. Kennet. Half way up Overton Hill, the Ridgeway crosses the Bath road at right angles.
West Kennet *White Hart* *Red Lion* inn inside the Avebury circle; 1619. Old well 80' deep.	79.25	Local building material is cob, chalk, water and straw moulded. The stone avenue leads to Avebury.
Pan Bridge		Cross the R Kennet
Silbury Hill	80.125	On r., remarkable barrow. At some distance is Avebury noted for its stupendous remains of a druid's temple [sic]
Beckhampton Inn P Stage change for all	80.75	On r., road to Highworth, on l., road to Devizes

At this point the road to Bath diverges and can be reached by going through Devizes. The Bristol Mail took the slightly faster and easier route through Calne and Chippenham while the Bath Mail turned south through Devizes and Melksham. At the point of divergence is found on the right the ***Waggon and Horses****.*

Continuing via Chippenham

Cross the downs to Cherril [Cherhill] The *Black Horse*. Haunt of highwaymen.	83.875	On l., at Cherril, a white horse cut out upon the hill, a remarkable landmark. It is visible for 30 miles, and the eye is filled with bottles set bottom up to sparkle. Oldbury Mound.
Quemerford [bridge]	86.125	Bridge over branch of R. Marden. Flax mill.
CALNE B P MH The *Waggon and Horses*, the *Lansdowne Arms* formerly the *Catherine Wheel* until the 19th C. when split level coach house built. Was an inn here from 1565. Facade Georgian. The *King's Arms*	87	781 houses 3,767 inhabitants. Mails arr 7.20am dep 8pm Once a wool town and noted for bacon; Harris's Bacon Factory founded 1770. Once belonged to Duchy of Cornwall.
[bridges]	88	Cross the Wiltshire and Berkshire Canal and the R. Calne.
		On r., road to Wooton Basset, on l, to Devizes.
Studley *Shelburne Arms*	89.75	Through Studley on l., is Bowood the superb seat of the Marquis of Lansdown. Grounds and garden well deserving the traveller's attention.
Derry Hill	90.125	
[bridges]	90.50	Cross Wiltshire and Berkshire Canal and a branch of R. Avon. On l., a road to Devizes

CHIPPENHAM B P [Bridge] The stately *Angel* and the *Rose and Crown* in stone and brick.	92.7s5	683 houses 3,366 inhabitants. Mails arr 8.10 am dep 7.05pm. Old Yelde Hall, 16th C building in middle of market place Mail coaches stop on the balustrade bridge, widened from medieval width to 20 arches in 1796. Maude Heath's causeway runs to Bremhill and is 4.5 miles long, built with bequest from Maude of Bremhill in 1474 to allow people to come to market despite flooding. on r., road to Malmsbury, on l., road to Melksham.
Pickwick	97	On l., road to Devizes
Box The *Queen's Head* and the *Bear*	99.75 **TG**	Village lock up next to the Queen's Head.
Ashley Green	100.375	Entrance of Bath Easton; on l., road to Devizes
Entering Somerset	TG	Crossing the By Brook, with vividly green hills all around.
Bath Easton	103.25	
Walcot Tollgate	104.625 **TG**	Toll gate
BATH C B P MH	105.75	4,463 Houses 32,000 inhabitants. Mail arr 9-30, dep 5.30 pm

Bath, via Devizes.

Follow previous itinerary as far as Beckhampton Inn

Beckhampton Inn		The downs studded with barrows and tracks, and the Wansdyke is crossed.
Site of battle of Roundway Hill		Royalists defeated Parliamentarians 1643. On left is pond with swans.
DEVIZES B P The *Bear*; a large bear over the porch. In Market Place. Also in Market Place, the *Black Swan*, 1737, the *Pelican* opposite and nearby the *Castle*.	88.125	898 houses 4,747 inhabitants. Mail arr. 7.30 am dep 7.15pm on r., road to Chippenham on l., road to Lavington. Cromwell destroyed the castle in 1645. Fanny Burney and Mrs. Thrale stayed at The Bear Inn in 1780 and noted the skill of the landlord's son at drawing. He was Thomas Lawrence. Market Cross 1814.
[bridges]	89	Cross Kennet and Avon Canal and see on right the 29 locks taking the canal up Caen Hill, completed 1807. [Note; the canal was completed in 1810 after 16 years building, Devizes locks being one of the last pieces.] Cross canal again. In a hard frost can skate on canal to Pewsey. 12 miles away.
Sumerham Bridge [bridge]	91.25	Over branch of the R. Avon. On l., road to Trowbridge
Selves Green	91.75	

Bower Hill	93.75	Entrance to parish of Melksham. On l., road to Warminster Springs found in 1815 and 3 large yellow stone buildings mark an abortive attempt to found a spa.
MELKSHAM P [church]	95.125	75 houses, 4,030 inhabitants. Mail arr 9.00 am dep 6.15pm Many local industries including tent and rope making from 1803
[bridge built 1809] Previous bridge destroyed in flood		Cross R. Avon. On r., road to Chippenham, on l., road to Bradford. Woods, and cottage orné and sign 'To the Guildhall, Bath, 7 miles Bath roads' there being an older road to the left over Kingsdown Hill and a newer via Box. We are following the older.
Shaw	96.875	On r., road to Corsham
Shaw Hill	97.75	
Attworth	98.375	
Blue Vein	100.875 **TG**	Toll gate. Name of hamlet refers to local rock type.
Kingsdown Hill The *Swan* on the Bath side.	102	On l., road to Melksham
Entering Somerset		
Bathford *The Old Inn*	103.25	
[ford]		Cross the Box Brook
		On r., road to Chippenham, on l., to Bradford, a little further on r., Fosse Way.

Bath Easton The *Lamb*	103.875	
Walcot	105.25 **TG**	Toll gate
BATH C P MH	106.375	4,463 Houses 32,000 inhabitants. Mail arr 9-30, dep 5.30 pm

The road through Box was developed because of how hard Kingdown hill was on horses.

Toll Charges

Person/carriage/livestock passing	**Toll**
For every horse, mule, ass or other beast except dogs drawing any coach, landau, barouche, chariot, chaise, chair, horse gig, curricle, whisky, cart, wagon, wain, timberframe, cart frame, drag or other vehicle when drawn by more than one horse or other beast, such a carriage having wheels less than 4½" width	4½d per horse
As above when drawn by one horse or other beast only	6d
As above when drawn by more than one horse or other beast with wheels 6 inches or upwards in width	3d per horse
As above when drawn by one horse or other beast	4d
As above with wheels between 4 ½ inches and 6 inches width with more than one beast	3¾d per horse
As above but only one beast	5d
For every horse, mule, ass or other beast drawing any cart with wheels of every breadth when drawn by any such animal NB 2 oxen or neat cattle drawing count as one horse	6d
For every dog drawing any truck, barrow or other carriage for the pace of 100 yards or upwards	1d
For every horse, mule, ass or other beast laden or unladen and not drawing	2d
For every carriage moved or propelled by steam or machinery or by any other power than animal power	1/- per wheel
For every score of oxen, cows or neat cattle and so in proportion for any greater or less number	10d [ie ½d per beast]
For every score of calves, sheep, lambs or swine and so in proportion	5d [ie ¼d per beast]
For every ridden horse	3d

The Stage-Coaches from London to Bath and the Inns from which they leave, and to which they return.

The first stagecoaches in the 17th century took 3 days to go from London to Bath. After the pike roads were built, the time dropped to between 14-18 hours, commonly, with some slower. The mail coach did it in 12-13 hours.

The places named are where they stopped to take on or set down passengers. Sometimes half an hour was allowed for dinner. If you were late queuing for the Jericho, or trying to swill down scalding hot coffee, the coach would go without you.
Particular coaches are named.

Costs are in general unknown but the lower end seems to start at 11d per five miles inside, and 6d per five miles outside, so starting at a guinea for the 103 miles, [21/- or £1/1/-] inside and around 12/- outside.

Angel Inn, St Clement's Street

By Calne and Chippenham; daily
dep 5.30 am, arr 10pm at White Lion
Leave Bath 5.30 am, arrives Angel 10pm

By Beckhampton Inn and Devizes, daily except Sunday. For families and invalids.
Dep 7.30 am, overnight Devizes arr Next Day 6 pm White Hart, Bath.
NB: *although Devizes is more than half way, half way is Newbury, where the country gets hillier and the going is slower if not to cause too much problem to the passengers.*
Leave Bath 7.30, arrives next day 6pm.

Belle Sauvage, Ludgate Hill

Bath and Bristol, through Marlborough, Calne and Chippenham
Daily 2pm

Bolt-in-tun Fleet Street

'The Post Coach' by Beckhampton Inn and Devizes, daily [not Sunday] dep 5am arr 10pm White Hart
Leave Bath 5am London, Bolt-in-tun 10pm

Bull and Mouth Bull and Mouth Street

For Bath, Exeter and Plymouth, daily except Sunday. Calls at Common Coffee House, Charing Cross, where parcels for carriage should be left.
Leaves 6 pm London, Bath 8 am following day, on to Exeter 8-30 pm and Plymouth Dock 6am following day.
Leaves Plymouth midday, reaches Exeter 8pm. Leaves Exeter 6am next day, Bath 6pm, to be in London 8am following morning
.

Fare,	London to Bath	£2/-/-
	Outside	£1/2/-
	London to Exeter	£3/10/-
	Outside	£2/2/-
	London to Plymouth	£4/10/-
	Outside	£2/12/-
	Bath to Exeter	£1/10/-
	Outside	£1/-/-
	Bath to Plymouth	£2/10/-
	Outside	£1/10/-

George and Blue Boar, Holburn

'The Volunteer' Bath and Bristol through Maidenhead, Reading, Newbury, Hungerford, Marlborough, Calne and Chippenham, daily
Leave 4pm, arrives 9am next morning, Lamb Inn [the Bush, Bristol 11am]
Departs Bristol 2pm, Bath 4pm arrives 'George' next morning 9am.

The overnight service suited a lot of people who were able to sleep in coaches. As this journey took 17 hours there was probably a stop at Maidenhead [which would be reached about 8pm] for dinner. Probably the coach used by Naval Officers reporting to Bristol.

Garrard's Hall, Basing Land, Bread Street: and Black Bear Piccadilly

Through Hungerford, Marlborough, Devizes and Melksham
Tues, Thur, Sat leaves 1pm arrives Christopher Inn next day 10 am
Departs Bath Sun, Wed, Fri, 1pm arrives next day 10am

'The Express', Bath and Bristol through Calne and Chippenham daily
5pm [Sunday 3pm] Bath arrives Midday? Bell Inn, Bristol 2pm
Leave Bristol 11am, arrives London 11am next day
[21 – 24 hours, I think 'The Express' was a bit of a joke]

Another overnight service, see remarks from previous.

Golden Cross, Charing Cross

Bath and Bristol by Beckhampton Inn and Devizes, daily [except Sunday]
Leaves 5am arrives 7pm White Hart, Bath, 9pm White Lion, Bristol
Leaves Bristol 5am, Bath 7am, London 9pm.

'the New Post Coach' Bath and Bristol through Beckhampton Inn and Devizes, every afternoon.
Leave 5pm, arrive 10am next day White Hart, Bath; midday White Lion Bristol.
Leave Bristol 4pm, Bath, 6pm, arrives London 9am.

Again, overnight.

Saracen's Head, Snow Hill

Bath and Bristol through Newbury, Hungerford, Marlborough and Chippenham, Daily.
Leave 2pm, arrives next day 8am Greyhound, Bath; at the London Tavern & Swan Inn Bristol 11am
Departs Bristol 2pm, Bath 5pm, arrives next morning 10am.

Saracent's Head, Friday Street, Cheapside

Bath and Bristol through Marlborough, Calne and Chippenham daily

Leave 2-30 pm arr. Next day 8am White Lion Bath, 10am White Hart, Bristol
Leave Bristol 12 noon, Bath 2pm, arrives London next day 8am.

The Swan with two Necks Lad Lane

'Royal Mail' for Bath by Beckhampton Inn and Devizes, daily
Leave 7-30 pm [Sun 5.45pm] arrives 9-30 am next day, Lamb Inn, Bath
Depart 5-30 pm arrives London 8am next day.

'Royal Volunteer' Bath and Bristol through Chippenham, daily
Leaves 3-45pm arrives Lamb Inn, Bath next day 11am, The Bush, Bristol 1pm.
Departs Bristol 2pm, Bath 4pm, arrives next day London 10am.

City of Bath from London Rd 1770

Chapter Two: where to stay and how to get around when you get to Bath.

Once in Bath, a place to stay is necessary, and the choices between staying in a noisy inn, or a hotel, or taking rooms or even a house must be made. Next a visit to the shops to purchase all that is needful to cut a dash at the entertainments. Knowing what is on to entertain one is also essential! And perhaps a visit to the Pump Room or to take a bath. Bath has many ways to meet other people, but beware, the rules are strict. If Midnight sounds in the middle of a dance at a subscription ball, the ball is over.
Most of the buildings in Bath are built from the attractive honey-gold Bath stone, which presents a warm and mellow appearance and invites one in to its attractive walls.

The Inns

The White Hart, Stall Street
The largest and most prestigious inn in Bath. Stylish and efficient. Near the pump room. Always busy. A white deer mounted over the entrance. Terribly noisy. Sometimes also known as the White Hart Hotel.

The Greyhound, Market Place

The Castle, Northgate St

The White Lion, Market Place

The Lamb, Stall St

The Christopher, Market Place

The Westgate Inn, 38 Westgate Street
Dates back to 1611, one of the original coaching inns. Stage-coaches came originally in 1657 from London, taking 3 days. Has a ghost.

The Bear

The Castle

The Saracen's Head 42 Broad Street

The Christopher, Market Place and St. Michaels W. Everitt, 1840, *Views of Bath and its Environs, PD*

The Three Tuns, Stall St

The Angel Inn, Westgate St

The Full Moon

Hotels

York House in York Buildings
Very large, elegant and commodious.

Belvedere Hotel, near Cambden Place
Foreign wine and spirit merchant. Gentlemen and families in good clean accommodation.

Sydney Hotel, end of Great Pulteney Street
Elegant apartments for gentlemen and families, with the advantage of the garden and rides.
Commodious coffee room, mews and coach houses and good stabling; post horses and drivers for hire.

Melun's Hotel

Other accommodations

Lodging Houses -
The price of these is regulated according to the situation and the number and excellence of the rooms and the elegance of the furniture. The prices in the heat of the summer are usually lower. Here are some average prices.

1st September to 21st May
½ guinea [10/6d] per week for best rooms
5/6d for servants

Summer, June, July, August
7/6d for best
5/6d for servants

However, many lodging houses let suites, so one is obliged to rent 5-6 rooms.

Boarding Houses can have single rooms at rates corresponding to accommodation to be expected [a few shillings a week?]. Many would only take gentlemen or families; some, like the Misses Kyan would accept ladies or gentlemen with proper references.

Mrs. Barrows kept a lodging house in St James' Parade.

Some Boarding Houses
Mrs Esdale, 11 Abbey St
Miss Laurence, 8 Bath St
Mrs. Faulkener, 16 Bond Street
Mr. Norket, I Church Street
Mr. Higgo, 18 Churchyard
Mrs. Bristow, 59 Gay St
Miss Kyan, 18 Henrietta St [but she moves a few times]
Mrs. Lautier, 32 & 33 Henrietta St
Miss Wilson, 42 Milsom St
Mr. Milsom, 2 Northumberland Buildings
Miss Brooks, 12 Northumberland Buildings
Mrs. Peack, 10 & 11 Orange Grove
Mrs. Petrie, 2 & 3 Pierpoint St
Mr. Bastin, Lower Walks

Houses might be rented or leased. A house in Edgar Buildings near the city centre with the usual offices and stable with a garden let for £105 per annum, plus ground rent of £4/15/-.
Often the remainder of a lease may be taken on if the leaser dies. Eg, no. 8 Milsom Street was leased for 99 years in July 1765 and the leaseholder died aged 79 in 1813. There was a tenant who paid £130 a year rent and the £4/6/- ground rent; the lease was for sale at £300, yearly building tax to be paid by the leaseholder.

In 1810, a furnished house was to let for a guinea and a half [31/6d or £1/11/6d] a week, probably in Charles Street or nearby where applicants were asked to apply with a post-paid letter. Charles Street was a bit off the beaten track, being to the West of the hub of the town. Even so, the yearly rent would be almost £82. It was still a respectable location.

In 1820, a neat compact house, no. 12 Russell Street was let furnished at 7 guineas per week, by the month or 6 ½ g per week for six months. Some new carpeting.

Eight-year lease on a house to be sold, genteel situation, garden behind, four sitting rooms, two attics, four garret, hall, kitchen, arches etc. rent only £53 pa. As seen above, a des. res. in a favourable position and a large property could be over £100 pa.

House prices started with a whopping £1800 for a house in the Royal Crescent, as assessed for insurance, down to a couple of hundred for a sadly unfashionable and poorly located building. The King's Circus appreciated in value since its building, on the whole; the Queen's Parade became less fashionable and the houses dropped in value from £1,350 in 1786 to around £1,000 by the end of the Georgian era. Of course, it depended too which side of a square on which one's house was situate; the north side had more sunlight so was more desirable than the south side, by as much as half as much again.

Rent of a medium sized house in an unfashionable part of London would be £12-£25 pa., for comparison.

Where *not* to live

Naturally the most desirable place to live is the parish of Walcot, to the north of the town.
Whilst it may not be given to everyone to live in The Royal Crescent, no girl of breeding wishes to lodge in an area which will mark her out as of no account; the Lower Town should be avoided, the Parish of St James is distinctly lower class. This is the southern end of the town, from Westgate Street and especially from Lower Borough Walls, and including St James' Parade and south. The completion of the Navigation of the Avon brought with it a cluster of warehouses, stables and small workshops around Horse Street and in this general vicinity; and too a large number of licensed alehouses. Horse Street had most, hosting 14 of Bath's 143 ale houses. Indeed, Stall Street, the continuation of Horse Street, had 11 alehouses and ran as far north as Westgate Street.
The exceptions to this are those addresses to the west of the Lower Town, such as West and East Green Park Place, bordering King's Mead and the other fine modern buildings between this and the Bristol Road.

Generally, the further north the address, the better it is, though Laura Place and Great Pulteney Street were acceptable addresses, unlike Henrietta St and Grove Street, paradoxically to the north of Gt. Pulteney Street, but very much part of the old Bathwick hamlet.

Locations to the east of the town are also undesirable; those near the river in both directions, south and east, though it is less clear cut to the east. Broad Street is not a genteel location, nor the area between Green Street and Cheap Street, to the south-east of Milsom Street, which is essentially the main shopping area, where one might find the grocers, tea merchants, butchers and all the other admirable, necessary and yet bourgeois trades. These are also locations of licensed ale houses, the most in Broad Street, which had 10.

Less desirable too are the Bladud Buildings, Paragon Buildings and Axfords Buildings along Vinyards, to the north of the town but being on the main London road rather too noisy for comfort, unlike such desirable residences as Camden Place, to the west of this road, sufficiently removed from the bustle to be suitable.

By the late Regency more building was going on off the London Road, with Hanover Square and the abortive Grosvenor Square; but the Walcot area along the London road was not high status. There was a poor house there...

Not undesirable, but inconvenient were the buildings of Lansdown Crescent, being somewhat out of town to the north-west of the city, and up a steep hill. Prices might be lower there for a large house because of the inconvenience.

Getting about Bath

It is more practical to get around Bath using the sedan chairs than in attempting to ride or take a carriage. The slopes and number of hills are detrimental to wheeled traffic. Anyone who is in Bath for their health, and are in a Bath Chair would do well to use one with the biggest wheels they can find, for less discomfort over the cobbled streets, or more correctly the sandstone setts.
Those people used to London cobbles will be used to the rounded stones set in accretion which give a noisy, uneven but moderately safe ride. Those people from the east may be more used to knapped flint, usually set in four inch squares, much like the decoration on the local churches there. Those used to small, round stones of greater depth than those used in London will find that walking is less painful than you are used to. Bath cobbles or setts are less slippery than flint in the wet, and are typically six to eight inches by four inches, but they are not tremendously evenly set, and wheels tend to catch on them – as do tired feet when walking! This is another good reason to take a chair, rather than wear ugly walking boots in town.

The Chairmen's fares are settled by magistrate:
For carrying one person from any place within the walls to any other place within the walls 6d
For carrying one person any distance not exceeding 500 yards... 6d
Above 500 and not exceeding 1173 yards [¾ mile] 1/-
Beyond 1173 yards and not exceeding a mile 1/6d
Beyond one mile and not exceeding one mile and 586 yards 2/-
Not exceeding one mile and 1173 yards............................. 2/6d
Not exceeding 2 miles 3/-
And for every 586 yards or part over that 6d

Any person may detain the chair a period of time without paying more as follows:
A sixpenny fare ....10 minutes
A twelvepenny fare ....15 minutes
An eighteenpence fare ....20 minutes
A two-shilling fare ....25 minutes
A half-crown fare ....30 minutes
A three-shilling fare ....35 minutes
Etc
Otherwise 6d for every 15 minutes wait.
All fares doubled after 12 midnight.

Distances for the chairs to travel

Measured from the Lower Assembly Rooms front door	
To N.E. [furthest] corner Queen's Square	508
To no. 5 Great Pulteney St., on the RH side	596
To no. 2 Great Pulteney St., on LH side	496
To the north door of Walcot Church:	1128
To the 1st house in Bladud Buildings	596
To the north end of Belmont Row	876
To the last house in Monmouth Street	702
To the corner house of King's Mead Square next Westgate	439
To the last house on North Parade	301
To the Pump Room	284

From the Pump Room	
To N.E Corner of Queen's Square thro Bridewell lane	521
To S.E Corner of Queen's Square thro Ditto	419
To No. 1 Great Pulteney St on the R.H Side	510
To the north door of Walcot Church	1074
To north end of Belmont Row	822
To last house in Monmouth St	513
To the last house of North Parade	492
To the last house of South Parade	542
To West Gate	253
To the Lower Rooms	284

From the Guildhall, Market Square	
To the last house on North Parade	455yds
To West Gate	291
To last house in Monmouth St	553
To N.W corner of Queen's Square	622
To upper end of Belmont Row	722

From the Abbey Church	
To S.E. corner of Queen Square, thro Bridewell Lane	515
To the same corner of the square thro Green Street	522
To the last house on the North Parade	302
To the first house in Bladud's Buildings	502
To the north end of Belmont Row	785
To the centre of Milsom Street	490
To No. 3 Great Pulteney Street, on the RH side	405

From the Upper Rooms	
To the centre house in the Royal Crescent	506
To the first house in Walcot Parade	720
To the first house in Charles Street on the LH	673
To the lower house in Bond Street	538
To the last house in Rivers' St on the RH thro' St. Margaret's Buildings	457
To the SW corner in Queen Square	520
To the Town Hall, through Broad St	700
To the last house in Queen's Parade	488

From the Octagon Chapel	
To the first house in Brock St, on the RH side	523
To the centre house in Westgate Buildings	400
To the last house in Belmont Row	534
To the first house on St James' Parade	517
To the first house in Axford Buildings	584
To the last house in New King Street	598
To no. 12 in Paragon Buildings	509

From the New Theatre	
To no. 1 on the North Parade	610
To no. 1, Alfred St	635
To no. 1 Pulteney St	651

Livery Stables

Robert's Livery Stable variously described as Cottle's Lane, the Crescent, and Back of Crescent. Was certainly there in 1810 and in 1819. Cottle's Lane ran from the middle of the back of the crescent through to Kingston Buildings.

Bell's Livery Stables, Barton St, Queen's Square was certainly open between 1810 and 1820.

J. Tasker of Pulteney Street in business there 1799-1819 see below.

Grey's Livery Stables, Rivers Street from 1811 to 1819; business taken on by J. Tasker who moved into the Rivers Street property.

Roper's Livery Stable, James St certainly there 1814 run by Sandy Roper, in 1817 from February it was being run by Mrs. Mary Roper, relict of Sandy.

Stevenson's livery stables and Riding School [also had a riding house for exercise in inclement weather]. Top of Russell Street from 1811. W. Stevenson died January 1820 after a severe illness.

Mews serving Edgar Buildings on George St., Mews facing St Andrew's Terrace on Bartlett St. Photo S.Waldock

The Mail

When living in Bath, naturally one wishes to know when the mail leaves and arrives from other places, and the cost. The cost of mail to London is 6d, despite the distance, because of the frequency of the mails; to other places, the rates on the cross roads are fixed according to distance.

Not Exceeding 15 miles, 4d; 30 miles, 5d; 50 miles, 6d; 80 miles, 7d; 120 miles, 8d; 170 miles, 9d; 230 miles, 10d; 300 miles 11d; 400 miles, 1/-; and +1d per 100 miles.

To and from London and points beyond

Goes out every evening except Saturday at 5pm; Comes in every morning except Monday 10am – 12 noon

To and from Maidenhead, Reading,Newbury,Hungerford, Marlborough, Calne, Chippenham, Devizes, Melksham, Trowbridge, Bradford etc.

Goes out every evening at 5pm, comes in every morning 10am-12 noon.

To and from All parts of Oxfordshire, Abingdon, Farringdon, Malmsbury, Swindon, Wotton Basset, Cricklade, Highworth, Lechlade, Fairford, Cirencester, Minchinhampton, Tetbury, Sodbury etc

Goes out every afternoon at 3pm, comes in every morning 9am-10am

To and from Cornwall, Devonshire, Wellington, Taunton, Bridewater, Wells, Somerton, Langport, Ilminster, Chard, Crewkerne etc

Goes out every morning at 9am, comes in every evening from 6pm - 7pm.

To and from Dorsetshire, Hampshire, Salisbury, Heytesbury, Warminster, Frome, etc

Goes out every evening except Sunday at 5pm, comes in every morning except Sunday from 9am-10am

To and from The North of Ireland, Wales, part of Westmoreland, Lancashire, Cheshire, Shropshire, Staffordshire, Worcestershire, Herefordshire, Monmouthshire, Birmingham, Stratford[on Avon], Warwick, Gloucester, Cheltenham, Stroud, Northleach, Newnham, Berkeley, Newent, Michel-Dean, Colford, Dursley, Wotton, etc

Goes out every afternoon at 3pm, comes in every morning 9am-11am

To and from Bristol, South of Ireland, Pembrokeshire, Caermarthenshire, Glamorganshire, Newport, Caerleon, Usk, Chepstow etc

Goes out every morning at 9am and every evening at 5pm; comes in every morning about 10am, and every evening at 6pm.

Chapter Three: Shopping in Bath

Now you have arrived, and are ready for the Assemblies and Galas and maybe even to drink the waters and bathe in the healing baths, so you want to look your best. Naturally you will be looking for haberdashers, milliners and other sundry shops. This is a guide to some of the shops who advertised in the newspaper.
Unless specified as readymades – which did exist – when a 'dress' is spoken of, this refers to a dress length of fabric. Generally, this is 4-6 yards depending on width; that's based on an ell width of 40" or so. Double for narrowcloth of 24" wide.
Fancy dress; probably dress ball gowns, as there were fancy dress balls and ordinary ball gowns.
Warehouse; a house or shop with wares in. Not the modern meaning.
This is by no means a comprehensive list but offers a good selection with the widest time period in business I could find.

Haberdashery and Millinary shops [often both together]

Samuel Slack, later S&W Slack
I have a very full history of this business!

In 1801 Samuel Slack was in Bath St. Selling cambrics, calicos, muslins etc. A few prices below:
Fine ell-wide India mulls 2/- a yard
Worked India muslin dresses 31/6d
Fine ell-wide India stripes 3/- a yard
Japan muslin dresses 18/- and 21/- [normally sold for 42/-]
Elegant worked dresses from 31/- to 42/-

In 1805
Samuel Slack opens a second shop in Milsom Street, no. 40 aka 'The Centre House'. As well as the muslins from India [stripe muslin dress lengths down to 12/- each] he has British muslins and French Cambrics
Also, printed furniture fabric and household linen:
Chintz furniture fabric 22d/yd
Stout furniture dimities 21d/yd
Damask and diaper table linens
Irish linen sheeting.

In 1807
India Jacconets were 2/- a yard
India Mulls 9/- a dress length [presumably an ell wide and needing under 4 yards]
Yard and a quarter wide [45”] India calicoes 13d/yd
India worked muslins
French cambrics from 33/- to 38/- per piece
He also had some 170 remnant pieces of waterstained cambric muslin at 6d and 12d per yd, a bargain as the water staining would wash out readily.

In 1811
S. and W. Slack advertise that they visited London and Manchester to restock their warehouse. Elegant Gordon and Dundee dresses, Merino crepes, lustres, Imperial nets, Bombazines, Gossamer etc; and from the East-India sales, several bales of curious muslins for dresses, particularly cheap, as well as tambour and satin-worked muslins as now universally worn in the first circles.
From Manchester, pieces of cambric and jacconot cambric muslins for dresses or cravats. Also long cloths, shirting calicoes, prints, dimities etc; a most extensive collection of rich printed furnitures [fabrics] in the newest designs, quilts, counterpanes, blankets etc.
Irish linens and shirtings imported by themselves from the most reputable bleachers in Ireland. Also S. & W. Slack have a warehouse in Clare-Street, Bristol
R. Price, trained by S. & W. Slack, ie has been shop assistant, opens a linen draper shop at 10 Old Bond St, and is joined by his wife from her shop in Rivers Street to take up millinery and dressmaking at her husband’s premises.
In 1816
In October, S. & W. Slack have retired from business, and leave it to Mr. W. Crocker from London.
In 1817
W. Crocker has the haberdashery in 40, Milsom St.

<u>Thomas Stroud</u>

Opens April 1811 in 6 Union Street
Linen draper, hosiery, sarsenets, laces etc
From 1817 Irish linens, sheeting, huckabacks, bed ticking 1/- per yard, coleranes [half-bleached Irish linen] ½d per yard.

Mrs. S. Vezey

Mrs. Vezey was rather a peripatetic seller of Lace, Muslins, furs, silk goods and haberdashery.
Before January 1805 she occupied 4 Argyle Buildings, but moved to Walcut to a premises adjoining Mr. Vezey's Coach Shop.
In 1807 she was back in Bath, in 4 Bath Street.
In 1816 she moves from Bath St to 19 Milsom Street, and advertises Parisian fashions
In March 1820 she retires.

E. & A. Laing's

Millinery, Pelisses, corsets and stays, dresses [readymade], spencers [do] Ornaments and fancy articles. Worked trimmings, caps, tuckers and habit shirts.
Velvet Pelisses from £3/13/6d to £7/7/-
Cloth Pelisses from 18/- to 42/-
Corsets and stays from 10/6d to £1/1/6d
In January 1805 moved from 9 George St to 34 Milsom St.
Laing's sold winter wear at a reduced rate in March, generally half price
In 1807 was advertising childbed linen
In 1810 advertising 'completely waterproof shoes, made of Vancouver's cement or Iron Glue.'

Miss Lovelock
In 1805, Millinery, Haberdashery, and lace. Rooms 34 Brook St, and No. 146 Cheltenham [St.].
Chip, straw and leghorn hats and bonnets, black and white lace cloaks, veils etc. New opera sarsenet for dress. Ribbons, gloves, feathers, flowers etc.
In 1812 still at 34 Brook St, and 311 Cheltenham [St.]

Lindsey Hewer
1818, Expanding from Cheltenham [Street?] at 41 Milsom Street.
Mechlin, Lisle and Valenciennes lace, Brussels lace dresses and veils, bobbin net veils. Real and imitation French blond lace, figured silks etc.

W. Exton

In 1807 in 18 Bath Street, selling fur, bear, and fox.
Bear muffs 12/-
Bear long tippets, 9/-
White long dress tippets 10/6d
Fur can be black, grey, Isabella [fawn or creamy colour], brown
Lace, Vandyke and plain.
1808 buff, limerick and dark kid habit-gloves 1/- pair
Figured cotton net sleeves, 16d a pair
Silk hemmed handkerchiefs 3/6d upwards
Shawls in imitation of India from 6/6d
In May 1812 moves to 14 Old Bond St, next door to Barett's library from Bath Street. Sale of stock in Bath St. shop
In 1814 Bobbin lace shawls 28/- each
In Feb 1816 moves to 16 Old Bond St.
White and other fur for trimming 6d/yd
Swansdown on sale 1/- per yd
White dress tippets 5/-
Muffs 20/-
Swansdown tippets 21/-
Velvet 12/- yard etc
October 1819, all items are on sale as Mr. W. Exton is selling off his whole stock of a declining business; including thread lace, bobbin net, velvet, cloths, lace veils, seling [?Saling? goat and camel from Turkmenistan 12" wide and 22 yards long], gloves, silk handkerchiefs, muffs, tippets, fur trimming, gauzes and other haberdashery.

Mrs. M. Langdon

In 1806 hosiery, lace and glove warehouse 11 Argyle St, opposite the chapel.
As well as the usual types of things she sells embroideries in chenilles, bugles, silk etc for dresses and her valuable collection of Georgiana, Trafalgar, Arrow and Parisian fans
Hassocks, stools, after the Grecian, Egyptian, Turkish and Ottoman style.
In April 1811 moves to 37 Milsom Streed, selling old stock by auction to restock. Selling millinery, readymade dresses, haberdashery and Imperial corsets as well as her embroidery which she also teaches. Certainly still there in 1818

George Towson [Late of Tully and George's]

From Jan 1807 Hatter, hosier, glover and man's-mercer
4 North Parade
Fleecy hosiery; funerals furnished
From Nov. 1807, now also a habit-maker
Feb 1808 advertised Vigona cloth embroidered *en chenille*. [Vigona is probably Vicuña, aka Vigogne in French]
September 1811 joins with Peter Ardenond in 24 Milsom Street. Peter Ardenond late of Abbey Churchyard is a woollen draper, tailor, habit maker. Funerals furnished. Moves out 1817, business taken on by Mr. Denie, woollen draper, then Thomas Flaherty in 1820, and takes over Mrs. Spornberg's at 27 Milsom Street in 1819 in addition.

Mrs. R, Spornberg
Milliner, mantua-maker fancy dress and pelisse-maker
Assortment of the newest patterns with flowers, feathers, trimmings, printed and plain kerseymeres etc for pelisses 'as now worn by the fashionable in the metropolis' in 1802 when she was at 5 Bond Street; she moved to 27 Milsom Street in Dec 1812, and was there until June 1819.

Madame Simeon later C. Simeon

Opens Sat. November 14th 1808, when the premises is complete; opening was delayed.
The original French Lace Warehouse and *Temple de Gout*, 31 Milsom St.
Ladies dresses, robes, pelisses, mantles and millinery made.
Cologne water, French laces, hosiery and haberdashery, umbrellas and parasols.
January 1811, declared Bankrupt, re-opens as C. Simeon in October, C. Simeon is male [her son? He has a brother in Bristol who supplies umbrellas.]

Lockwood and Porter

1807 Linen draper, hosier etc 12 Milsom St
Tambours and satin-worked muslins etc from 8/- to 4g the dress length
Embroidered robes 12/- upwards
Embroidered train 21/- upwards
Muslin leno [open-weave] dresses worked in winter colours
Plain India muslins from 20d/yd to 20/- per yard
Decca works [Indian patterns] 20/- the dress length
Cambric muslin from 16d/yd and up
Jacconet cambric for men's handkerchiefs from 17d to 7/- per piece
Scotch cambric 10/- to 42/- a piece for handkerchiefs [one piece makes 9 handkerchiefs]
Furniture dimities from 1/- per yard
Quilts, counterpanes, blankets, Scotch ticks, Welsh flannel et.
1808 silk shawls from £1/5/- to £4/14/6d
Mulls and Jacconets 18d/yard upwards
India decca-worked muslins 25/- dress length.
Cossaes [Cassas, a soft fine Indian cotton with slack-twist yarn] 5/4yard [45"] wide, 15d/yard
Ell-wide cambric muslins 13/- the piece of 12 yards
6/4 yard [54"] wide ditto from 15d per yard.
Imitation figured velvets
Furniture dimities 13d/yard
Quilts, counterpanes, bed-ticks, Welsh and Lancaster flannels, Blankets from 5/- to 63/- a pair. All forms of household linen.
May 1812 James Lockwood moves from Milsom Street to 1 Westgate place. Here he becomes sole agent for Lowe's patent British Shirting Cloth, warranted equal to the best Irish linen in durability at half the price. The superior kind of texture which is peculiar to this fabric renders it most pleasant, comfortable and economical kind of shirting cloth ever manufactured. It washes beautifully.
7/8th yard [31.5"] at 2/4d per yard [Irish linen 4/-]
Yard wide 2/6d to 3/- per yard [Irish linen 4/2d to 6/-]
May 1813 unfortunately James Lockwood, draper, is declared bankrupt. Maybe that shirting wasn't all it was claimed to be ...

Joseph Pearson
For many years, hosier and Lace manufacturer in Stall Street opposite the pump room.
1816 moves to 15 Northgate Street.

Mr. C. Foreman
From 1804 or earlier, at 42 Milsom Street. Hosiery and gloves, lace, handkerchiefs, furs, modes [aka alamode, plain, glossy light silk fabric usually dyed black for mourning scarves and lining] and pelongs [aka pelang, pealong, pelin; a Chinese silk in plain or satin weave. Usually white or plain colours, sometimes a patterned weave. Pieces were 16 to 20" wide and 10 yards long.]
Muffs, tippets and ribbons.
In 1817 he was in 41 and 42 Milsom Street.

S. Clark
1816 fashionable straw hats, 11 Green Street.
Fine split straw, foreign chips, Dunstable, Imperial etc etc
Family mourning hats in foreign or imperial chip on short notice; hats altered to any shape, cleaned, dyed.

James Taylor, Hatter, later Alexander and Gould
Hatter, Hosiery, gloves and Undertaker, 3 Bridge Street for many years
18th June 1819 James Taylor died, aged 52, he was a deacon of the Independent Chapel for 21 years and was uniformly obliging and upright. His assistant Mr. Charles Gould and brother-in-law, Mr. William Alexander incorporated to carry on the business.
1820 Alexander and Gould have an elegant selection of Ladies' and Children's beaver bonnets and hats. Gentlemen's fur hats, silk and cotton hosiery, gloves etc.

Joseph Cooper Boot and Shoe Maker
Of 15 Bath Street
In June 1816 opens a second shop at 1 Bridge Street; the old shop will be open for a while, selling old stock.

Other shops; perfumers, hair cutters, jewellers

As well as fabrics and dresses, one needs perfume, hairdressing and jewellery
It must be pointed out that perfumers usually also held makeup, hair care products, soap, face cream and a selection of patent nostrums.

The Rocking Horse and Golden Fleece
No 8 George St, Bath.
Owned by Warren and Rosser, perfumers, of 5 Skinner Street, Snow Hill, [prior to 1808 at Cheapside, London and 36 Warwick St Golden Square, London
From 1808 also in Bath.
Milk of Roses, Cream of Roses, Imperial Powder Royal, Liquid of Violets and Jessamine, Lavender water.
Also selling British Tooth Powder etc.
Feast's Vegetable Lily Paste for restoring the skin soft, white and delicate, removing freckles, tans, redness, heat, wrinkled and signs of ageing, in pots 5/- each or 2/6d for smaller. Preserves the skin from the bad effects of cold winds, sharp frosts, hard water &c.
In March 1806 Mr. Warren died, John Mason held the premises and licence until 1811
1811 No. 7 George St appointed Mr. Spreat
And at No. 5 York Street Mrs. Marriot
Both to sell Warren's Milk of Roses, purified Honey Soap and Vegetable Lily Paste.

Mr. J. Spreat
Perfumer, toy and fancy goods turner, jeweller. [toys mean small valuable items, ornaments, snuff-boxes, etui boxes and things ornamented in silver, silver-gilt etc]
1811 out of the Rocking Horse and Golden Fleece no. 8 George St where he purchased the lease for 20 years.
New and fashionable assortment of Tunbridge and Morocco workboxes and many kinds of fancy articles, all kinds of French and English finery.
19th July 1812 Mrs. Spreat of George St dies – is this his mother or his wife? Age not given.
26th November 1812 Mr. John Spreat marries Miss Parkes.
By November 1813, Mr. John Spreat is a bankrupt and the more valuable of his stock is sold to cover his debts: including 18 years of unexpired

lease to the premesis. 70g a year rent, and £24 a year ground rent. The situation is undeniably the best in Bath for a genteel trade, being the principal thoroughfare to the most elegant parts of the city.
Sold, [giving us an idea of his stock] gold, silver, amethyst, opal, cornelian and coral lockets, brooches, necklaces, seals, snuff boxes etc; elegant tortoiseshell, rose-wood and Morocco Ladies' work boxes, writing cases, caddies &c, &c. A great variety of Tunbridge ware; dissected puzzles; toys and turned articles of every description.
In 1814, Miss Spreat, sister of Mr. John Spreat, married Mr. Moore, clock and watchmaker of Backwell. Mr. John Spreat lives at No. 30 Milsom Street, and has restored his business as the Rocking Horse and Golden Fleece. In December the emblem of the Golden Fleece was stolen!
1815 Spreat given a licence to sell Atkinson's vegetable dye to change grey or red hair to auburn, brown or black. Prices 5/-, 7/6d, 10/6d and 1g [licence also to Mrs. Marriott and Joseph George in Bath as well as Messers Cruttwell, Binns, Wright and Cuff, reputable perfumers]
Also Atkinson's curling fluid for dressing the hair, keeping it glossy, removing scurf and keeping it in curl. Bottles 3/6d, 10/6d and 1g. Atkinson's Ambrosial soap, 1/- a square; Atkinson's vegetable paste for washing the face. 2/6d a pot.
1815 sold under licence Mrs. Vincent's Gowland Lotion, a pleasant and effectual remedy for all complaints to which the face and skin are liable, by removing every kind of coarseness, eruption and unpleasant appearance and rendering the skin clear, smooth and transparent.
1816 gains licence to sell Butler's vegetable tooth powder [and other reputable perfumers] also Butler's scouring drops for taking grease out of silks, stuffs, woollen cloths etc 1/- the bottle.
1818 the Rocking Horse and Golden Fleece still in Milsom St. Miss Spreat is conferred the honour of teaching Her Royal Highness Princess Elizabeth, the 7th child and 3rd daughter of King George III and Queen Charlotte. the new and fashionable art of purse making.

Mrs. Marriott

5 York Street 1806, moved around 1811 to 1 York Street, also identified as corner of York Street, warehouse of perfume and snuff.
1811 under licence from Warren and Rosser of London to sell their products [see above]; over next few years licenced by others like Atkinson, Mrs. Vincent, and Butler as under Mr. Spreat.
Also a romantic herbal essence for use in crowded rooms and public

places to remove the unpleasant inhalation caused by animal heat and cures nervous headaches.
The Indian Soap or fragrant balsamic washing paste, 2/-, prepared in Dehli. Removes every blemish etc. From 1810
Russia oil for gentlemen to dress the hair from 1811
Carrington's vegetable life pills [a panacea for everything including coughs, colds, stomach ailments, depression, female complaints and sufferings brought on youth by solitary vice] 4/6d a box 1815.
Certainly still in York Street in 1817.

Joseph George

Hair cutter/Hair dresser and perfumer, 2 Argyle Buildings, a bow-fronted shop window.
Held a licence for Atkinson's curling fluid and dye from 1813.
Friday 20th October, 1815 Joseph George's body was taken out of the river at the bottom of the North Parade; he had been in a despondent state of mind and left home the previous morning. He left a wife and 5 children. Inquest found insanity.
F. George, his widow, continued the business. She received patronage from His Royal Highness the Duke of York.
Ownership of the property she leased was sold in 1816
In 1818 she moved her perfumery warehouse from no. 2 to no. 10 Argyle Buildings, where she has an excellent assortment of Genuine Perfumery, tortoiseshell and ivory combs, hair-brushes etc which she continues to sell at the London prices. Also Watson's celebrated Horse Medicines.

Mr. Gould, Civet-Cat, perfumer and hair-cutter

From 1807 and still in place in 1820, no. 4 Milsom Street.
A large assortment of ornamental hair, toys and cutlery.
Ladies' dress wigs, common colours £1/11/6d
Ladies' crop ditto £1/1/- [1g]
Paris fronts 5/-
Borders 5/6d
Toppings 2/6d
Rounds from 10/6d to 15/-
Fronts 3/6d
Bands from 10/6d to £1/1/- [1g]

Gents' wigs from £1/5/- to £1/11/6d
Trotter-oil pomatum and Russia oil to prevent the hair from falling and promote its growth.
1812, William Gould is a bankrupt.
1820, Mrs. Gould is the sole agent of Richardson's improved patent rug skins of various rich and durable colours for all kinds of carriages, doors, French windows, halls etc. Sold at the Perfumery and Snuff warehouse, Civet Cat, 4 Milsom Street.

Sundry others described as perfumiers

Cruttwell, Binns, Cuff and Hunt of Bath, who also had licences to sell many of the above goods, also sold Dr. Fothergill's Female Pills, advertised as helping to deal with the Green Sickness or Menstrual Obstruction. Female obstruction was also a euphemism for pregnancy, and as it happens, most remedies for sluggish courses are also abortifacients. Cruttwell Binns, Cuff and Robinson also carried Dr. Sibly's Lunar tincture at 4/6d for disorders to the Female Sex.
Also Cruttwell sold Rymer's tincture for cardiac and nervous disorders and disorders of the stomach and bowels, headache, confusion etc etc.
Rhymer's cough drops and Pectoral medicine.
Cruttwell, Binns, Meyler and Keens sold the Cordial Balm of Gilead, for weakness and debility.
Cruttwell also carried Leake's genuine pills for Venereal disease. He was the sole seller of Velnos' Celebrated Syrup in Bath for all manner of ailments...
Cruttwell was also a printer, Binns was a bookseller, it was not uncommon to sell patent beauty products and nostrums on the side, nor for printers to sell books.

Mr. Cuff is listed also as a chemist, and in 1819-20 at least lived in no. 15 Milsom Street. As he has appeared through the years in adverts for patent nostrums it is reasonable to suppose his services were available for the same with some perfume.
1819 holds eau de rose, or double-distilled rose water, new tamarinds [lozenges?], Imperial powders for making ginger beer, agent for Schweppe's soda water

Mr. Pitter

4 Bath Street
Gold laceman, jeweller and perfumer; gold and silver rich spangled laces for dresses, tiaras, flowers and bandeaus for the hair, tambour threads and spangles.
Perfumery, rouge tablets for ladies, rouge in pots in great variety
Fans.
He doesn't quite fit in with haberdashery or jewellery so here he is all on his own.

Jewellers

S.N. Riviere and sons

Goldsmith, Jeweller and Watchmaker of 63 New Bond St, London to His Royal Highness the Duke of Gloucester
From Nov. 1803 Riviere would come to Bath for the winter, take a short lease for the winter season from November to May. In May he goes to Cheltenham for a while opposite the George Hotel.
His addresses in Bath, being from November to the following May:
1803-4 at 32 Milsom Street
1804-11 at 29 Milsom Street
1811-1818 at 1 Old Bond Street
September 1813 his infant child died.
May 13th 1815 Mr. John Smith Riviere, respectable jeweller, brought a defamation suit against Alexander Kelty, a jeweller in Cheltenham, who impugned his financial integrity. An apology was obtained.
1815 the shop in Cheltenham is now also open during the winter [presumably under one of the 'and sons']
In 1820 at 19 Old Bond Street.
With a stock of superb and elegant Jewellery, Watches and Plate.

John Riviere and his fellow jeweller, Mr. Lautier of Bridge Street were members of the Bath Guardian Society which was a kind of Neighbourhood Watch of shopkeepers. In 1818 both jewellers were subject to fraud and obtaining under false pretences by a man calling himself James Phillips, a man of almost 20 years, 5'8" dressed in black. A reward of 10g from Riviere, 5g from Lautier and 5g from the Guardian Society.

Mr. B. Lautier - watch and clock maker

1811, Benjamin Lautier, late of Union St, dissolves partnership with Peter Vigne, and goes into business on own account at no. 6 Pulteney Bridge
In 1818 he is in Bridge Street.

Wm. James, Watchmaker, goldsmith and Jeweller

1813 moves to 2 Old Bond St from Pulteney Bridge.

Basnett Jeweller and Goldsmith

May 1811, stock sold from his premises at Bond Street to by auction to permit improvements.
November 1811 moves to 23 Milsom Street
Ster 1819, S. & J. Martin takes over the business as Jeweller, silversmith and watchmaker in 23 Milsom Street.
Silver articles, such as waiters, tea and coffee pots and biggins [coffee pot with separate area for heating water and coffee], candlesticks, sugar basins, saucepans, elegant epergne dish-stands, toast racks, and plated articles, tea and coffee urns, bread baskets, liquor and bottle stands, dish covers and heaters, tureens, sugar and cream basins, butter coolers, cruet and egg frames, chamber candlesticks, supper branches, caddies etc.
Jewellery and trinkets in neck-chains, ear-rings, brooches, bandeaux, toothpick cases, snuff boxes, etuis etc. Paper and Japan tea trays, mathematical instruments, pocket books with instruments etc.

And for those times of trouble:

J.L. Joseph, Pawnbroker
May 1820 moves from 4 Church Street, Abbey Green to 12 York Street.

For cheaper goods or to sell in times of need, also:

Auctioneers

Abraham Nonmus, at Nonmus Auction Rooms, New Bond Street
Personal address 20 Green Street. In November 1813 he also commenced the business of pawnbroker.

Mr. Evill, Great Rooms 18 Milsom Street

Mr. Stafford, auctioneer and upholsterer, paper hanging.
20 Milsom Street new auction rooms in 1816.

C. Pritchard auctioneer and upholsterer
12 Westgate St.

Some auctioneers were also upholsterers and decorators; there were also others to decorate the newly-occupied rooms taken for the season.

John Stafford's Upholstery Warehouse

John Stafford was also an auctioneer and was in no. 20 Milsom Street from 1816.
1818 sells Crease's Washable Paper hangings, which may be washed with soap and water.
Body grounds from 4d per yard and upwards
Satin grounds 11d a yard.

Baily's Upholstry and Cabinet Rooms

Benjamin Baily, Nos. 6 and 7 Bath Street
From March 1816 the widow Eliza Baily continues the business in no. Street, selling furniture, carpets and paper hangings, very good second-hand furniture too. Draper and other bedlinen.
In December 1820 Eliza Baily carries on business in no. 6 Bath Street, having let no. 7 and is looking to reduce the stock to fit in one premises.

Charles Pritchard Upholsterer to his Majesty and auctioneer

In 1810 at no. 8 Westgate Street
Selection of chairs, sofas, chaises longues etc. executed after drawings from the antique.
1811-1816 he is merely given as Westgate Street
No. 12 Westgate Street
1817
1818 has an elegant and fashionable display of ell-wide chintz furnitures.
1819 has a fresh supply of Turkey carpets, fashionable stock of paper hangings and borders and London floor cloths.
1820 had fresh imported Turkey carpets, also Turkey stair carpet, 3 feet wide.
Paper hangings and borders, well-seasoned London floor cloths of the best patterns and various widths.
C.P. recommends the patent broom machine for sweeping rooms and carpets without the least dust rising. [first ever sweeping machine patented by James Hume in England, a box containing a brush turned by a pulley.]

G. Tucker Painter and Glazer

In February 1813 Tucker moves from his shop in Orchard Street to a new oil, colour and glass warehouse at 37 Horse-Street. Oils and colours ready prepared for house-painting in general.

D. Russel, China, Glass and Staffordshire

Moves into 9 Bridge Street in 1811 and was certainly still there in 1815
In 1814 he had a sale by auction to restock.
Splendid sets of dinner, supper and desert services, elegant enamelled gold-edge and other sets of tea china, rich pencilled bowls and basins, beautiful chimney ornaments and wax-light figures mounted in ormolu and bronze. Sugar stands, pudding moulds and stands, cream ewers, sandwich sets etc.
Jugs etc for chambers
Assortment of Brosely Nottinghamshire and other brown ware.
Glass: cut-glass trifle dishes and stands, decanters and bottles, salts and mustards, jugs, sugars, hyacinth glasses [for growing hyacinth bulbs], lamp glass, smelling bottles etc.

Random other shops

Jonathan Salter, Lyncombe Hill Nurseries

In 1812 in Argyle Street; nurseryman, florist and seedsman to her Majesty Queen Charlotte
Dutch Roots, Hyacinth and Narcissus [for the hyacinth glass from D. Russel], sweet-scented tulips, double and single jonquils
Best prize pinks
In 1812, the new geranium, Geranium Scitamina from 3/- to £1, around which there was a scandal over who created it, who threw out his creation and who subsequently profited from it. Nowadays it is Geranium zingiberales, or ginger-scented geranium
Pelargonium graveolis, a rose-scented geranium from South Africa in 1774
Other geraniums
Vegetable seed warranted good
Flower seeds and everything in the flower way.
In 1820 at Wells Road Nursery near Devonshire Buildings, 14 the Abbey Churchyard and 15 Cheap Street; has just received from Italy a large assortment of tube roses.
A treatise on the flower garden by J Salter 3/- to be had in his shop.

Dealy's paper and stationary warehouse

No 3 Westgate Street, old established.
In 1816 M. and E. Dealy are successors to their late father, Cornelius Dealy
1818 Still present at this address.

Henry Gye and son, writing papers of every description

1810 printing books of sermons also mentioned as a stationer.
1811 also sold tickets for the theatre.
1812 selling also blacking by Day and Martin [as is Cruttwell the perfumer] at 1/6d per bottle
In 1815 -1820 at 13 Market Place
Wove and laid, 1/- per quire

Fine Bath hot-prest post stamped 11d/quire
Bath vellum 11d/quire, 12/- per ream; gilt edged 11d /quire, 13/- /ream
Superior ditto 1/- /quire, 19/- /ream; gilt edged 1/2d/quire, £1/1/- /quire
Superfine Bath vellum stamped 1/2 per quire, £1/2/- per ream
Gilt edged 1/4d per quire, £1/5/- per ream
Black edged 1/2d per quire, £1/1/- per ream
Good yellow wove post 6d per quire, 10/- per ream
Foolscap paper 1/1d per quire, £1 per ream
Superfine foolscap 1/6d per quire, £1/8/6d per ream
Best vellum note, 4d/quire, 6/- /ream, 6d/quire & 9/6d/ream black or gilt.

Almanacks, printing, patent pills, account books of various ruling.
In 1818 selling attornies' papers of various qualities, ladies' curling papers 6d/quire, 9/- /ream , large curling papers 9d/quire 14/-/ream
Cartridge, drawing, brown, whited brown, tissue and all other papers.
In 1819 advertises Morrell's improved and warranted black lead pencils for engineering and outlining, H, HB, S, BB, M.
In 1820 Henry Gye is calling himself 'Stationer' and is also licenced to sell London Genuine Tea.

Stationers seem to have carried random other goods as well like nostrums, or locally printed books.

Confectioners

Confectioners also often had tea-shops where one might drink tea and partake of cakes, ices and so on, after the manner of Gunter's in London.

S. Flint, later, from 1818 Fisk and Fortt, successors to S. Flint.
Confectioners, 39 Gay Streeet. Also no. 18 Walcot Buildings. They sold out in August 1820.

1811 Mr. Bedford's Confectioners, Northumberland Place

Sally Lunn's 4 North Parade Passage

Sally Lunn's shop, photo S. Waldock

Sally Lunn's shop is the oldest house in Bath, built in c1482 though the lowest floor level dates to the reconstruction of the Abbey after a fire in 1137; it was originally part of the abbey range.
The famous buns are part cake, part bread, part brioche, rich with cream and eggs, and are trencher bread still popular when first Sally, supposedly a Hugenot refugee in the 1680s, started making them there. Trencher bread takes its flavor from whatever is served on top. Half a bun with a topping is a full meal.

1812 the premises of 6 Bridge Street sold including moulds, ice cans, etc – the premises has an Ice House, oven, hot-stoves and stew holes for a confectioner and pastry cook.

Mrs. Mollands, Milsom Street
In 1810 she prepared the gala supper for the Harmonic society. In May 1813 she died at an advanced age.

1811 J. Tulley, late cook at Molland's
Started his own shop in the premises formerly run by Mr. Rose, confectioner, no. 3 Argyle Street where he will carry on that business with cook and pastry cook.

John Fricker cook and confectioner
In York Street until April 1813 when he moves to Kingston Buildings. Here in addition to his other wares he has fitted up a commodious soup room where the London and Bath papers may also be found for the use of any eating there.

Grocers

John Gibbons, Tea Dealer, Grocer and wax chander, 18 High Street.for your candles and a good cup of tea.

Evans, Grocer, tea dealer etc
Walcot Street

T. Cook, from Mr. Evans, Walcot St
Moved into the shop of Mr. Baylis near the turnpike in Claverton Street in November 1811.

Milsom Place, Milsom Street. Photo S. Waldock

Markets
The principal market days are Wednesday and Saturday, and they are plentifully supplied with every kind of provision. Fresh butter is brought in from the country every morning.
Fish markets
Monday, Wednesday and Friday. These are thought to excel those of any inland town in the kingdom, as well as in the goodness and quantity of sea fish and fresh fish from the River Avon.

So, if you have a toothache from all that confectionary, or break your reading glasses or catch a cold, you need…

The Medical Profession

Physicians, listed in 1807
* Fellow of the Royal Society + Royal College of Physicians
^ Members of the London Corporation of surgeons

Dr Harrington, 4 Northumberland Buildings
Dr. Falconer, 29 Circus, *+
Dr. Lee, 2, Seymour St *+
Dr. Parry, 27 Circus+
G.G. Brwon, Mill [Fellow of Royal Col. Physicians, Edin]
27 Marlborough Buildings
Dr. Moodie, 8 Galloway Buildings
Dr. Gibbs, FRS Circus
Dr. Gillum, 7 Axford's Buildings
Dr. Crawfor, 41 Rivers Street *
Dr. Davis 15 Pierrepoint St
Dr. Fellowes [physician to the Regent] Axford Buildings
Dr. Birkit, 3 Trim St
Dr. Haygarth, 15 Crescent
Dr. Merry, 10 Fountain Buildings
Dr. Robertson, 14 Paragon Buildings
Dr. Murray, 12 Bladud's Buildings
Dr. Langworthy, 43 New King St
Dr. Broderin, FRTC, 6 Green Park Buildings
Dr. Wilson, FRTC 6 Bladud's Buildings
Dr. Hayward, 3 Upper Church St
Dr. Steward, 13 Axford's Buildings
Dr. Boisragon Green Park Buildings
Dr. Sherwin, Chandos Place.

Mr. Phillott, 30 Milsom Street
Mr. North, 14 Queen St ^
Mr. Creaser, Gay St ^
Mr. Norman, New King Street
Dr. Perry, 6 Queen Square
Dr. Day, 5 Westgate Buildings

Dr. Goldstone, Northumberland buildings ^
Dr. Grant, also apothecary, 7 Edgar Buildings
Mr. Cam, 6 Wood St
Mr. Tudor, Army surgeon and surgeon extra to the Princess of Wales, Gay St.^
Mr. T.W. Cruttwell, St James' Street
Mr. Watkins, also apothecary, Alfred St
Mr. Edwards, Walcot
Mr. G. Kitson, 4 Belmont

Dr. Dunn, Oculist, Member of the Royal College of Surgeons

In 1810 at 3 Abbey Green
For all cases of blindness, deafness, cancer etc
Especially successful with all eye disorders, giddiness, convulsions and nervous disorders.
A huge list of things he can cure.

Mr. Whatford, Surgeon
In 1818 at Chandos House Bath
Diseases of the eyes, deafness and dentistry
The poor attended gratis every morning 8am-10am.

Dr. Muttlebury 1820

Charles Henry Parry, MD, FRS etc

Physician to Bath General and Casualty Hospital and the Puerperal Charity
1818-1820

Isaac Wilson, Dentist
In 1816 at 13 Paragon buildings
Constructor of artificial teeth

Dentists
Mr. Sigmond, surgeon dentist, York Buildings
Mr. Goldstone, Northumberland Buildings
Mr. Breuer, Broad Street
Mr. Shew, surgeon Dentist, 12, Belmont Row
Mr. Parkinson Gay Street.

Jo. Abraham, optician

From 1810-1820 at 8 Bartlett Street, near the Upper Rooms.
Makes spectacles of all kinds, and also all kinds of optical toys and instruments, as well as other precision instruments like barometers. Will accept part payment in optical instruments.
In 1813 took out advertisement that someone was impersonating him.
In 1819 he is now Optician to his Royal Highness the Duke of Gloucester and His Grace the Duke of Wellington.
From 1805 - 1815 J. Cole Chiropodist to Her Royal Highness, the Duchess of York. No. 5 Abbey Green. Has a peculiar method of extracting corns, and particularly the removal of nails sunk into the toes is allowed the safest mode ever adopted.
By 1816 it is Miss H. Cole, Chiropodist, who has taken over from her late father as a Ladies Only Chiropodist.
Having attended many Ladies of the first distinction and numerous others. Those afflicted with corns, bunions, nails sunk into the quick and other painful conditions to the feet and hands may expect complete satisfaction. Still at 5 Abbey Green near the Post-Office.
The Chiropodial Lotion or Chilblain Wash prepared by H. Cole and by her alone and sold at 5 Abbey Green and by appointment at the Union Bazaar in Union Street in bottles at 3/6d each. It heals rapidly and cures effectively the most inveterate kides or chilblains, whether on the hands or feet, and immediately allays the most painful inflammation occasioned by the disorder. Prevents further attacks.

Chapter Four: The Inhabitants of Milsom Street

Whilst researching the shopping, I was coming across Milsom Street quite a lot, and it is mentioned in a sufficiency of novels that I became interested in who lived there and for how long.

Built in 1762, by Thomas Lightholder, Milsom Street is mentioned in most novels about Bath, as a centre for shopping for fabrics, jewellery and clothes. As seen in the list of shops, it was not the exclusive centre of shopping, but certainly it contained many shops. The other main shopping streets were George Street, New Bond Street, Old Bond Street and Bath Street. Originally Milsom Gardens, it was leased by Chas. Milsom to the City to 'Build a Street 53 feet wide from House to House' leased for 99 years. At 4/- for every foot of front. It was originally intended as private dwelling with the exception of Stockley's Bank, but shops were gradually allowed until it became one of the most famous shopping streets in Europe.

Milsom Street is an amazing street. It contains buildings which are detached, and others which are terraced. But those which are terraced are grand terraces, like Somerset Buildings, 37-42. Grand frontages with columns, bowed centres and in-your-face Palladian architechture turns a block of five houses into something which would not be out of place as the residence of an earl, if only placed into a country setting, not on the street.

Numbering of Milsom Street is also not as we are used to; even and odd do not denote the side of the street. Instead, the numbering starts with no. 1 on the west side of the street at the northern end – where a number of roads like Old Bond Street start – and numbers up the western side to no. 23 on the corner of George Street. Immediately opposite no. 23, numbering recommences with no. 24 and runs down to no. 47, opposite no. 1.

The buildings are, on the whole, 4 storeys, with basement as well, and often double-bayed. Many of them are broken up into multiple occupancy, typically with shops and the rooms behind them on the ground floor, and residences or boarding houses above. Most boarding houses offer 'rooms for gentlemen or families'; single ladies rarely mentioned, only by the Misses Kyan of no. 42

Note; there were supposed to be 5 confectioners in Milsom Street including Mrs. Molland, mentioned by Jane Austen, who died at her lodgings at an advanced age in 1813. She was named as a pastry cook and confectioner of Milsom Street.

Those houses whose occupancy I have not been able to trace may be presumed to be private dwellings or boarding houses which advertised by word of mouth rather than through the newspapers. Where I have a lodging-house in 1807 I cannot prove how long it was held.

West Side

1 In April 1816 White's Pianoforte and Music Warehouse (also on 5 George Street)
Speculated: the un-numbered Music Warehouse of Mr. William Loder, band-leader and violin maestro of the Theatre-Royal, who has a music warehouse in Milsom Street from 1815. [it is opposite his private dwelling]
Numbers 2-22 are a terrace named Portland Place

2 May be a bank; Loder's Music Warehouse is 'Next door to the bank'

3 Mr. Godwin, lodging house [1807]

4 Premises called Civet-Cat, occupied by a Mr. Gould, a perfumer and hair cutter, who also provided wigs and hair pieces. It is to Mr. Gould that one requests information on letting a cottage with 5 acres on the Kennet and Avon, 3 miles from Bath, which a daily packet boat service to and from the city. Did he own it?
1812, William Gould, Perfumer, is a bankrupt.
A Miss Ann Gould of Milsom street [his daughter?] married the

Rev. John Williams of Chester at St George's Hanover square London, on Thursday 6th August 1818.
1820 Mrs. Gould is still trading.

5 Mr. Partridge, lodging house [1807]

6 Mrs. Jarman, lodging house [1807]

7 1794-1804, owner-occupier J. James, fine muslins and table linen. He moved and let the premises.
Until March 1817 Thos. Sheppherd and Jas. Trinder, woollen drapers, hatters and undertakers; in March 1817, they dissolve the partnership and Thomas Sheppherd continues alone. Also Mr. Sheppard kept a lodging house; he had been there in 1807 with the lodgings.

8 Leased for 99 years in summer 1765; the occupant dies age 79 in 1813, the lease being for sale for £300, plus yearly ground rent £4/6/-. There was a tenant-at-will Mr. John Howell who paid the ground rent and £130 a year rent. He also kept a lodging house.

9 1803 E. Sandys, child-bed and ready-made linen warehouse. In Feb 1817 the leasehold dwelling house and shop were for sale. Miss Sandys ran a lodging house.

10 Jan 1801 sold by auction. The centre house of Portland Place. By 1811 Bally and Bartrum, auctioneers, also letting-agents, ie doing the job we should now call estate agents. Mr. Bally also kept a public library with reading rooms. Still there in 1820. November 1820, the house was being let, furnished, by the year or less; Bally & Bartrum were still operating out of their 'Great Rooms' there which is now numbered 'number 5, Central House, Portland Place'.

11 Mr. J. Bally Lodging house 1807.

12 Mr. Henry Bowen until 1806 when the premises was sold to cover his bankruptcy. In 1807 he was still there, running a lodging house.
1807 Lockwood and Porter linen draper, leave May 1812.
1815-1820 Public Library, C. Duffield Bookseller and publisher.
Also from Nov. 1816 Mr. Kay, cutler, jeweller and plated goods.

13 Unknown until the 1820s when it became Jolly's Bazaar, and is still Jolly's department store to this day, under the House of Fraser.

14 In 1812 it was a lodging house, to be let; the shop frontage and shop separate. Presumably Mrs. Faulkener mentioned 1807
1813 J. Earl of the North Parade, woollen-draper, tailor etc has entered the premises with an assortment of hats from London,

hosiery and gloves etc, fancy goods, beaver hats for ladies as well, gentlemen's dress hats, regulation caps, liveries etc, funerals furnished.

15 Mr. Cuff, Chemist and perfumer and in 1807 he was also running a lodging house. He was still there in 1820.

16 Up to 1809 P. Nonnet, Jewellery, perfumery, wigs etc Tunbridge-ware, selling up stock May 1809 to move to London. Mr. Reeves was running a lodging house 1807.

17 Mr. Woodroffe, lodging house 1807

18 Mr. William Evill, auctioneer, upholsterer, appraiser, undertaker and letting office.
Also 1815 Mr. Kay, auctioneer.
Also 1816-1818 at least William Bell, Upholsterer.

19 1801 Charles Smith Bookseller and Lodging House.
1804 Mrs. Mary Smith, relict of Chas. Smith, with her brother Henry Godwin Bookseller and stationer.
1808 H. Godwin moves out with his business to Public Library to No. 43. Did Mary die?
1816 Mrs. Vezey moves from Bath St.; Haberdashery. Gives up business 1820
From Feb 1820 Abraham and Levy, jewellery.

20 From January1816 new auction rooms, Mr. Stafford, auctioneer, upholsterer, paper hanging. Still there in 1820

21 Sold in April 1807. Probably lodging houses in upper floors; given as address of Mr. Elliston, actor, first staying temporarily in 1811 and then permanently.
1811 [probably the ground floor] Mr. Webb auctioneer [possibly later in partnership with Mr. English]. Upholstery, carpets, paper hangings.
1818 Messrs English, English and Becks, Auctioneers, same 1820.

22 Mr. Ellen Lodging house 1807.

23 Prior to 1795 E. Mackinnon held a perfumery here, but sold out on quitting the business. Mrs. Molland lodging house 1807.
Russel and Brookman, silks, velvets, gloves etc; dissolve partnership July 1811.
November 1811 bought by Mr. Basnett, Jeweller and Goldsmith, formerly of Bond Street.
After alterations, Oct 1819 shop bought S&J Martin, jeweller, silversmith and watchmaker, conducting business on the first floor until alterations on the ground floor are to their satisfaction.

East Side

24 1807 Mr. Marshall lodging house
Oct 1811 Peter Ardenond moves in from Abbey Churchyard. Woollen Draper, Tailor, Habit Maker. Apartment to be let at will. Moves out to the Colonnade House, 9, Bath St., October 1817, to set up a bazaar. With George Towson late of North Parade, hatter, glover and man's mercer. Funerals furnished.
Unknown time, Mr. Denie – presumably 1817-1820
1820 Thomas Flaherty, successor to Mr. Denie, Woollen Draper, Habit maker, Tailor, second premises; also uses no. 27.
Possesses baroque details not seen on other buildings.

25 Owned by 'a lady' who died early 1812
By December 1812 bought by Terry and Dutton chemists and druggists who have every medicine and dispense prescriptions

26 Unknown

27 1807 Mr. Evans Lodging house.
From Dec 1812 Mrs. R. Spornberg, Milliner, mantua-maker until June 1819.
1819 Thos. Flaherty, see no. 24

28 1807 Mrs. Sharp, lodging house.
Dec 1811 Mr. Basnett first advertises, is certainly there 1813; goldsmith and jeweller, continuing from his father.
Also July 1818 Mr. Holbrook selling large furniture removing to Catherine place – probably in second occupancy with Mr. Basnett?

29 1805-1811 S.N. Riviere [moved in from no. 32] Jeweller also Mr. Bond, with lodging house.

30 1807 Mr. Phillot, physician.
1813 J Spreat perfumer bankrupt, formerly at the Rocking Horse and Golden Fleece 7 George St.; in 1815 operating as perfumier here again under the sign of the Rocking Horse and Golden Fleece.
Jan 1818 J Spreat, perfumer, toy and fancy goods, Jeweller
In June 1816 address of Miss Thomas who runs a dancing academy. She leaves January 1820.

31 From Nov. 1808 Mme Simeon, French Laces, bankrupt Jan 1811. Later 1811 C. Simeon, French Laces [her son?]

32 1801 S. N. Riviere Jeweller [of 63 Bond Street London] until 1805 when moves to no. 29 q.v.
1807 Mrs. Adams, lodging house.

1820 the whole house with exception of two parlours to be let.

33 1801 Frederick Albrecht, stays, habit and garter-maker to Her Highness Duchess of York. Moved from 7 George St.
Mrs. Albrecht to help the ladies. Also a lodging house.
1819 R Thompson's Warehouse pharmacy – lavender water, isinglass, powdered ginger, ginger beer powder etc also prescriptions.

34 Jan 1805 -1810 [at least] E & A Laing, Millinery, Haberdashery, dresses and pelisses.

35 Prior to 1793 Mrs. Prynn, private occupier; sold June 1803
1815 occupied by Mr. Fasana who was running a lodging house in 1807.

36 1811-1815 at least, Mr. Fasana, repository of arts, silver, plated goods, oil paintings etc. As part of his repository of arts, Mr. Mackie, teaching ladies shoe making. 1807, Mrs. Thomas, lodging house.

Numbers 37 - 42 are a terrace called Somerset Buildings. An elegant central bow.

37 1802 Mr. Daniel, Miniature painter
1805 Mr. Andras, booking pleasure boats also 1806
1811 Mrs. M. Langdon moves from Argylle St.; Hosiery, millinery, dresses, haberdashery and Imperial corsets. In 1817 Mrs. Thos or Mrs. John [there is some confusion] Langdon is teaching embroidery and painting on velvet.

38 1807 Mr. Holbrook Lodging house
From June 1819 J&R Spornberg, milliner, mantua-maker; moved from no. 27 which was sold out from under them when the owner went bankrupt.

39

Numbers 39 and 40 were owned by a Mr. W. Glover, sold 1801

40 AKA 'The Centre House'. By 1805 Messers Slack Haberdashery who sold to Mr. W. Crocker in 1816, who was still there in 1820. In 1817, when the whole upper house was let as 'having been and suitable for a boarding house'. [The upper rooms were a boarding house.]
1820 Mesdames Urry and Huffown were keeping a boarding house, successors to Mrs. Bless.

41 AKA Wellington House. May have been sold by Mr. Glover to someone initialled A.B.
1802 Sheffield plate warehouse, mirrors, Japanned goods etc, said to be 'at Glover's'.
1807 Mr. Foreman is running a lodging house.
Up to Oct. 1817 Mr. Charles Foreman, haberdashery and fine French laces. Stock sold, shop let separately to house, the house is very elegant with patent water-closets. See also no. 42
1817 part to let; taken on by Mr. Crocker, drapery, silks, shawls, still there 1820 [shop?]
1818 Mr. Hodgson Auctioneer Wellington House.[House?] Formerly of Kay and Hodgson, 7 Union Street. Also 1818 Lindsey Hewer, lace seller.

42 1801 Miss Wilson, quits premises in May but is there in 1807 with a boarding house.
By 1804 C. Foreman; Hosiery and Gloves also see no. 41
From October 1807 the Misses Kyan's Boarding House, having moved to a larger house from Henrietta Street. Would take ladies or gentlemen with proper references. Purchases boarding house in Cheltenham as well, 1808 and at 19 Circus, Bath 1811 Weymouth 1816, when she is still living at 19 Circus, Bath.
Sept 1810 unexpired lease for sale for 11 ¾ years, rent £136/1-/- per annum.
1810 Mr. and Mrs. Bloss take on boarding house buying 11 ¾ years of lease left @ £136/10/- p.a.; it has been newly papered.

In 1820 a Mr. Brod lived in Somerset Buildings; number unknown.

43 1807 Mr. Marret lodging house
Circulating Library and Reading Room; H. Godwin, bookseller, printer, publisher, moved in1808 after leaving no. 19. [he printed the original of the map of Bath in the front of this book]
In 1811 also lived here J. Randolph, Solicitor.

44 1807 Mesdames Moore & Hale lodging house

45 In 1807 Mr. Godwin is running a lodging house, it is Mr. Loder's private address by 1815 [and separate to his music warehouse]

46 1807 Mr. Bretton Lodging house.
Before 1813 Mr. Bretton; jewellery. Quits business June 1813. There is an arched entranceway to no. 46 which also gives access to the Octagon Chapel. In 1817, a Miss Cranefeldt advertised her

dancing academy opening here.

Octagon Chapel. Not numbered as such.

47 Detached building, massive 4-bay frontage with pillars. Currently a bank and looks as though it was built either to be a bank or some civic building.

A Mrs. Mirvan lived in Milsom Street in 1816- 1818 but I have not tracked down which number.

Looking down Milsom Street. Photo S. Waldock.

The residents of Milsom Street petitioned to be provided with gas lighting in 1818.

In 1817 the following inhabitants of Milsom Street displayed a Crown and the letters C.R. as part of the illuminations to express the joy at the safe arrival of the Queen and Princess Elizabeth.

Mrs. Vezey	Mr. Earl
Messers Crocker	Mr. Evill
Mrs. Langdon	Mr. Duffield

Chapter Five: Available Entertainments

As well as the Upper and Lower Assembly Rooms where balls, concerts and card games may be found, there is the theatre, and music every morning in the New Pump Room. There are also some balls at the Bath City Assembly Guildhall, some concerts at the Sydney Gardens Vauxhall, as well as breakfasts and galas over the summer.

The general Winter Season venue is as follows:

Monday: Ball at the Upper Rooms
Tuesday: Ball at the Lower Rooms & Theatre
Wednesday: Concert at the Upper Rooms
Thursday: Fashionable Ball at the Upper Rooms & Theatre
Friday: Harmonic Society, Theatre occasionally
Saturday: Fashionable night at the Theatre

In Summer there were the races, and galas and concerts and fire works as well as public breakfasts variously at Sydney Garden Vauxhall

Details of the Upper and Lower Rooms and Sydney Gardens will be examined in detail in other sections.

Until 1771, when the Upper Rooms opened, though the Lower or Harrison's [later Kingston] Rooms remained, the former second set of rooms, The Wiltshire Rooms aka Gyde's Rooms, became a warehouse, unable to cope with the competition. [note; both the Lower Rooms and the Wiltshire Rooms were licensed ale houses]. For those interested, Gyde's Room was 86' long, 30' wide and 30' high, with a cove ceiling and a portrait and a bust of Richard Nash esq., and many landscape paintings. There were also antechambers for cards and concerts. Mr. Glyde's nights for balls were Mondays, Wednesdays and Fridays.

Regular entertainments:

Annual foot races are run in July around the hills of Ammerdown.

Concerts of the Harmonic Society and the York-House Catch-Club.
The Harmonic society is under the patronage of the Prince of Wales. The Earl of Leven and Melville is President, and Walsh Porter esq. is Vice President. The society meets every week during the season, when songs,

duets, catches and glees are performed before and after supper. Two entertainments are given every year by the Society to the ladies, consisting of concert, supper and ball. These meetings are usually held at the Lower Assembly rooms, and are attended by the best performers who can perform.
The Catch Club is held at York House every Friday Evening during the season where the members sup together. The third Friday of every month is called a lady's night, when each member has the privilege of giving two tickets to the '*fair ones of his choice*'. On this occasion the meeting is held in the concert room of the New Assembly Rooms. Feltham says "*The Entertainment, however, on these evenings, is merely for the ear, the gentlemen being of the opinion that the ladies can provide occupation for their mouths better elsewhere.*" The men sang to entertain the ladies, who were not expected to join in.

The Pump Room and Baths
The Kingston Pump Room where the hot spring waters might be drunk at £1/11/6d per year, 15/- per quarter or 7/- per month. Dr. Wilkinson's Analysis of the waters is in the press. See chapter on the Pump Room and Baths

Other Gardens:
See end of chapter on Sydney Gardens

This section includes:
Boating
Swimming
Lessons in sundry skills
Lectures
Libraries
Panoramas
Sundry other entertainments

Boating

A boating service of packet and pleasure boats on the Kennet and Avon Canal began on Monday April 6th 1807, from the boat warehouse, North-East side of Sydney Gardens. The coal packets land their coals in the same place, and will receive orders for delivery. However, in 1805, 'The Royal Charlotte Yacht' was a named pleasure boat, with every convenience for dinner [luncheon] and tea parties, hireable privately on Mondays, Wednesday and Fridays. On other days the boat leaves Bath precisely at 10am and returns at 4pm having left Bradford at 2-30 pm . Accommodation on board for Dinner [luncheon] and Tea. State rooms 2/6d, steerage 1/6d.

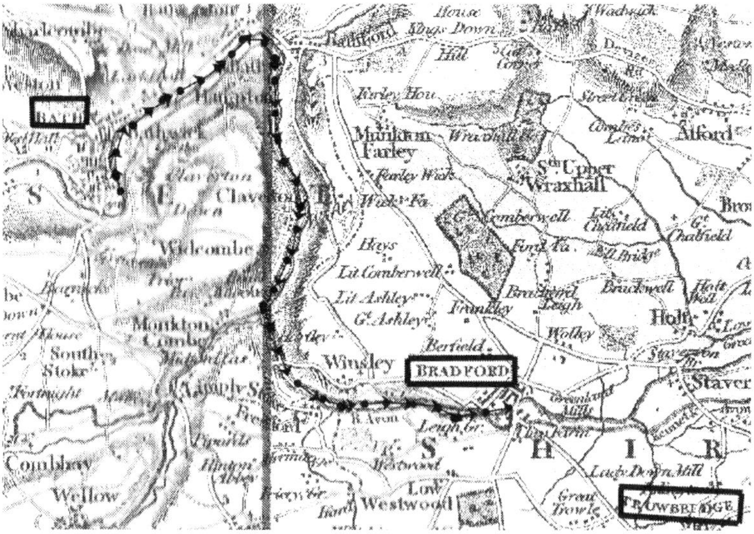

The Trading Packet left Bradford every morning at 9am, and returned from Bath in the evening at 5pm for the conveyance of passengers and parcels. A light, covered cart set off every morning from the George, Trowbridge at 8-30 am for the boat at Bradford, and will return in the evening. On the trading packet a cabin is 1/6d, steerage 1/-
By 1815, 'The Royal Charlotte' was still running, and so was the packet, together with the cart on to Trowbridge.

In 1805-06 one enquired of booking from Mr. Andras in Milsom Street but in 1815 it was from Mr. Bedford in Northumberland Court. Previous to this one might have particulars from the Castle and Bull inn.

One of the features of riverside housing is access to the river, and is given as a selling point. Being able to step onto the pleasure or packet boats as they passed your garden was also a selling point. From Christmas 1810 the Kennet and Avon Canal was completed and formed a means of transport around the region. Boats were often advertised for sale.

Bathing Pool or Pleasure Baths

On Thursday 13th July 1815, a notice in the 'Bath Chronicle and Weekly Gazette' informing the public that a piece of ground near the marl pits had been secured for the purpose of forming pleasure baths with apartments for dressing. 'The object in view is to provide a place in connexion with the River, where those who swim and those who do not will be alike accommodated' which is a roundabout way of saying that it will be shallow enough to be safe. The notice goes on to state that the plan will depend on the first subscriptions, and gentlemen asked to subscribe. A book for subscriptions could be added to at James Evill and sons, Messers Bourne and Austin's, Market Place and the Kingston Pump Room. No money was to be taken until sufficient names had been put forward. This notice was repeated the week after.
Apparently it went ahead with the same speed most public works manage, and the notice on Thursday 24th April 1817 that it would be ready by the 1st of May that year.
The notice released on May 4th 1818 reads:

"THE PLEASURE BATHS
On the banks of the Avon, near Sydney-Gardens
ARE NOW OPEN
THESE BATHS are replete with every accommodation, considerable improvements having been made since last season."

Unfortunately, in August 1818 a lad named Lionel Sampson aged 15 went with two companions to bathe, but it had been emptied [for maintenance?] so though an inexpert swimmer decided to swim in the river. One of his companions tried to save him when he was in trouble and both sank, but the companion managed to get away. A gentleman named Bourne swam towards him with corks, but he had sunk. The Humane Society's drags, poles and boat were at hand and the body was drawn out within ten minutes and the best surgical aid procured, and resuscitation efforts were tried for an hour and a half but in vain.

The only other mention in the news of the Pleasure Baths was an indictment brought against the proprietors in August 1818 for stopping up an ancient footpath in that part of Bathwick designated as the 'Villa Field.'

In 1825 the Pleasure Baths were to be sold by private contract. The advertisement of sale was repeated in June 1826.

A further accident occurred in August 1828, when a Mr. Hooper with Miss Harriet Heath and Miss Ann Norvill took a boat at the Pleasure Baths. This appears to have been on the river, but hired out by the owners of the Bath. The current was faster than they expected and they were thrown over the weirs at Pulteney Bridge, and the boat was upset. Miss Heath grabbed the hatches [of the weir] and remained for a considerable time in this perilous situation until a boat was brought to her rescue, Mr. Hooper clung to the boat, and was also saved, but Miss Norvill 'sunk, to rise no more'. She had just had her 15th birthday. A verdict of accidental death was returned at inquest.
STOP PRESS! The next issue of the Bath Chronicle and Weekly Gazette posted that the boat in which this fatal accident occurred was *not* hired at the Pleasure Baths [though presumably boats could be hired there] and no accident has occurred during the season.

Ladies of course would not swim but might take a boat hired by the bathing pool with their gentlemen escorts.

Lessons in Sundry Skills

Music and Singing

Looking good at soirées in being able to show off accomplishments is important for a young lady hoping to contract a suitable marriage.

1817 Mrs. Ashe's Musical academy at 35 Belvedere.
An academy for musical instruction. Classwork: 1 hour given to each pupil by themselves of which half is tuition in singing with Mrs. Ashe and the remainder on either harp or pianoforte with Miss Ashe.
For 3 months £8/8/- for two lessons a week
For 1 month £2/3/-
Mrs. Ashe gives private lessons as usual at 10/6d each.
Mr. Ashe instructs on flute at 10/6 per lesson. Miss Ashe teaches harp and piano at 1g for four lessons.
The Ashe family performed regularly at the Theatre Royal.

November 1817 Signor Anelli, late tenor of Princess Borghese's private music and attached to the Court of Portugal gives lessons in Italian singing. Applications at Loder's music warehouse Milsom St, or his residence no. 5 Abbey Street.
November 1819 Signor Anelli, professor of music to the King of Portugal purposes to fix his residence here and impart instruction to those ladies and gentlemen who are desirous of attaining an accomplished and elegant style of Italian singing. Teaching over the winter and returns 1820.
Harp-lute and Spanish guitar taught by Mr. Davis, 1 St James St, Abbey Green.

1810 Mr. T. Light teaches Harp-Lute and Apollo Lyre and Pedal Harp No. 4 Green Park Place West. Mr. T. Light is the son of the inventer of the Harp-Lute; still teaching in 1812.

Dancing

A vital skill in order to be well-prepared for the Assemblies; not all young ladies or gentlemen had the advantage of being trained in this social art by a governess or tutor, nor had a visiting dancing master if they went to school.

1810 opens in no 1 [Orange] Grove, January 17th, Mr. Webster's academy for dance. Teaching days Wednesday and Friday mornings, for ladies from 10am to noon, for gentlemen from noon to 2pm. Evening academy on the same days 8pm to 10pm for those who cannot attend in the morning.
Nov. 1810, by popular request, for private practise on Wednesday and Friday evenings from 8pm to 10 pm during the winter session. The morning academy as usual.
Sept 1811 open Wednesday and Friday 11am to 2pm, evening academy opening October 2nd. Boarding Schools attended. Teaching the most fashionable style of Scotch[sic] Irish and Cotillion steps, waltzes [3-step country dances] and dancing in general.
December 1812 will keep academy open during the vacation.
Terms for the vacation 1g
Private tuition, for one lady or gentleman for 4 lessons of one hour each 1g
In families where there is more than one, 3 lessons for 1g
Academy terms per quarter, no entrance, £1/11/6d. Ladies, Thursday and Saturday mornings 11am-2pm, gentlemen Wednesday and Friday mornings ditto.
1813 term recommences Wednesday July 28th
1814 term commences 2nd August Tuesday. Same days, same time. December 1814 address given as Orange Grove for first time [presumably a local name change?] An academy during vacation, and the evening academy on Wednesdays and Fridays from 8pm-10pm
December 1815 academy open during vacation from noon - 2pm for young people holidaying in Bath.
Decamber 1819 opening during the vacation as usual, quadrilles and waltzing etc.
1820 the same.

Jan 1811 Dancing taught by Mr. Ashley, late apprentice and assistant to Mr. Metralcourt [retiring from Bath]. Ladies and gentlemen may take private lessons either at their own homes or at no. 11 Old Bond Street. Academy days, Tuesday and Saturday. Schools attended.
Dec 1815 still there.

January 1811 Mr. Dowland is succeeding Mr. Metralcourt in that worthy's dancing academy no. 8 St Andrew's Terrace.

January 1815 Mr. E Second has removed his dancing academy from Abbey Street to the large room lately occupied by Mr. Metralcourt in St Andrew's Terrace near the Upper Assembly rooms
Mr. Metralcourt's retiral seems to have led to a bit of a dogfight between dancing masters.

Miss D.C. Rundall ran a dancing academy for years and in June 1816 sold the concern to Miss Thomas of 30 Milsom Street, a former pupil of Mrs. Elliston and Miss Rundall and M. D'Egville.
1820 Miss Thomas has the latest French dances, and has moved from Milsom Street to 13 Gay Street.

Dec 1814 M. Barrée, professor of dancing and ballet-master late of the Opera House, Paris and the Opera House, London assisted by Mlle Barrée and M. Barrée's son. Lessons given in Bath, Bristol and Clifton. Apply no. 6 George Street or by post to his residence, Carlton Place, Tiverton, Lower Bristol Road, nr Bath.
1817 specifies 3 lessons a week, Mondays, Thursdays and Saturdays, one of those days for Quadrilles and Waltzing only. Young Gentlemen admitted from 10am to noon, young ladies from noon until 3pm. Private lessons continue as usual with assistance from his son and from Mlle Barrée his daughter.

1817 Miss Percival's Dancing Academy 5 Trim Street.
For young ladies. Young children under 12, boys admitted. Schools attended.

1817 October, opened Miss Cranefeldt's dancing academy, 46 Milsom St.

The Misses Giroux have a dancing academy for children at 14 George Street.

Painting and Crafts

Velvet Painting

August 1813 Miss Viner has the honour of announcing to ladies that she continues [so presumably the lesson was available before] to give lessons in the elegant and highly fashionable art of flower and fruit painting, on paper and velvet. The latter is after Mr. Town's approved method. Miss V. Recommends her very superior liquid velvet colors, which for softness, richness and brilliancy she feels confident need only a trial to ensure them a preference, also her velvet and brushes. NB, borderings for Ladies' Dresses, bell ropes and all kinds of Ornamental Decorations in Velvet Painting for Drawing Rooms executed to order.
No 2 Burton Street. Four lessons for one guinea.
In May 1815 she moves to 3 New Bond Street.
In January 1817 she is to be found at 3 Wood Street, Queen Square.

Mrs. Langdon, embroidery and later Paintings on Velvet.

October 1811 she is instructing ladies in embroidery and fancy work, supplying every material for that purpose.
Dec 1817; Variously given as Mrs. Thos. Langdon and Mrs. John Langdon, giving lessons to Princess Elizabeth and continuing to instruct ladies in every New and Fashionable work at her house, 37 Milsom Street where one may also see her superb embroideries.

In 1818 Mrs. and Miss Warner's boarding school for young ladies, at Dursley, Goucester, was offering painting on velvet for 4g/year and an entrance of 10/6d. Plainly it was very fashionable.

J. West, Landscape Painter and Drawing Master North Parade

Jan 1811 publishes a set of progressive lessons in imitation of chalk, selling for 1g the set, containing 6 numbers, 36 plates. There from at least 1807.

Dec 1814 Academy of Painting

Mr. Thomas Barker purposes opening his gallery on Sion Hill as an academy of painting on Wednesday 8th February 1815 where the higher principles of art will be taught under his own immediate superintendence and direction. The Barkers were there from 1807 at least. Mr. Thomas

Barker on Sion Hill, B. Barker Bathwick St, J Barker, Miles Buildings.

February 1814 Mr. J.A. Sanders, landscape painter and professor of the science of perspective etc

Gives lessons in drawing in black-lead pencil and painting in oil colours etc. 19 Kingsmead Street Bath and Clifton Place, Clifton. Ladies and Gentlemen's schools attended. In 1807 in Green Park buildings.

1811-1815 The Repository of Arts 36 Milsom Street

Mr. Mackie teaches shoe making to ladies.

The new and fashionable art of purse-making

Taught before and during 1818 by Miss Spreat of 30 Milsom Street to ladies. [Miss Spreat is the daughter of J. Spreat of The Rocking Horse and Golden Fleece shop of perfumes, toys and fancy work.]

Foreign Languages

November 1811 Mr. Cherubini of Rome will instruct pupils in Italian; those who know French will receive their instructions in French. He will give lessons at his house on Mondays and Thursdays at 6-00 pm, at two guineas the quarter, the first to be beforehand, and a guinea entrance. 7 Queen Street, enquire within or at any of the libraries. He teaches over the winter.

November 1812 he is at 2 Broad Street.

In October 1814 he has moved back to 7 Queen Street, teaching Wednesday and Saturday at 6pm at 3g per quarter.

After the 1815 spring session, Mr. Cherubini was afflicted by a long illness and returns to teaching in November 1817 where he attends pupils in their own houses.

January 1817 M. La Bigne instructs in the French language in his clients' own homes, 6 lessons 1g.

His French Academy 17 Beauford Square opens on the 23rd January for gentlemen, 3 days a week, Wednesday, Friday, Saturday. The first lesson from 7-30 am to 9-30 am, and from 6pm to 9pm in the evening.

One lesson per week, 1g per quarter

Two lessons per week £1/11/6d [1 ½ g]
Three lessons per week £2/2/- [2g]
January 1818 Monsieur de la Bigne continues to give lessons in the French language, schools also attended. No. 2 New King Street.
October 1820 gives a morning class for ladies at his residence, now 4 Harington Place, Queen Square on Mondays and Thursdays from 10am to 12 noon and an evening class for gentlemen on the same days from 7pm to 9pm.

January 1818 Signor Angelini of Rome gives advanced lessons in French and Italian, commencing Monday Feb 2nd 1818 for one hour, two shillings per session. No. 2 Chandos Buildings.

November 1817 French Academy teaching grammar, pronunciation etc using the primitive sounds of the consonants. Mrs. Dourlen's Academy, no. 2 Chandos Buildings

Nov 1817 Rev. S. Lyon teaches Hebrew at his academy 7 York Street every Monday, Wednesday and Friday from 10-00 am to noon, 24 lessons.

Other

February 1812, Mr. Jones, scientific reformer of illegible writing [in eight lessons only] will teach penmanship, applicable to persons from 10 to 70 years of age. 7 Queen Street.

1810 Mr. George Viner instructs young ladies in writing and arithmetic from 12 noon until 1pm at his academy for young gentlemen no. 15 Green Street.

1816 Dr. Wilkinson purposes to open a Chemical Institution on Tuesday November 5th for instructing pupils in the mode of analysing soils, minerals and mineral waters. The laboratory is provided with every necessary apparatus and each pupil will have an opportunity of performing a great number of Chemical Experiments. The instruction will be given every Tuesday and Thursday from 1pm to 3 pm. 2g per month.

1811-1820 W. Stevenson, stable keeper and purveyor to his Royal Highness the Duke of York, - riding school and livery stable at the top of Russell Street. With Mr. Smith as a riding master, to instruct ladies and gentlemen in the polite art of riding gracefully and properly managing their horses.
Half-broke horses trained for every purpose. Families supplied with corn, hay and straw of the best quality on moderate terms.
As a livery stable one might stable one's mount there, hire a horse or purchase any put up for sale through the stable.
October 1816 the services of Mr. Munn to superintend the school.
January 1820, Mr. Stevenson died after a severe illness. The school is still named Stevenson's Riding School in November.
Has a riding-house for indoor exercise in inclement weather.

1818 mention of Mr. Meade's riding school.
1820 purchases riding school premises Upper Bristol Road and moves there with his school. Has a riding house for exercise in inclement weather.

Lectures

1810 Dr. Wilkinson on Experimental philosophy, 9th March at 12 noon a series of 12 weekly lectures on electricity, galvanism, pneumatics, hydraulics, light and colours, magnetism, mechanics, geography and astronomy. Subscription to the course [1g?] single lectures 2/6d; tickets at Dr. W's house Kingston Buildings. Private instructions on any of the subjects of Natural Philosophy and Chemistry
Kingston Buildings, entrance in Church Street.

30th April 1810 7pm lecture on Education at the theatre, by Mr. Lancaster. Tickets; Boxes 3/-, pit 2/- and gallery 1/-

1810 Monday December 31st for 12 weeks every Monday and Friday at 1pm, Dr. Wilkinson on Atmosphere, Electricity, Galvanism [medically employed] etc. 2/6d per lecture or 12 transferrable tickets £1/1/-

1811 Thursday May 23rd, 1pm Dr. Wilkinson will deliver a lecture on the construction and economy of the hoof of a horse. All prepared by Mr. Clarke whose ill health prevents him from delivering the lecture himself. At the Lower Rooms, tickets 3/-

1811 Monday 25th and Friday 29th November at 1pm, two lectures on galvanism by Dr. Wilkinson. On the following Wednesday, 4th December, a lecture on the Bath Waters. Admission 3/-. Lecture room in Church St, adjoining Kingston Baths.

1813 Wednesday April 21st, Friday April 23rd and Monday April 26th on the principles of electricity by Dr. Wilkinson, held at the Lower Rooms. Transferable tickets for the course, 10/-, single lectures 4/-.

1813 Friday morning at noon 15th January at the Lower Rooms. Commencing a course of 3 lectures by Mr. Lloyd on Astronomy beginning with the diastroiodon or grand transparent orrery. 3 lectures, 10/6d, non subscribers 5/- each lecture. Subscriptions received at Meyler's library where may be had an epitome of the course with a

particular account of the comet of 1811, price 1/-; with plates 1/6d. Following lectures Friday 22nd and Friday 29th January at noon.
Repeated 2 evenings and one morning, Fri 22nd and Sat 23rd January at 7pm and Mon 26th at 12 noon.

1814 a series of 12 lectures by Dr. Wilkinson at the pump room, 12 tickets £1/4/-, 6 tickets 15/-, admission to each lecture 3/-

1814 Dr. Wilkinson regrets that the lectures on Tue 12th and Fri 15th April are unavoidably postponed to Wed 20th and Fri 22nd of the month at 7pm when he will deliver two lectures on electricity with experiments.

1814 commencing Wedesday 2nd November at 1pm a course of 26 lectures by Mr. Cherubini on the most admired Italian authors ancient and modern, and every succeeding Wednesday at the same time at his apartments no 7 Queen Street, corner of Quiet Street. Subscriber to 26 transferable tickets £1/11/6d, non subscribers for each lecture 2/-; 2 subscribers, tickets non-transferable £2/2/-; one subscriber non-transferable £1/5/-

1814 Dr. Wilkinson at the Pump Room commences a course of 10 lectures on Monday December 5th at 7pm on the usual subjects of electricity, galvanism, hydraulics, pneumatics etc.
10 transferable tickets £1/4/-. Single ticket 5/-

1815 Dr. Wilkinson commences a course of 8 lectures on electricity, galvanism, optics, astronomy, pneumatics and hydrostatics at his own home in Kingston Buildings every Monday, Wednesday and Friday commencing Monday 1pm February 20th. 8 transferable tickets £1/2/-, single lecture 3/6d

1815 Sat 20th, Mon 22nd and Tue 23rd May commencing 12 noon, Mr. Lloyd will give Astronomical lectures with his orrery in the Lower Rooms.
3 lectures 10/6d, tickets transferable, non-subscribers 5/- per lecture: repeated on Thur 25th, Fri 26th and Sat 27th May in the evening at 7pm.

1816 at Kingston Lecture Rooms on Friday 19th January and Monday 22nd January at 1pm, Dr. Wilkinson's lectures on electricity. Wednesday 24th and Friday 26th January the lectures will be on galvanism. Entrance 5/-

1816 series of 4 lectures on the principles of perspective and their applications in drawing. Commencing Tuesday January 23rd at 1pm at Dr. Wilkinson's lecture rooms, Kingston Buildings, by Mr. G. Ward, F.S.A. using a large apparatus with models and drawings. Tickets 1g for the course. The following lectures will be on the following Thursday, Saturday and Monday mornings [at 1pm.]

1816 Dr. Wilkinson at the Kingston Lecture room commencing Wednesday 6th March at 1pm a course of 10 lectures on the more interesting parts of chemistry arranged for those whos avocations may not have admitted any attention to these pursuits; illustrated with experiments. Transferable tickes £1/1/-, single lectures, 3/-
Delivered every Wednesday and Friday at the same hour. Free to members of the Bath Philosophical and Literary society.

1816 Mr. Robert Bakewell, mineralogical surveyor will commence a course of lectures on Monday 18th March in the Kingston Lecture Room. The course will consist of 7 lectures each illustrated by drawings, chemical experiments and mineral specimens. The lectures will introduce the natural history of the Earth and its mineral production, the arrangement, structure and succession of rocks and strata, the formation of metallic veins and other mineral repositories; the organic remains of unknown animals found in the upper strata, the phenomenon of earthquakes, volcanoes and meteoric stones; the laws of crystallisation etc. A more particular view of the geology of England made from Mr. Bakewell's observation. Tickets for the course £1/1/-, a family ticket admitting one gentleman and his wife or daughter £1/11/6d.

1816 Dr. Wilkinson purposes to open a Chemical Institution – see lessons.

1816 Dr. Wilkinson commenced a course of 10 lectures in optics, astronomy and other interesting branches of experimental philosophy commencing Wednesday November 13th at 1pm. Tickets for the course

1g, single admission, 3/-; lectures to be delivered every Wednesday and Friday.

1816 Lectures on Geology and Mineralogy, Dr. W.H. Gilby of Clifton, will give a course of 9 lectures at the rooms of the Bath Literary and Philosophical Society. The first on Monday the 23rd of December at 1pm and the course will be continued 3 days every week on Mondays, Wednesday and Fridays. Wednesday 25th being Christmas Day, the second lecture will take place on Thursday 26th December. Tickets 1g each with a syllabus of the course.

1817 Friday February 14th at 2pm commencing a course of 7 lectures on history as connected with the most celebrated architectural remains throughout the world, from the earliest period to the present time, illustrated with numerous drawings, maps and plans. It will be at Mr. Saunders's Great Rooms 3, [High]gate Buildings by Mr. John George Wood F.S.A.
Transferable tickets for the course 1g, single lecture 4/-

1817 lectures from 10am to noon every Monday, Wednesday and Friday by the Rev. S. Lyon on the Hebrew Language at his Academy 7 York Street, in sets of 24 lectures per set of pupils.

1817 Mr. Thelwall's lectures in the Kingston Assembly rooms, Thursday June 5th commencing a short series of lectures on Milton and Shakespeare. Doors open at 8pm, lectures begin 8-30pm, admittance 3/6d. Private lessons in Elocution during residence of lecturer at Mrs. Wyld's, 5 The Walks

November 1817 Mr. R.E. Lloyd, the astronomical lecturer's 23-year-old daughter died.

1817 Dr. Wilkinson on Experimental Philosophy starting Friday 26th December a series of 10 lectures as usual. Monday, Wednesday and Friday

1817 Monday and Tuesday December 29th and 30th, Mr. Sams exhibits an examination with 4 young gentlemen and 4 young ladies under his new system of Mnemonics. Admission 1/- to go to charity. Examined on all manner of subjects. A course of lectures on Mnemonics at Mr. Sams's house, 8 Ashford Buildings to commence Thursday January 1st 1818

1819 an instructive course of 6 lectures on history, connected with the architectural remains of antiquity and illustrated by numerous drawings and maps, commencing Monday Feb 1st, by Mr. Geo. Wood, F.S.A. lecturer at the Royal Institute. Admission to each lecture 4/- or tickets for the course, 1g. Time and place to be decided.

1819 Monday 15th February at 1pm Mr. Boner will begin a course of lectures on perspective at no. 3 Great Bedford Street, St James' Square. Subscription for 6 lectures £1/1/-
Mr. Boner gives private lessons in French, German and Italian and in Mathematics, Navigation, Fortification, Astronomy, Geography and History, and Mrs. Boner has opened a Preparatory School for young gentlemen under 10 years old.

1819 Mr. Wood's Evening Lectures on illustrations of History, exemplified by drawings of the remains of ancient architecture will commence with a lecture on Egypt, its history, antiquities etc at 7-30pm on Friday 12th February at 3 Westgate buildings. Admission to each lecture is 4/-. Mr. Wood's Morning lectures on History are delivered at 1pm on Monday, Wednesday and Friday, and on perspective on Thursday, Saturday and Tuesday at 2pm.

1819 on Wednesday April 28th and Monday May 3rd to begin precisely at 1pm, Mr. Renou, Member of the Royal College of Surgeons, intends delivering two lectures explaining the process of digestion, absorption and the influence of the nerves on the digestive organs; calculated to elucidate this part of the science of Physiology and to render it generally useful and interesting.
Freemasons' Hall, York Street; tickets 5/- each.
The second lecture was unavoidably postponed and Mr. Renou intends delivering it on Mon 10th May.

1819 Mr. Ogilvie to deliver a course of lectures on Oratory at the Upper Assembly Rooms at 1pm Friday November 19th the first of two discourses. No charge made for admission. Repeated Friday 3rd December and in January 1820. *There was a long bit of guff. He sounds like a pompous idiot.*

1820 Saturday May 6th 1pm for the last time in this city, Mr. Lloyd will close his grand transparent orrery. Freemasons' Hall. This being Friday's evening lecture postponed.

1820 Mr. Addams will give a course of 12 lectures on Philosophy commencing Monday 23rd October at the Kingston Rooms. The lectures will be delivered on Mondays, Tuesdays, Thursdays and Fridays at 12 noon, each lecture repeated at 7pm.
This course includes the sciences of Electricity, Chemistry, Mechanics, Hydrostatics, Galvanism, Geoloty, Pneumatics, Optics and Astronomy. To be exhibited a splendid transparent orrery, Bramah's hydraulic press, steam engines of different constructions, Newman's blow-pipe apparatus, models of pumps and diving bells, a beautiful working model of Montgolfier's water ram, patent blowing machine, model of an apparatus for gas illumination, wagons and wheels of different kinds. Dissected model of the eye, and every other instrument requisite for the elucidation of various laws and phenomena of nature.
12 transferrable tickets £1/4/-; to a single lecture 3/- syllabuses gratis at the libraries.

Libraries

Mr. Bally's library Milsom Street

At least 1810 - 1820 Mr. J Barratt's Library, Bond Street
1810 - 1820 Mr. Bally's Library and reading room, 10 Milsom Street at the Upholstry warehouse and house agency office.

1807-1820 Mr.H. Godwin's Library, 43 Milsom Street, bookseller; as bookseller still there in 1844 Mr. Charles Godwin.

1810 – 1816 ?? Mr. Gibbons; library Argyle Street, opposite 13 Argyle Buildings. Just on the other side of Pulteney Bridge from the main city.

1810- 1820 Mr. Meyler's and son's Library, literary and reading tooms, bookseller and printer, 5 Abbey Church Yard [still there in 1844]. Adjoining the Pump Room.

Mr. John Savage's Library, also bookseller and stationer, 12 Argyle Buildings. Circulating library and reading room
Subscriptions: Per year, 15/- ; Per quarter 7/6d;
Per month 3/6d; Per week 1/6d
The reading room is furnished with Bath, Bristol and London daily newspaper, reviews etc. Folios of caricatures lent for the evening.

1810 - 1820 Mr. J. Upham's Library, The Walks.

Musical Library and musical instrument warehouse
J. Lintern, music seller to their RH the Duke and Duchess of York. 15 The Grove. New and second-hand instruments, music to lend.

1810 Buchan's Musical Libary, Northumberland Place

The painting still visible on this library in Milsom Street, This is Mr. Godwin's Library at no. 43

Sundry Other Entertainments

Panoramas

Mr. Bennett's Panorama was a relatively short lived phenomenon, and having seen how infrequently it was changed, I have to say that it was likely to have been through indifference to the spectacle which led to its demise. Other panoramas in other places did extremely well.
The principle behind a panorama is that a huge painting on canvas was made, to encompass a circle of considerable diameter. The first exhibited was in 1791, a view of London from the roof of Albion Mills, and London had a permanent building for exhibiting panoramas, which continued to be shown for the next 70 years there. The 360 ° view was painted in a slightly distorted style to appear realistic to those viewing it, typically on a platform set one storey or so up from the ground, to maintain the illusion of being in the centre of the painting.
Alas for Mr. Bennett, whose panoramas were not quite as large as those in London, nor changed as frequently in Bath, which was probably the real mistake. His first exhibit was in January 1810 and by 1815 he had gone bankrupt, and his land and the panorama building were being sold to cover his debts. The diameter of the Bath panorama would have been something around 40 feet, the circumference being 120 feet. The rooms of the wooden building in front were 12' high, and it was 40' x 20' and included a shop of memorabilia, guides and was where the artist also painted portraits and miniatures from 1813 to defray expenses.
The first season was a more makeshift affair however!

The Panorama, when being shown, was open 9am to dusk. Ladies and Gentlemen 1/-, children 6d

4th January, 1810, the advertisement appeared that a panorama view of Brighton would be displayed in York Street, near the Abbey Church Yard.
"1500 sq. Ft. Of pictures to represent the principal part of the above celebrated and beautiful watering place."

This exhibition was taken down for the Bristol Fair at the end of August; it is not clear whether he meant to exhibit it there, but it seems likely.
It is back in November 1810, now in a slightly different location, in the corner of Orange Grove. The Panorama of Brighton goes back on display,

as well as a large painting of the Battle of Alexandria and the patriotic drivel about a smaller number of British forces winning against all odds hides the disaster this battle was, for the glory of Sir Ralph Abercrombie who got his silly self and a lot of other people killed unnecessarily. The painting showed portraits of principal officers and the death of Sir Ralph, as well as distant views of the City of Alexandria, forts etc.

This panorama and painting persisted until May 1812 when a spacious and purpose built building was erected next to the Post Office, Abbey Church.

May 1812: 'A view of the city, fortress and harbour of Havannah in the West Indies, with fine open sea, beautiful bay, a graceful procession of the host by the water, great variety of shipping, barges, boats etc. This painting was made from accurate drawings made on the spot, forming a complete circle 1600 square feet of picture, which will be found on inspection to be one of the most pleasing panoramas ever offered.'

Jan 10th 1813 was to be the last showing of the view of Havannah. Allegedly.

The new picture was to be the Conflagration of Moscow, interspersed with great numbers of Russian, Cossack and French soldiers.

However, in April 1813, the view of Havannah appears to be reinstated, though in November 1813 the Conflagration of Moscow returned. This was still advertised in February 1814; the next mention of the panorama is the filing of Mr. Bennett as a bankrupt and his goods for sale in September 1815.

Maybe it's something in a name; Lizzie Bennett's father was lax in his attentions to good financial practice too.

That's 3 panoramas and one big painting over 5 years. It just lacked sufficient variety.

Illuminations

It was common from the reign of Charles II and through the entire Georgian period to exhibit illuminations to celebrate some patriotic endeavour deemed worthy of it. Early illuminations were no more than lit windows, but as time went on, more elaborate displays were desired. Coloured lanterns strung up outside house were common, and wealthy people or businesses would often mount scaffolding with pictures painted on glass, lit from behind. Even more modest households could paint on 'silver paper' a very fine white paper, which was used by jewellers to wrap trinkets in. It was used as overlays before tracing paper came from

France to England. If painted and then treated with a varnish made of Canadian balsam dissolved in aqua vitae it would be nearly transparent.
These illuminations were shown for such things as the defeat of Napoleon Bonaparte in 1814; the *real* defeat of Napoleon Bonaparte in 1815; the arrival of the Queen and Princess Elizabeth in Bath in 1817 and the popular support for Queen Caroline in 1820. They were generally displayed by all loyal subjects.
Bath also had an exhibition of illuminations at the grand galas for the birthdays of the king and the Prince of Wales in Sydney Gardens, which will be found in the chapter on Sydney Gardens.

Illuminations in Bath Friday April 13th, 1814
Every house contributed its share to this popular expression of delight over the restoration of peace. Some of the more striking edifices gave all that could be combined of brilliant and tasteful decoration.

The Guildhall was elegantly decorated with coloured lamps arranged in pyramids, stars, anchors, G. R. and crown, in the centre the word *Alexander* in blue lamps and over the entrances to the market on each side rows of flambeaux.

MessersClement and Co's Bank; *Blucher* in variegated lamps.

The Greyhound Inn had a transparency representing the conversion of the implements of war to those of agriculture. Surmounted with a dove and olive branch and the motto:
The useless lances into scythes shall bend
And the broad falchon in a ploughshare end

The Christopher Inn - the front ornamented with wreathes of laurel and [artificial?] flowers and a transparency representing Brittania seated on a rock welcoming the return of peace and commerce.

The White Lion – a transparency exhibiting a temple, the columns labelled 'Lords', 'commons' 'the dome' 'the constitution' surmounted by a crown, Britannia seated in the temple supported by a lion, the sun rising from the ocean in the background; and in the rays, the words 'Peace! Peace!'. Ships sailing to and from Britain. On the right, a hand from the clouds holding a message 'England Expects [etc]'; on the ground a husbandman with a flail in his hand. Etc.

The Lower Rooms presented in the centre a full length figure of the Duke of Wellington, in the background a view of Salamanca, with a demicircular piece representing Britannia seated on a rock; the royal arms of France circled with rays of glory. A landscape of the advance of the Cossacks and retreat of French army into Paris. On each side views of Lisbon and Madrid. The whole encircles with a double wreath of laurel and surmounted with the flags of the Allies and the Prince's plume of feathers.

The Theatre illumination was wholly composed of variegated lamps forming G. R and a crown with stars and the word 'Peace'. The Royal Arms and lyres at the top were adorned with variageted lamps and over the entrance a portrait of the Duke of Wellington.

Pump Room decorated with stars and festoons formed by lamps.

Many private buildings had such transparencies as Britannia embracing Peace, portraits of Wellington, and patriotic expressions. Mr. Sensley Lilleput Alley had a star formed of 300 lamps.
And many, many more.

Tuesday July 5th Guildhall Order regarding Illuminations from the Right Worshipful Mayor and Justices
It is forbidden to bring guns or pistols, throwing-squibs or crackers at any illuminations for fear of alarming anyone. Or any fire works. Anyone doing so will be apprehended by Police Officers and constables.
Presumably the April Illuminations were disrupted by unwonted and indeed unwanted detonations.

April 1815 not so much illuminations re peace but the coming of gas lighting to Bath and some shops under brilliant illumination. I can find no account of general illuminations in Bath to celebrate the victory of Waterloo. Only a grand Military Gala at Sydney Garden with appropriate illuminations and a representation of the Battle of Waterloo.

Monday 3rd November 1817 arrival of Queen Charlotte at Sydney Place with Princess Elizabeth. Public respect was expressed with general and splendid illuminations.
The front of the Guildhall was a resplendent mass of light, beautifully opposed by the elegant arrangement of lamps at Messrs Clement, Tugwell

and McKenzie's Bank on the other side of Market-Place. The arch within the oval inclosure[sic] produced a striking effect; and at the other end of Pulteney Street Mr Parish's house [as usual upon every public occasion] shone with superior brilliancy. A beautiful transparency representing her Majesty on a pedestal, on whose panel Fame appeared, recording the triumphs of the present reign, added much to the effect of this gentleman's tasteful decorations; while a band of music stationed before his house complimented her Majesty as she passed with "Godd save the King" and continued playing during the evening.

The Theatre – at the box entrance in the Sawclose, three columns of coloured lamps, the centre bearing a crown. On the north side a superb crown, on either side a star and beneath "VIVAT REGINA" in letters of immense size and dazzling lustre.

Upper Assembly Rooms – the windows in Alfred Street hung with festoons of lamps and underneath a most superb C.R. and crown.

Kingston Assembly Rooms – neatly lit at the ball entrance

The King's Pump Room – an immense C.R. surmounted by a crown and decorated with stars

The Yeomanry Office – a star of variegated lamps and a festoon round the door with the arms decorated.

The Rectory – displayed two gothic arches supporting one of a broader span, and surmounted with C.R and a crown.

Sydney House – the columns entwined, and the entire front decorated with variegated lamps; C.R. crown and star

Mr. Erskine's at New Sydney Place was elegantly decorated with C.R. and a crown. All the houses in this noble pile were ornamented with lozenges of lamps and festoons of lamps were also tastefully hung along the whole range.

Messrs Evill and Sons, jewellers to their RH the Duke and Duchess of York, Market Place – a brilliant crown with C.R. and a row of lamps, the whole of which had a striking effect.

Messrs Meyler, Abbey Church Yard – a well-executed full-length transparency of Beau Nash, holding in his hand the plan of the General Hospital and the motto:

Welcome to Bladud's realms, thou best of Queens;
For thee once more Nash quits Elysian scenes
Long may these healing springs thy life preserve,
Their bracing virtues renovate each nerve.
-Ere I return, oh! May old Englsnd see
Another branch shoot from her royal tree

On the right of the figure, a transparency of the Bath Arms, with the motto *"Hail, honour'd Happy City."* On the left the King's Arms with the scroll *"God bless our Queen."*
Mr. Furvoye, painter to her Majesty and the Princesses, Argyle Buildings, gave an elegant repast, a ball and a chosen band of music to his friends, in congratulations of the Queen's safe arrival and exhibited three beautiful Chinese lamps with a crown, star and C.R.
Many other illuminations ...

After Queen Caroline was cleared of wrongdoing in November 1820, on Monday 13th November the audience at the theatre refused to sing 'God Save the King' but substituted the word 'Queen' for 'King' between the play and the farce, despite the Manager trying to stop this.
On Thursday 16th an Illumination took place in the City of Bath which was more general than had been anticipated. The evening was ushered in with many peals from the different church bells and there was gaiety in the streets. Many houses were adorned with coloured lamps and the letters C.R. with a crown of white lamps. At Mr. Brod's house on Somerset Buildings, Milsom Street a transparency representing Mr. Brougham trampling under foot the Bill of Pains and Penalties, and holding in his right hand a scroll with the words "*The Queen's Shield; Truth, Honour, Justice and the People. When righteousness prevail the city rejoiceth and when the wicked are overcome, the people shout.*" The letters in his shop window were lighted with gas.
The areas of New Sydney Place were tastefully hung with lamps. Mr. Wilson in Milsom Street and Mr. Block in Argyle Buildings had her Majesty's portrait. Mr. Marks on the Bridge displayed a transparency in which the perjured Majesty formed a conspicuous figure; other transparencies of equal moment were displayed.
Apart from some panes of glass broken at Mr. Hobb's in Market Place, all was quiet until about 11pm when the conduct of the populace became so turbulent it was judged necessary to call out the troop of the 16th Lancers, whom the magistrates had, as a measure of precaution sent for from Bristol. They were greeted with groans and whistles. Some panes of glass at the Guildhall were broken and at 12 midnight, the Chief Magistrate, John Wiltshire esq. read the Riot Act, which had the effect of compelling the crowd to return to their homes. Nearly 40 people were arrested for breaches of the peace, some of them respectable inhabitants! Some were discharged, others will answer charges at the Quarter Sessions.

Harmonic Society

Friday 7th April 1820 the Bath Harmonic Society gave a splendid Gala Fête at Kingston's Rooms. To the ladies, in honour of the Accession of their August Patron to the British Throne. The selection of glees opened with an Ode, most admirably set by Mr. Clifton. Supper refreshments supplied by Mr. Tulley. The lower entrance of the rooms was brilliantly illuminated and a military band played during the evening. After the *Non Nobis Domine* was sung, His Majesty's health was drunk followed by other healths. After *God Save the King* was sung, the Contre Dance and Quadrille Rooms were thrown open and dancing was kept up with great spirit until three o'clock.

The Panharmonicon February 1815

A panharmonicon on view at Mr. Evill's exhibition room, Milsom Street. This piece of machinery from Vienna consists of 210 instruments all on view performing music by mechanical power; the most favourite compositions of Mozart, Haydn, H.R. Bishop etc.

Commencing 1pm and continuing until 4pm with 8 pieces of music in each hour; and in the evening from 7pm.

Admission 2/-, children 1/-; evening, admission 1/6d, children 1/-/

Also on display a time piece called the AULORGANON that plays at pleasure, by mechanism, a variety of pieces of music;

Also a Merlin's Weighing Machine, by which the company may be weighed and measured.

The Temporary Theatre

At Mr. Webb's auction room, 21 Milsom Street

Monday 16th, Tuesday 18th and Friday 20th December 1811

Signor Belzoni will commence with an exhibition of several Italian, Scotch [sic], English and Irish airs on the musical glasses. He will then conduct several philosophical experiments in hydraulics and the power of water.

Signor Belzoni, commonly called the ROMAN HERCULES will display several striking attitudes from the most admired antique statues, including Fighting Gladiators, Labours of Hercules, Instructions of Achilles etc,

demonstrating grace and physical strength. The whole to end in carrying a group of SEVEN MEN! He will also play the Spanish Guitar.
A grand display of optical illusions will be exhibited.
Door open 5-30pm commencing 6-30pm, concludes 8-45pm. Also Tuesday, Thursday and Saturday at 1-30pm to 3pm. Admittance 2/6d, children 1/6d/

Beautiful Sculptured Alabaster from Italy 1820

Mr. Stafford has the honour to announce to the nobility and gentry, amateurs and patrons of the polite arts that he has received advice on an importatation of sculpture in alabaster comprehending a brilliant display of genius.

A beautiful group of the Graces of fine symmetry;
A figure;
Apollo de Medicis;
A pleasing goup;
L'Amour et Psyche
A small miniature group;
The Rape of the Sabines;
Canova's Hebe;
With several other allegorical subjects.
Also splendid Etruscan and Medicean vases, lamps and elegancies of the first class, the whole to be sold by Auction at the Rooms, no. 20 Milsom Street on Wednesday and Thursday 29th and 30th March 1820, beginning each day at 12 noon precisely.
AN EXHIBITION of the sculptures will be given to the public on the Monday and Tuesday preceding the sale; and the whole will be illuminated on the evening of the same days, when their inimitable transparency will be manifested.

In October 1811
The pictures now exhibiting [gratis] at Wise's room, 18 Union Street.
Vandyck 'Christ curing the Demoniac'
Murillo 'The Beggar Boys'
Velasquez 'The Beggar Man and dog'
Caravaggio, two matching fruit pieces

Circus

1810 January Moritz's troop to the circus in Corn Street, bottom of St James's Parade. Displays of horsemanship and burlesque.
Feb 9th a variety of new performances containing Phantasmagoria, philosophical deceptions, feats on the tight rope, horsemanship etc. The inimitable Miss Saunders will exhibit several feats on the single horse, and equilibriums on the slack wire. By request there will be a Saturday performance at 1pm. Continues to the 3rd week in February.

Open Friday March 8th 1816 at Stoke's Riding School, Monmouth Street the new popular Harlequin pantomime of the life, death and re-animation of the High-Mettled Racer, the pantomime commencing with a real horse race.
A real Fox chase with hounds, horses etc.
Mlle Quantreliette from the circus, Paris, will make her appearance on horseback; the foremost female equestrian in France.
M. Ducrow will perform elegant feats on the tight rope.
The Wonderful Poney [sic] will lay down, sit up, fetch and carry like a spaniel, ungirth his saddle and pull it off, leap through a hoop 24" in diameter, through a balloon etc on word of command.
Still Vaulting by the Troop of Flying Phenomena.
The equestrian hero, Master Woolford will go through his elegant performances on horseback.
Slack rope by Mr. Blackmore.
Doors open at 6pm, performance at 7pm, boxes 2/-, pit 1/-. Gallery 6d. Monday, Wednesday and Friday.
March 21st 1816 announced that the above circus will continue open for a short time, three nights a week, Mondays, Wednesdays and Fridays. The performance consists of Equestrian Exercies and to conclude with the HIGH-METTLED RACER.

1816 August Equestrian Circus at the bottom of Grove Street, opening Monday August 5th. M. Godeau performs feats on the tight rope. Also Mlle Louis, the female equestrian from the circus of Paris and London.

Barker's Picture Gallery

Mentioned as being set up in 1805; no other information. Presumably to exhibit the paintings of Thomas and Benjamin Barker, brothers, the Barkers of Bath.

Tennis court next to one of the two riding schools for young men to frequent.

1819 12th August a grand match of cricket on Captain Thornhill's grounds, Lower Bristol Road, between the two elevens of Bath and Bristol cricket clubs. Many bets are depending on the game.

Annual Flower Feasts

1818 Annual Carnation Feast held 23rd July at Gloucester Inn, Walcot. A fine show of flowers. First prize for carnations to Mr. John Howell of Bath for his 'Boyles Lord Ashbrook', 'Metcalfe's Miss Saunders' and 'Young's British Hero;
1818 at the Annual Carnation and Gooseberry Feast at the White Hart Inn, Widcombe, on the 27th July, first prize in carnations to Mr. Collins of Bathwick for his 'Perrin's Queen Charlotte', 'Howell's Seedling' and 'Webbe's Lord Wellington.' 2nd to Mr. Howell
Gooseberries first price for the 6 heaviest berries to Mr. Webb of Brokington. weight of 6 berries, 40z, 6 pennyweight 10 grains. Types, 'Sportsman', 'Jubiliee' and 'Crown Bob.'

1819 3rd August the annual carnation and gooseberry feast at the White Hart Widcombe. There was a large show of flowers and gooseberries, rarely equalled for beauty and perfection. Mr. G Bargess of Willsbridge won the carnation cup and Mr. Brown of Marlborough won first price for the six heaviest berries; the largest weight upward of 4g, the 6 weighing 6 ounces. The largest was 4 ¾" about.

Churches

Walcot Church, St Swithin's
On the Paragon, Walcot, was erected on a site of worship dating back to the 10th century. It was built between 1777 and 1790. It is classical in style and serves those who live at the northern end of Bath.

St James', Weymouth St at the end of St James' Parade
A fine modern style of building, being rebuilt in 1768-9; a ring of 8 bells. Serves the Southern end of town.

St Michael's, between Broad and Walcot St
Known as St Michael's Without, being outside the original walls, when exiting the north gate. The parish is St Michael's with St Paul's. The west tower fronts Northgate Street. Rebuilt in 1742 on Medieval original [and to the disappointment of the time-traveller, the current church is Victorian]. Divine service Sundays, prayers Wednesday and Friday at 11am and Saturdays 4pm, and morning prayers 11am on Saints Days.

The Octagon Chapel, Milsom Street
Divine service every Sunday at 11am and 5pm, and prayers Wednesdays and Fridays at 11am.

The Abbey, aka the Church of St Peter and Paul.
This building having fallen into disrepair in the 15th Century was rebuilt at the orders of Bishop of Bath and Wells, Oliver King, who had s dream in which he saw Angels ascending to heaven by means of a ladder and a voice crying, "Let an Olive establish the Crown and let a king restore the church." Carvings of these angels may be found on the West Front. The beauty of this church is beyond description in a short paragraph, but the fan vaulting in the nave is a most beautiful example of its kind, and the proportions are graceful and elegant. It has a ring of 8 bells.
Divine service is celebrated twice a day, at 11am and 4pm.

Some of the ladder climbing angels: photo S. Waldock

There are other chapels in which to worship, and also provision for non-conformists.
The Presbyterian Meeting House is in Frog Lane
The Quaker Meeting House is at the upper end of Merchant's Court in the Market Place.
The Anabaptist Meeting House is in Horse Street.
A Methodist Tabernacle is in Harlequin Row.
The Catholic church is the Bell Tree House in Bell Tree Lane

Fairs and visiting exhibitions
Attending fairs is always enjoyable, because they are less predictable than common shopping, and as well as the stalls, there are often exhibits, entertainments and other spectacles.

The city of Bath has two annual fairs which are 'of very trifling note'.

Lansdown Fair
This is held on or near the 10th August annually, save when this falls at a weekend being a fair for cheese, horses, and most kinds of merchandise. 1811 the fair was on Monday 12th August.
Cattle, sheep and lambs also shown.

In August 1810, the Polito's Royal Menagerie was on display at the fair, including an elephant, an ostrich, a lion and lioness, a 'tyger and tygress' [sic] a pair of Kangaroos, a male panther, a pair of leopards and the Ursine Sloth. Also a wolf, a jackal, a hyaena, the civet and genet, racoons, the Ichneumon [Mongoose], an emu, a cassowary, pelicans, Bellearike or royal crown birds, the adjutants or giant cranes, the black swan, the condor, a vulture, Great Horned Owl, spoon bill and other birds. 1/- admittance.

Beware of the notorious George Groves and his boy pickpockets. Groves is a notorious villain who likes to dress well and ride upon a good horse. He haunts fairs and races for victims to rob.

Further afield was the Devizes Spring Fair, held on or around 20th April; this moving to Saturday 21st if Good Friday fell on that day as in 1810.

[NB further menagerie exhibitions were heldfrom Monday 13th January 1812 at the bottom of Henrietta Street, with an elephant, tiger, kangaroo with joey, quagga etc.
Also in February 1815, in Walcot Street, Polito again with all as described at the fair, also the Zebra and the Nilghan or Horned Horse.
Also in April 1817 in Racey's Yad, Walcot St. With young lions and rhinoceros, leopard, hyaena etc. Admittance 1/-
Also in 1820 in March in the George Inn yard, Walcot Street, with a black tiger and white lion, elephant, lions, etc etc; ladies and gents 2/-, childen and servants 1/-, feeding time 9-30pm for 2/6d .]

Chapter Six: Lower Assembly Rooms

AKA The Kingston Rooms from 1810 [first, Harrison's Rooms, then Simpson's Rooms]

The Lower Assembly Rooms are to be found on Terrace Walk off North Parade.
During the day, one can walk there and meet people. Stone walks and terraces surround the building where people may gather. Also walks in the ballroom in inclement weather.

Remains of the Lower Assembly Rooms with North Parade in the background. Foreground is Parade Gardens, formerly St James; gardens. View from across river. Photo S. Waldock.

Balls on Tuesday
Concerts on Friday

From Nov. 1811, promenades and card assemblies every Friday too. Seasons begin November and end February with some other occurrences.

Master of Ceremonies from 1811 Mr. Francis John Guyenette; from 1815 Mr. James Heaviside to Feb 1818 [moves to Upper Rooms]; Charles H Marshall from Feb 1818 to spring 1820/

The Kingston Rooms were the first public place to welcome gas lighting on Wednesday 21st April, 1819 with five elegant pyramidal lustres containing 22 Argand gas burners, and two in the orchestra which produced a most brilliant and undiminished light during the whole evening.

Rules voted on Nov. 1810

- Subscribers are to preserve decorum and maintain respectability at the balls in these rooms.
- Anyone hoping to be a subscriber must be introduced by a subscriber.
- All transferable tickets of subscribers admitted to these balls shall be written the name of the lady admitted and the same endorsed by the person transferring this ticket.
- No gentleman resident in Bath shall be admitted to these balls without being a subscriber.
- The balls shall be on Tuesday nights; the rooms shall be opened at seven o'clock; and that dancing shall eight o'clock and end at twelve o'clock precisely even in the middle of a dance.
- Ladies intending to dance Minuets do give notice thereof to the MC the day previous and be in the rooms punctually by eight o'clock.
- In order that every lady may have an opportunity of dancing, gentlemen shall change their partners every two dances.
- The Upper Benches be reserved for peeresses and that ladies of precedence do take their places; those who stand up after a dance has begun shall take their place at the bottom of the dance and not be permitted to sit down until the dance be finished.
- No lady shall permit another to come in above her after she has taken her place in the set.
- No gentleman shall be admitted to the balls in boots, excepting officers with uniform and on duty.

- The MC on receiving information of any person acting in opposition of these regulations shall signify to such a person that as MC it is his duty to see the orders of the subscribers properly enforced.
- That every person shall, on admission to the ball pay 6d which will entitle them to tea.
- The tea-room will be opened at nine o'clock and continue until 12 o'clock.

Concerts

£2/2/- subscription will be entitled to admission tickets for 12 concerts transferable to a lady only.

£1/1/- will be entitled to admission tickets for any five concerts following such subscriptions.

Non-subscribers tickets at all times 5/-

All transferable tickets to be endorsed by the subscribers with the name of the person to whom such tickets shall be transferred, and in case of the absence of the subscriber, any lady or his or her family is authorised to endorse the same to ladies only. Subscribers with their families removing from Bath during the concerts, their tickets for the remainder of the concerts are not transferable. No transferable tickets will be admitted at rehearsals.

There will be 12 subscription concerts *[not always adhered to.]*

Winter balls

£1/6/- subscription entitled to 3 tickets for each of the 24 balls, two of which will be transferrable to ladies only and one not transferable.

£0/-14/- subscription will be entitled to one ticket, not transferable

The season begins in November and continues to last Tuesday in May

A number of Royal Deaths occurred in this decade; it was customary to eschew theatre performances and entertainments until after the funeral, when mourning would be worn.

In details of the balls below, numbered balls and concerts are subscription balls or concerts.

1810

oOoOo

Mr. G Lanza is MC? Messrs G and F Lanza also will give lessons in Piano-Forte and Singing during their stay in Bath
12 concerts and 24 subscription fancy balls announced.

Fri Nov 2nd Death of Princess Amelia

Tues Nov 6th 1st Fancy Ball probably cancelled for death of Princess Amelia

Tues Nov 13th 2nd Fancy Ball cancelled
Tues Nov 13th Funeral of Princess Amelia

Tues Nov 20th 1st Fancy Ball

Fri Nov. 23rd First Concert of 12 Madam Bianchi to sing

Tues Nov 27th 2nd Fancy Ball

Fri Nov 30th 2nd Concert, Signor Tramezzani's and Signora Bianchi's last performance

Tues Dec 4th 3rd Fancy Ball

Fri Dec 7th 3rd Concert

Tues Dec 11th 4th Fancy Ball

Fri Dec 14th 4th Concert

Tues Dec 18th 5th Fancy Ball

Fri Dec 21st 5th Concert

Fri Dec 28th 6th Concert. Trio with Mr. Bishop, Mssrs G and F Lanza. Mr. Harrington a concerto on oboe. New overture, Beethoven; a glee; Aria; song; duetto buffo, grand trio for 3 performers on 2 pianofortes etc. Act II, Grand symphony by Mozart, glee, Irish ballad etc

1811

Tues Jan 1st 6th Fancy Ball

Fri Jan 4th Benefit Concert, principle vocalists Mrs. Bland of Drury Lane, Misses Stephens and Pouchee, Mr. Lea, Mr. Lacy and Mr. Lanza
Signor Spagnoletti on violin and Mr. Harrington on oboe.

Tues Jan 8th 7th Fancy Ball

Fri Jan 11th 7th Concert

Tues Jan 15th 8th Fancy Ball

Fri Jan 18th 8th Concert

Tues Jan 22nd 9th Fancy Ball

Fri Jan 25th 9th Concert. Miss Hughes. Mr. Harrington a concerto on oboe, and Mr. Guichard a concerto on piano-forte

Tues Jan 29th 10th Fancy Ball

Fri Feb 1st 10th Concert

Tues Feb 5th 11th Fancy Ball

Fri Feb 8th 11th Concert

Tues Feb 12th 12th Fancy Ball

Fri Feb 15th 12th Concert

Tues Feb 19th 13th Fancy Ball

Tues Feb 26th 14th Ball

Tues Mar 5th 15th Ball

Tues Mar 12th 16th Ball

Tue Mar 19th 17th Ball

Tue Mar 26th 18th Ball

Tue Apr 2nd 19th Ball

Good Friday April 12th

Tue Apr 23rd MC's Benefit Ball. New Grecian lamps lit for the first time, and are elegant and brilliant. The rooms to be kept open during the summer months

Tue Apr 30th 20th Ball

Tue May 7th 21st Ball

Tue May 14th 22nd Ball final Ball and end of winter season.

Thur May 16th Subscriptions for the summer season now open.
15/- entitles 1 ticket for a gentleman non transferable and 2 tickets transferable to ladies for 12 Balls including 4 in race week
A single subscription 7/- non transferable.
Non subscribers 5/- per Ball.
Tea to be paid for as usual. Tea room open 10pm and shut 11pm

Fri May 17th Card assembly

Thur May 23rd at 1pm Dr. Wilkinson will deliver a lecture on the construction and economy or the hoof of a horse

Wed May 29th First of 12 summer balls

Fri Jun 28th Card assembly as usual

Wed Jul 3rd 1st Race week Ball

Thur Jul 4th Concert in race week with Mme Catalani who gives her services to raise money for British prisoners in France

Fri Jul 5th MCs summer benefit Ball

oOoOo

Thur Oct 17th notice of the Old Assembly Rooms opening for the season, and the opening of the Ball-room for newspapers and cards on a similar plan to the New Rooms to open 1st November.
Promenades and card assemblies every Friday. New MC, Mr. Guyenette.

Tues Nov 5th 1st Ball
Fri Nov 8th Promenade and card assemblies commence

Tue Nov 12th 2nd Ball

Tue Nov 19th 3rd Ball

Fri Nov 22nd 1st Concert

Tue Nov 26th 4th Ball

Fri Nov 29th 2nd Concert

Tue Dec 3rd 5th Ball

Fri Dec 6th 3rd Concert

Tue Dec 10th 6th Ball

Fri Dec 13th 4th Concert

Tue Dec 17th 7th Ball

Fri Dec 20th 5th Concert

Fri Dec 27th 6th Concert

Tue Dec 31st 8th Ball

1812

Fri Jan 3rd 7th Concert

Tue Jan 7th 9th Ball

Fri Jan 10th 8th Concert

Tue Jan 14th 10th Ball

Fri Jan 17th 9th Concert

Tue Jan 21st 11th Ball

Fri Jan 24th 10th Concert

Tue Jan 28th 12th Ball

Fri Jan 31st 11th Concert

Tue Feb 4th 13th Ball

Fri Feb 7th 12th and Final Concert

Tue Feb 11th 14th Ball

Tue Feb 18th 15th Ball

Tue Feb 25th 16th Ball

Tue Mar 3rd 17th Ball

Fri Mar 6th First Card assembly and promenade of summer season, every Friday except good Friday

Tue Mar 10th 18th Ball

Fri Mar 13th Card assembly and promenade

Tue Mar 17th 19th Ball

Fri Mar 20th Card assembly and promenade

Tue Mar 24th 20th Ball

Good Friday Mar 27th

Tue Apr 7th 21st Ball

Tue Apr 14th 22nd Ball

Tue Apr 21st 23rd Ball

Tue May 5th 24th Ball

Fri Jun 5th Card assembly and promenade admission to non subscribers 2/6d, tea included. Subscribers entitled to admission to the balls in race week.

Fri Jun 12th Card assembly and promenade

Races on Wed 17th, Thur 18th and Fri 19th June
Races on Mon 22nd, Tue 23rd, Wed 24th June incorrect
[Both sets of dates given].
Balls and a concert Mme Catalani to sing.

Fri Jun 26th Card assembly and promenade every Friday until Fri Sept 25th

oOoOo

Wed Sep 30th notice given that subscriptions to winter balls are open. There will be 26 balls exclusive of the MC's balls.
Promenades and Card Assemblies will begin first Friday in March each Friday until the last Friday in September. Same subscription as to balls, and both cover the balls in Race week. Non-subscribers 2/6d each night

November A contretemps between Mr. King of the Upper Rooms and the Lower Rooms, over a benefit concert for a Mr. Hobbs which was to have taken place.

Tues Nov 3rd 1st Ball

Tue Nov 10th 2nd Ball

Tue Nov 17th 3rd Ball

Tue Nov 24th 4th Ball

Tue Dec 1st 5th Ball

Fri Dec 4th 1st Concert

Tue Dec 8th 6th Ball

Fri Dec 11th 2nd Concert

Mon Dec 14th concert and promenade arranged for benefit Mr. Hobbs by his friends, Mr. Field will preside on piano-forte. Doors open 7pm, concert begins 8pm. A subscriber of 10/6d will receive 3 tickets transferable, non-subscribers, tickets 5/- each. The celebrated band of the Leitrim Militia will perform several martial pieces, Irish and Scotch tunes &c before the concert begins and during the Promenade.

Tue Dec 15th 7th Ball

Fri Dec 18th 3rd Concert

Tue Dec 22nd 8th Ball

Tue Dec 29th 9th Ball

1813

Fri Jan 1st 4th Concert

Tue Jan 5th 10th Ball

Fri Jan 8th 5th Concert

Tue Jan 12th 11th Ball

Fri Jan 15th 6th Concert

Tue Jan 19th 12th Ball

Fri Jan 22nd 7th Concert
News, Jan 22nd 1813 the members of the Kingston Club have opened the large room on the left of the old entrance as a card club; the public card room only to be opened on Ball-nights.
Terms of admission £1/1/- per year or 10/6d for two months, and the usual consideration of £2/6d to the waiter.

Tue Jan 26th 13th Ball

Fri Jan 29th 7th Concert

Tue Feb 2nd 14th Ball

Ash Wednesday Feb 3rd

Fri Feb 5th 8th Concert

Tue Feb 9th 15th Ball

Fri Feb 12th a Ball in aid of the fund for the relief of the suffering Russian Peasants. Tickets 5/-

Tue Feb 16th 16th Ball

Fri Feb 19th 9th Concert

Tue Feb 23rd 17th Ball

Tue Mar 2nd18th Ball

Fri Mar 5th Cards & Promenade

Tue Mar 9th 19th Ball

Fri Mar 12th Cards & Promenade

Tue Mar 16th 20th Ball

Fri Mar19th Cards & Promenade

Tue Mar 23rd 21st Ball

Fri Mar 26th Cards & Promenade

Tues Mar 30th 22nd Ball

Fri Apr 2nd Cards & Promenade

Tues Apr 6th 23rd Ball

Fri Apr 9th Cards and Promenade

Tue Apr 13th 24th Ball

Good Friday April 16th

Fri Apr 23rd Cards & Promenade

Tues Apr 27th 25th Ball

Fri April 30th four musical prodigies perform a miscellaneous concert. Master Smith performs on Violin Piano-forte Violincello and Harmonic Glasses. Miss Smith who is only 11 years of age performs on the above instruments and is the first juvenile female violin performer in Europe. The two younger Misses Smith aged 6 and 3 and already proficient on Violin, Piano-forte and Harmonic Glasses. Tickets 5/-

Tue May 4th 26th and Final Ball

Bath and Somerset Grand Musical Festival Tues 22nd Jun – Fri 25th Jun at Abbey Church and Lower Assembly Rooms; with Mme Catalani as chief vocalist

Wed July 7th, Thur July 8th and Fri 9th Race week Balls

Fri Jul 9th Mme Catalani a grand concert. Tickets 8/-

oOoOo

First Ball generally early November on Tuesdays

First Concert generally first week in December on Fridays

1814

Generally 10 0r more balls up to May on Tuesdays

Generally 5 or more concerts up to end February on Fridays

First Friday in March generally begins card assemblies and promenades

Good Friday April 8th

Tues Apr 19th Mr. Guyenette's Ball after the concert at the Abbey Church

Mon 27th June a Ball

Races Wed 29th, Thur 30th June Fri 1st July; Balls

Fri 1st July The Master of Ceremonies Summer Ball

oOoOo

Subscriptions for the year recommence on the 1st November. The large room on the ground floor is exclusively appropriated for cards, the other large room above stairs is the reading-room. There is to be chess and backgammon in a room exclusively for these games and also a Commerce game room on the same floor. The reading-room is liberally supplied with the popular publications and furnished with atlases, maps etc. These rooms form a convenient and cheerful suite of apartments, distinct from the ballrooms and each department having its own entrance. Terms of subscription: year, £1/6/-. Six months: £1/-/-

Thur Nov 3rd Grand exhibition of ventriloquism &c by Mr. Charles at 8-30 in the evening. Admission 5/-

Mon Nov 7th Second exhibition of Ventriloquism as above.

Tues Nov 8th First Ball of the season

Tues Nov 15th 2nd Ball

Tues Nov 22nd 3rd Ball

Tues Nov 29th 4th Ball

Tues Dec 6th 5th Ball

Fri Dec 9th Concert

Tue Dec 13th 6th Ball

Fri Dec 16th Concert

Tue Dec 20th 7th Ball

Tue Dec 27th 8th Ball

1815

Tue Jan 3rd 9th Ball

Fri Jan 6th Concert

Tue Jan 10th 10th Ball

Fri Jan 13th Concert

Tue Jan 17th 11th Ball

Fri Jan 20th Concert

Tue Jan 24th 12th Ball

Fri Jan 27th Concert

Tue Jan 31st 13th Ball

Fri Feb 3rd Concert

Tue Feb 7th 14th Ball

Fri Feb 10th Concert

Tue Feb 14th 15th Ball

Fri Feb 17th Concert

Tue Feb 21st 16th Ball

Tue Feb 28th 17th Ball

Tue Mar 7th 18th Ball

Tue Mar 14th 19th Ball

Tue Mar 21st 20th Ball

Good Friday March 24th

Tue Mar28th 21st Ball

Tue Apr 4th 22nd Ball

Tue Apr 11th 23rd Ball

Tue Apr 18th 24th Ball

Wed May 3rd Concert of vocal and instrumental music tickets 5/-

Races Wed 28th, Thur 29th and Fri 30th June: Balls on race days? Fri Jun 30th Balls

oOoOo

Wed Nov 15th James Heaveside elected MC and the name 'Kingston Assembly Rooms' be officially adopted not Lower Assembly Rooms.

Tues Nov 21st 1st of 24 Balls

Fri Nov 24th Benefit Concert of Miss Mortimer tickets 5/-

Tues Nov 28th 2nd Ball

Tues Dec 5th 3rd Ball

Tues Dec 12th 4th Ball

Tues Dec 19th 5th Ball

1816

Tues Jan 2nd 6th Ball

Mon Jan 8th Benefit Ball, tickets 5/-

Tues Jan 9th 7th Ball

Tues Jan 16th 8th Ball

Tues Jan 23rd 9th Ball

Tues Jan 30th 10th Ball

Tue Feb 6th MC's Ball

Tue Feb 13th 11th Ball

Tue Feb 20th 12th Ball

Tue Feb 27th 13th Ball

Tue Mar 5th 14th Ball

Tue Mar 12th 15th Ball

Tue Mar 19th 16th Ball

Fri Mar 22nd tickets for the [Gallery?] for the Harmonic Society are issued at the Kingston Rooms between one and four in the afternoon; please bring silver as the secretary cannot provide change.

Tue Mar 26th 17th Ball

Tue Apr 2nd 18th Ball

Tue Apr 9th 19th Ball

Good Friday April 12th

Tue Apr 16th 20th Ball

Tue Apr 23rd 21st Ball

Tue Apr 30th 22nd Ball

Tue May 7th 23rd Ball

Tue May 14th 24th Ball

Race days Wed 3rd and Thur 4th July; Balls during week

oOoOo

Tue Nov 19th 1st Dress Ball

Tue Nov 26th 2nd Dress Ball

Tue Dec 3rd 3rd Dress Ball

Tue Dec 10th 4th Ball

Tue Dec 17th 5th Ball

1817

Tue Jan 7th 6th Ball

Tue Jan 14th 7th Ball

Tue Jan 21st 8th Ball

Tue Jan 28th 9th Ball

Tue Feb 4th 10th Ball

Tue Feb 11th 11th Ball

Tue Feb 18th 12th Ball

Tue Feb 25th 13th Ball

Tue Mar 4th 14th Ball

Tue Mar 11th 15th Ball

Tue Mar 18th 16th Ball

Tue Apr 1st 17th Ball

Good Friday April 4th

Tue Apr 8th 18th Ball

Tue Apr 15th 19th Ball

Tue Apr 22nd 20th Ball

Tue Apr 29th 21st Ball

Tue May 6th 22nd Ball

Tue May 13th MC's Spring Ball

Tue May 20th 23rd Ball

Tue May 27th Final Dress Ball

Thur Jun 5th Mr. Thelwall commences a short series of lectures on Milton and Shakespeare, with readings, recitations and oratorical illustrations, and discussions on characters as represented by famous actors and actresses. Doors open at 8, lectures begin 8-30pm. Admittance 3/6d

Thur Jun 12th another lecture?

Thur Jun 19th another lecture?

Tue July 1st, First of two Balls in Race week

Wed July 2nd First Race day

Thur July 3rd Second of two Balls in Race week second Race day.

oOoOo

James Heaviman resigns

One of the rooms to be hired by M. Barree, professor and dancing master from the Opera House, Paris. From 20th October, open for young ladies and gentlemen. Three lessons a week, Mondays, Thursdays and Saturdays, one of those days for waltzing and quadrilles only. Young gentlemen from 10am- noon, young ladies from 12 noon until 3pm. Private lessons also available with his son and daughter as assistants.

Thur Oct 23rd A vocal concert of Hebrew melodies. Tickets 5/-

Nov begin the Subscription Balls on Tuesday but death of Princess Charlotte of Wales on Thur. 6th November halts them until her funeral on Nov. 19th

Dec begins the Subscription Concerts on Fridays

Fri Dec 26th and subsequent evenings at 8pm Mr. Ardenond's exhibition of the views of: The City of Damascus: Island of St Helena: a Beautiful View in Holland, comprising the Hague; a view of Moscow. Tickets 2/- each, children half price. Mr. Ardenond will accommodate private parties at any hour of the day by receiving one day's notice. [Speculating that this is magic lantern.]

Sat Dec 27th ditto

Mon Dec 29th ditto

Tue Dec 30th Ball

1818

Tuesday Balls January to April or May
Subscription concerts January-February

Tues Jan 27th MC's Ball; MC is Charles Marshall

Wed Jul 8th – Thur Jul 9th, balls in the week common

oOoOo

Wed Oct 7th the subscriptions for the ensuing season are to be renewed.

Tue Nov 10th first Ball. The practice of quadrilles will be on that and every Tuesday at 1pm precisely.

Tue Nov 17th 2nd Ball which probably goes ahead though Queen Charlotte died, as it would take time for the news to percolate.

Tue Nov 24th 3rd Ball Cancelled

Tue Dec 1st 4th Ball Cancelled

Wed Dec 2nd the Queen's funeral

Tue Dec 8th 3rd Ball

Tue Dec 15th 4th Ball

Tue Dec 22nd 5th Ball

Tue Dec 29th 6th Ball

1819

Tue Jan 5th 7th Ball

Mon Jan 11th a meeting starting at 1pm to raise subscription for Mr. Simms, who was ruined by standing surety for Cavenagh and Browne's Bank who were Bondsmen for Mr. Edward Bowen who absconded with all the property tax for 1815.

Tue Jan 12th 8th Ball

Tue Jan 19th 9th Ball

Tue Jan 26th 10th Ball

Thur Jan 28th at 2pm and in the evening at 8 pm, M. and Mlle Chabert, the two wonderful Russian fire-proof phenomena. A display of fire works around M. Chabert until his outer garment be destroyed. A band of music also. Admission 3/-, back seats 2/-, children half price

Tue Feb 2nd 11th Ball

Tue Feb 9th 12th Ball

Tue Feb 16th 13th Ball

Tue Feb 23rd 14th Ball

Tue Mar 2nd 15th Ball

Tue Mar 9th 16th Ball

Tue Mar 16th 17th Ball

Tue Mar 23rd 18th Ball

Tue Mar 30th 19th Ball

Fri Apr 2nd Mr. Garbett's concert

Fri Apr 6th 20th Ball

Good Friday April 9th

Tue Apr 20th 21st Ball

Tue Apr 27th 22nd Ball

Tue May 4th 23rd Ball

Tue May 11th 24th Ball

Wed Jul 7th & Thur Jul 8th Race week, 2 Balls

oOoOo

Wed Oct 27th Notice that subscriptions due.

Tue Nov 9th First Ball; practise of quadrilles Tue afternoons CANCELLED.

Thur Nov 11th A rebuttal that seditious papers were taken at the reading room.

Tue Nov 16th First subscription Ball. Practise of quadrilles on Tuesday afternoons as scheduled.

Tue Nov 23rd 2nd Ball

Tues Nov 30th 3rd Ball

Fri Dec 3rd Mr. Ogilvie's first lecture on oratory at 2pm precisely; the lecture followed by the recitations of a select passage of poetry with criticisms.

Tues Dec 7th 4th Ball

Tues Dec 14th 5th Ball

Tues Dec 21st 6th Ball

Tues Dec 28th 7th Ball

1820
Tue Jan 4th 8th Ball

Tue Jan 11th 9th Ball

Tue Jan 18th 10th Ball

Tue Jan 25th 11th Ball

Tue Feb 1st MC's Ball rescheduled owing to the rescheduling of the MC's Ball at the Upper Rooms, the Tuesday of the following week being the eve of Ash Wednesday.

Tue Feb 8th MC's Ball MOVED to Feb 1st and suspended owing to the death of George III.

Mon Feb 14th Demonstration of the teaching methods of M. Guiot in the French language using the Dufief system.

Good Friday March 31st

Charles Marshall goes to Cheltenham as MC - elections.

A Literary and Philosophical institution to be founded.

Thur June 29th [second Race day] Mr. Mathews 'at home' with his entertainments 'Mail Coach Adventures' and 'Delineation of Nature.'

Thur July 6th Mr. Flemmington, successful rival of Mr. Mathews will be 'at home' for the second time for his Characteristic Lecture. Admission 3/- doors open at 7-30 for 8pm start.

oOoOo

Thur Oct 5th open to receive the season's subscriptions

Tue Nov 21st First Ball

Thur Dec 7th Mr. Mathews 'at home' with his enterainment 'Country cousins and the sights of London.'

Burnt down Thursday 21st December, 1820 about 11 o'clock, smoke seen issuing. The engines of the different fire offices were brought, but water could not be procured in time, and the flames overcame the building. The six windows of the great room burst between one and two o'clock. From the end of North Parade, the surrounding hills seemed tinged with red, and columns of sparks ascended to a great height. The fire raged until almost six o'clock when the whole fell in on itself. Providentially there was no wind to carry the flames. Leader of the band Mr. Loder and Mr. Cooper risked their lives to rescue Mrs. Mills and her children. The Rifle Corps also bore much assistance.
Insurance for the premises £4000; furniture £4000; Mr. Mills' private effects £2,400

Chapter Seven: The Upper, or New Assembly Rooms

These rooms are situated at the east end of the Circus, between Bennet and Alfred Streets. They were completed in 1771.
The ballroom is 105 x 43 feet [31.5m x 12.9m] and 42'6" high [12.75m]
One of the card rooms is octagonal, with a portrait of Captain Wade, by Gainsborough; the other is 70 x 27 feet [21m x 8.1m] with a picture of Mr. Tyson, late Master of Ceremonies.
Master of Ceremonies: Mr. James King d 1816 October
Captain Wyke until beginning of 1818
James Heaviside from February 1818

The Upper Assembly rooms, photograph S. Waldock

Public Amusements in the New Assembly Rooms during the season
Monday night Dress Ball
Tuesday night, Card assembly
Wednesday night, A concert
Thursday night, Fancy Ball

Balls and Concerts which are numbered are subscription balls and concerts.

Absence of specific dated occurences does not mean they did not take place during the season [November or December to February] only that there is an absence of evidence.

The rooms open every day except Sunday for card playing. Every other Sunday evening, a Promenade. Non-subscribers may be admitted to the Sunday promenade, gentlemen 1/-, ladies 6d, tea included.

Card Room, photo S. Waldock. Wide angle distortion

Subscription 10/6d for gentlemen and 5/- to ladies to walk in the rooms, and play cards and take part in the Sunday promenades. No person not subscribed is permitted to walk in these rooms.

Fancy Balls were fancy dress occasions, and some of the costumes could be quite outrageous; men in short, Roman tunics for example. Many aristocratic young ladies had little better to do than to devise fancy costumes.

Subscription and rules for balls:

- £1/6/- for the season for the Dress balls for gentlemen, conferring 2 tickets transferrable only to ladies.
- 12/- for the Dress Ball for the season for one ticket, non-transferrable.
- Subscription for fancy balls is 12/- for the season, the ticket not transferrable. Non-subscribers pay 5/- each time.
- Young ladies and gentlemen at school vacation will be admitted if introduced by a subscriber.
- Dress and Fancy balls begin as soon as possible after 7pm and finish at 11pm even if in the middle of a dance.
- Admission 6d for tea.
- Ladies of precedence given reasonable time to take their place at the top of the dance, but if tardy must go to the bottom of the dance. No lady is to permit another ahead of her after she has taken her place in the set.
- Ladies who intend dancing the minuet to wear lappets. Minuets open the Ball.
- The three front seats at the upper end of the room reserved for ladies of precedence being Peeresses.
- No gentleman in boots or half-boots to be admitted on Ball nights or public card or concert nights.
- No person admitted on Dress-Ball nights without a ticket. No ticket required for entry to the card-rooms on Fancy-Ball nights from such persons as subscribe to the walking subscription.
- 26 Dress balls and 30 Fancy balls to be provided annually.
- No person may take up play with cards left by another.
- No hazard or other unlawful games, nor any card games on Sunday.
- At Dress balls, only country dances are danced; at Fancy balls, two cotillions are danced, one before and one after tea.

The band for the balls was to consist of 12 performers, including harp, tabor and pipe, each to be paid a half guinea for his playing for each night.

Between 800-1200 people attend most balls.

As well as the ballroom there are card rooms, billiards rooms, concert rooms and coffee rooms.

No entertainments on Ash Wednesday, Good Friday or Jan 30th, the date of the execution of Charles I, observed by the church as a fast day. A number of Royal Deaths occurred in this decade; it was customary to eschew theatre performances and entertainments until after the funeral, when mourning would be worn.

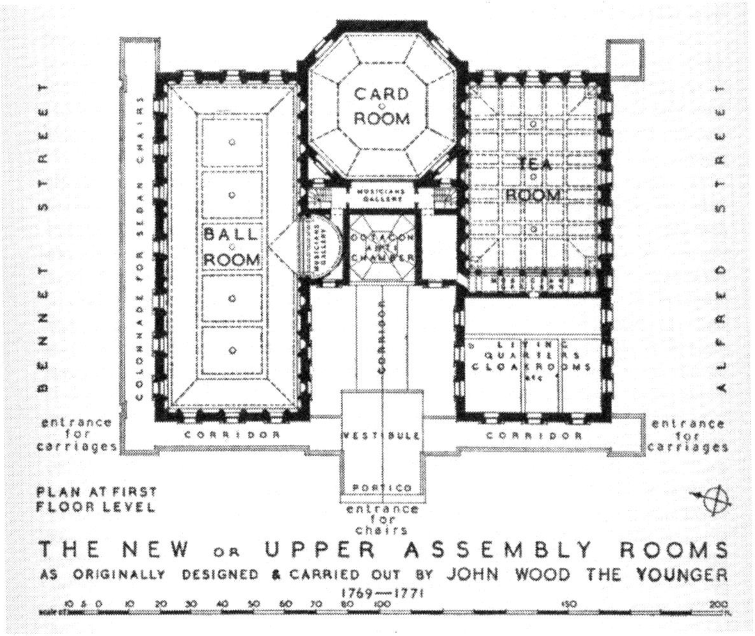

Special Concerts New Assembly Rooms

There are 9 subscription concerts and 3 choral nights in the winter season. 3 guineas and a half [£3/13/6d] subscription entitles entry to all, non-transferrable. Purchase of a second ticket transferrable to ladies only. Non-subscribers pay 7/- each time.
£5/15/6d will be entitled to 3 tickets for each concert transferable to ladies only.
£4/10/- will be entitled to two tickets for each concert transferable to ladies only.
£3/13/6d subscription entitles entry to all concerts, one ticket to each, non-transferable.

Subscriptions will be received for part of the concerts on the following terms;
£3/3/- will be entitled to three tickers for each of the four concerts following such subscription transferable to ladies only.
£2/6/- two tickets transferable to Ladies only for each of four concerts.
£1/6/0 an admission ticket transferable to a lady for the four concerts after this subscription.

Tickets for non-subscribers 7/-

Tickets to be had at the libraries, York House, and music shops as well as at the Rooms and anyone for whom the concert is a benefit concert.

Concerts start 7.30pm

1810

Wed Jan 3rd 6th Concert, Mrs. Dickons will sing 3 songs

Wed Jan 10th Benefit Grand concert of vocal and instrumental music, principal vocals Mrs. Dickons. Concerto violin Mr. Yaniewicz. Haydn, Glee, Mozart, solos, Handel. Gallery available. Mr. Braham to sing

Wed Jan 17th 7th Concert with Mr. Braham singing

Sat Jan 20th, Miss Darby's morning concert, Mrs. Ashe, Mr. Magrath etc; celebrated Signor Pucci will perform a concerto on the pedal harp. Tickets at Messrs Ashley's, Lintern's and Philpott's music shops, Godwin's Library Milsom St, and Miss Darby, 3 New Bond St.

Wed Jan 24th 8th Concert

Wed Jan 31st 9th Concert last of season. The second choral night. A grand selection from the Messiah with Mr. Braham. Act II, selection from Haydn, Mozart, Rauzzini and others.

Wed Feb 7th Miss Sharp's benefit grand concert, tickets 5/-

Wed Mar 7th Ash Wednesday

Good Friday April 20th

oOoOo

James King is MC

Sun Nov 2nd Death of Princess Amelia

Mon Nov 5th First Dress Ball of the season Cancelled

Thur Nov 8th First Fancy Ball of the season Cancelled

Tues Nov 13th Funeral of Princess Amelia

Mon Nov 19th First Dress Ball

Tues Nov 20th First Fancy Ball

Wed Nov 21st first of nine concerts. Principal vocalist Madame Catalani who will be singing at all 9 concerts. Also Signora Bianchi and Signor Tramezzani.

Mon Nov 26th 2nd Dress Ball

Tue Nov 27th 2nd Fancy Ball

Wed Nov 28th 2nd Concert

Mon Dec 5th 3rd Dress Ball

Tue Dec 6th 3rd Fancy Ball

Wed Dec 7th 3rd Concert

Mon Dec 10th 4th Dress Ball

Tue Dec 11th 4th Fancy Ball

Wed Dec 12th 4th Cconcert

Mon Dec 17th 5th Dress Ball

Tue Dec 18th 5th Fancy Ball

Wed Dec 19th 5th Concert

Mon Dec 31st 6th Dress Ball

Ballroom at Upper Assembly Rooms showing gallery above door from vestibule.

.

1811

Tue Jan 1st 6th Fancy Ball

Wed Jan 2nd 6th Concert

Mon Jan 7th 7th Dress Ball

Tue Jan 8th 7th Fancy Ball

Wed Jan 9th 7th Concert

Mon Jan 14th 8th Dress Ball

Tue Jan 15th 8th Fancy Ball

Wed Jan 16th 8th Concert

Mon Jan 21st 9th Dress Ball

Tue Jan 22nd 9th Fancy Ball

Wed Jan 23rd 9th Concert

Mon Jan 28th 10th Dress Ball

Tue Jan 29th 10th Fancy Ball

Mon Feb 4th 11th Dress Ball

Tue Feb 5th 11th Fancy Ball

Wed Feb 6th Benefit concert of Mr. and Mrs. Windsor of vocal and instrumental music.

Mon Feb 11th 12th Dress Ball

Tue Feb 12th 12th Fancy Ball

Wed Feb 13th Mr. and Miss Richards Benefit concert of vocal and instrumental music.

Mon Feb 18th 13th Dress Ball

Tue Feb 19th 13th Fancy Ball

Mon Feb 25th 14th Dress Ball

Tue Feb 26th 14th Fancy Ball

Wed Feb 27th Ash Wednesday

Mon Mar 4th 15th Dress Ball

Tue Mar 5th 15th Fancy Ball

Mon Mar 11th 16th Dress Ball

Tue Mar 12th 16th Fancy Ball

Mon Mar 18th 17th Dress Ball

Tue Mar 19th 17th Fancy Ball

Mon Mar 25th 18th Dress Ball

Tue Mar 26th 18th Fancy Ball

Wed Mar 27th Concert for the relief of our brave countrymen at present languishing in the dungeons of a vindictive enemy. Tickets 5/- Miss Sharpe and Mr. Magrath will sing in public only for this charitable occasion. A grand selection of Sacred Music

Mon Apr 1st 19th Dress Ball

Tue Apr 2nd 19th Fancy Ball

Mon Apr 8th 20th Dress Ball

Tue Apr 9th 20th Fancy Ball

Good Friday April 12th

Wed Apr 17th Grand Concert under direction of Mr. Ashe, with Madame Catalani

Fri Apr 19th Grand Concert under direction of Mr. Ashe, with Madame Catalani

Mon Apr 22nd 21st Dress Ball

Tue Apr 23rd 21st Fancy Ball

Mon Apr 29th 22nd Dress Ball

Tue Apr 30th 23rd Dress Ball

Mon May 6th 24th Dress Ball

Tue May 7th 24th Fancy Ball

Mon May 13th 25th Dress Ball

Tue May 14th 25th Fancy Ball

Mon May 20th 26th and final Dress Ball

Tue May 21st 26th Fancy Ball

4 Fancy balls in Race Week [end of June]

oOoOo

Wed Nov 27th 1st of 9 concerts with Madame Catalani and Mr. Braham for all.

Wed Dec 4th 2nd Concert

Wed Dec 11th 3rd Concert

Wed Dec 18th 4th Concert

Ballroom at upper rooms photograph S. Waldock

1812

Wed Jan 1st 5th Concert

Wed Jan 8th 6th Concert

Wed Jan 15th 7th Concert

Wed Jan 22nd 8th Concert

Wed Jan 29th 9th Concert

Fri Feb 7th Grand Concert of vocal and instrumental music, for the benefit of the Bath City Infirmary and Dispensary, Mr. Braham chief vocalist with Messrs Comer, Garbett, Magrath and Ashe; Mrs. Ashe, Misses Wood, Comer and Sharp. Tickets 7/-

Wed Feb 12th Ash Wednesday

Wed Feb 19th Mr. Magrath's benefit, concert of vocal and instrumental music, tickets 7/-

Wed Feb 26th Mr. & Miss Richards benefit concert of vocal and instrumental music. Fantasia upon piano-forte & grand chorus Tickets 7/-

Wed Mar 11th Miss Fryer benefit concert with a selection of scarce and valuable music from Haydn, Giordani, Handel and Prortogallo.

Mon May 25th in the morning, a Grand Concert of vocal and instrumental music. For the benefit of a fellow musician who has lost the use of his limbs. First act sacred music. Tickets 5/-

Good Friday April 16th

oOoOo

Wed Dec 2nd 1st of 9 concerts

Wed Dec 9th 2nd Concert

Wed Dec 16th 3rd Concert

Wed Dec 30th 4th Concert

1813

Wed Jan 6th 5th Concert

Wed Jan 13th 6th Concert

Wed Jan 20th 7th Concert

Wed Jan 27th 8th Concert

Wed Feb 3rd Ash Wednesday

Wed Feb 10th 9th Concert

Good Friday April 16th

oOoOo

Wed Dec 1st 1st Concert

Wed Dec 8th 2nd Concert

Wed Dec 15th 3rd Concert

Wed Dec 29th 4th Concert

1814

Wed Jan 5th 5th Concert

January Madame Catalani will sing for 4 of the 5 remaining Subscription concerts. An amicable arrangement with the lower rooms who ceded the engagement of Mme Catalini to the upper rooms.

Wed Jan 12th 6th Concert with Mme Catalani, with Signors Bianchi and Tramessani their second appearance this season.

Wed Jan 19th Concert

Wed Jan 26th Concert

Wed Feb 2nd Concert

Wed Feb 9th Concert

Wed Feb 23rd Ash Wednesday

Good Friday April 8th

Mon Apr 18th Grand Miscellaneous concert

[Tues Apr 19th Grand selection of sacred music in the Abbey Church to begin promptly at 6-30pm to permit the company to go to the Ball at the Lower Rooms. To be brilliantly lighted with lamps to light the gothic architecture to best advantage.]

Wed Apr 20th [morning, at the Abbey Church, a selection of music from 'The Creation' by Haydn and compositions of Handel, Mozart etc.]
On the same evening at the Rooms - A Grand Concert

Thurs Apr 21st [Morning at Abbey Church Sacred Oratorio of the Messiah.]

Principal vocalists, Madame Catalani, Misses Nash, Wood and Mrs. Salmon, Messers Braham, Magrath, Garbett and Tinney and the Messers Schuncke from Berlin by permission of the Prince Regent. Mr. Loder leader of the band.

Tickets; a subscriber of £2 will receive 6 tickets, one to each performance, which are transferable to a lady or a gentleman. Non-subscribers' ticker 8/-
Church door to open at 9-30 am, performances from 11am, the Rooms to open every evening at 6pm, concerts at 7pm.

Tea Room

oOoOo

Frid Nov 4th Ladies card assembly and every Friday during the season

Mon Nov 14th First Dress Ball

Thur Nov 17th First Fancy Dress Ball

Wed Dec 14th First Concert

Wed Dec 28th 2nd Concert

1815

Wed Jan 4th 3rd Concert

Wed Jan 11th 4th Concert with the celebrated Mr. Kalkbrenner, pupil of Haydn. Will perform his own composition on piano-forte. Mr. Bartleman will sing several favourite songs. Tickets for non-subscribers 8/-

Wed Jan 18th 5th Concert with the much celebrated Madame Sessi, who will sing several grand arias &c

Wed Jan 25th 6th Concert with Madame Sessi singing several grand arias; and Mr. Weichselle plays a concerto on violin

Wed Feb 8th Ash Wednesday

Wed Feb 22nd Benefit Mr. Loder, concert, vocal and instrumental music. Mrs. Ashe, the Misses Wood, Bartlett and Nash, Messers Cooke, Garbett, Oder, Comer and Rolle. Mr. Loder on horns
Mr. Percival a concerto on violincello, Master Field will play Beethoven's grand fantasia on Piano-forte with full band and chorus. Tickets 7/- from Mr. Loder, 45 Milsom Street or his musical warehouse, 1 Milsom St.

Good Friday March 24th

Fri Apr 7th Benefit morning concert for Miss Wood, principle vocal performers Mrs. Ashe, Miss Bartlett, Miss Wood, Mr. Loder, Mr. Garbett and Mr. Comer. To begin at 12-30pm precisely, tickets 7/- each.

Vestibule of the Upper Assembly Rooms looking left towards the Ballroom. Photo S. Waldock.

1816

Mon Jan 22nd MC's Ball – POSTPONED owing to illness of Mr. King.

Mon Jan 29th MC's Ball.

Wed Feb 14th Concert

Wed Feb 28th Ash Wedesday

Wed Mar 13th Mr. Loder's Annual Concert of vocal and instrumental music. Misses Wood and Bartlett, Mrs. Shaw, Messrs Loder, Garbett, Comer, Winter and Rolle. tickets 7/-

Good Friday April 12th

Mon April 15th The MC's Spring Ball

Wed Apr 17th in Easter week Annual Benefit Concert; the new musical play of *Guy Mannering* and other songs, from *Midsummer Night's Dream*. The Misses Ashe will perfor a grand duet on harp and Piano-forte. To begin 7pm

oOoOo

October, voting for new MC after death of James King.

Wed Nov 13th Grand Concert of vocal and instrumental music. Miss Harding to sing after the manner of Mme Catalini.
Tickets 7/-

Wed Dec 18th 1strd Concert

1817

Wed Jan 1st 2nd Concert with the Demoiselles De Lihu and Miss Tremearn

Wed Jan 8th 3rd Concert

Wed Jan 15th 4th Concert

Wed Jan 22nd 5th Concert

Wed Jan 28th 6th Concert

Wed Feb 5th 7th Concert

Wed Feb 12th 8th Concert

Wed Feb 19th Ash Wednesday

Wed Feb 26th 9th Concert

Wed Mar 5th 10th Concert

Wed Mar 12th11th Concert

Good Friday April 4th

Mon Apr 7th MC's Spring Ball

Wed Apr 9th, in Easter Week, Benefit concert for Mrs. Ashe. The celebrated Desmoiselles Delihu will sing new duets and songs. Miss Tremearn on violin. Tickets 7/- each

Sat Apr 12th Mr. Cole's Benefit Concert with that interesting child, Matilda Hook. Tickets 5/-

oOoOo

6th November Death of Princess Charlotte of Wales

19th November Funeral of Princess Charlotte

Wed Dec 10th 1st Concert

Wed Dec 17th 2nd Concert

Wed Dec 31st 3rd Concert

1818

Wed Jan 7th 4th Concert with much celebrated M. Bochsa on harp

Tue Jan 13th the first private subscription assembly with lady patronesses Lady Fitzgerald & Mrs. Bissett.

Wed Jan 14th 5th Concert. Gallery available

Mon Jan 19th MCs Ball

Wed Jan 21st 6th Concert

Mon Jan 26th 2nd Private subscription assembly; lady patronesses Mrs. Richardson and Mrs. Pigou. Quadrilles will commence promptly at 9pm.

Tues Jan 27th Will be the Card assembly not Fri 30th, the Friday being the anniversary of King Charles's Martyrdom

Wed Jan 28th 7th Concert with the Demoiselles De Lihu and the celebrated Signor Puzzi on the French Horn; M. Bochsa on harp and duet for harp and horn with these gentlemen

Fri Jan 30th 7th Concert

Wed Feb 4th Ash Wednesday

Fri Feb 6th 8th Concert the last night of Mr. Perceval and the De Lihus. Mrs. Ashe, Miss Wood, Mr. Pearman and Signor Vercellini

Fri Feb 13th 9th Concert

Sat Feb 14th In the morning, concert of vocal and instrumental music. Vocal performers Miss Poole, Mr. Pearman, Mr. Garbett, Mr. A. Loder, Mr. Bedford and Mr. Rolle. Mr. Downes and Sig. Anaia will perform on Harp-lute and Spanish guitar. Tickets 7/-

Tues Feb 17th 3rd Private subscription assembly. Lady Patronesses Lady O'Brien & Mrs. Cope. The musicians will attend at the rooms on Mon 16th at 1pm for Quadrille practice.

Wed Feb 18th 10th Concert, the gallery fitted up for ladies who prefer it.
Good Friday March 20th

Fri Mar 27th [Friday after Easter] Public assembly for the pupils of the Misses Giroux. Tickets 5/- from the Misses Giroux' Academy at 14 George Street.

Wed Apr 1st Mr. Percivall's Benefit concert

Wed Apr 15th Mr. Cole's Annual

benefit concert, tickets 7/-

Wed Apr 22nd First Philharmonic Society concert [Frederick Loder, secretary]

Wed May 6th Second Philharmonic Society concert

Wed May 13th Third Philharmonic Society concert

Wed May 20th Fourth Philharmonic Society concert

Wed Jun 3rd Fifth and final Philharmonic Society concert

Mon Jun 1st –Fri Jun 5th the 6th Bath and Somersetshire Grand Musical Festival at the Upper Assembly Rooms and Abbey Church. Principal vocal performer Miss Corri, Miss Williams, Miss Carew [from Covent Garden] Mr. Sirrail [from the oratorios] Mr. Braham, Messrs Thorn and Sinney, leader Mr. Loder. The Abbey Church will be splendidly lighted under the direction of Mr. Mills, Kingston rooms. Doors for all evening performance open at 6pm, and commence 7pm; for morning performances doors open at 9-30 am and begin at 11am.
A subscriber of £2/10/- will be entitled to two tickets for each performance, transferable to lady or gentleman; a subscriber of £1/1-/- wil be entitled to one ticket to each performance, transferable to lady or gentleman. Non Subscribers, tickets 7/- each.

Mon Jun 1st Evening, at Upper Assembly Rooms a grand miscellaneous concert

Tue Jun 2nd Evening, at the church, a manuscript Miserere by Winter and a selection of sacred music

Wed Jun 3rd Evening at upper assembly rooms, a grand concert

Thur Jun 4th Morning at the Abbey Church, the first part of the Creation, an extract from a grand mass by Beethoven and a selection from ancient composers

Fri Jun 5th At the Abbey Church, The Messiah, chorus of more than one hundred and twenty performers.

Tue Aug 18th -Thur Aug 20th Salisbury Musical Festival at Upper Assembly Rooms and Cathedral with Mme Fodor Tickets for Morning performances 9/-; for evening

10/6d. Morning performances begin at 11sm, evening at 7-15pm

Tue Aug 18th Evening in the assembly rooms grand miscellaneous Concert and Ball

Wed Aug 19th Morning at Cathedral, grand selection of sacred music
Wed Aug 19th Evening, select vocal concert

Thur Aug 20th Morning at Cathedral, The Messiah

Thur Aug 20th Evening at Assembly Rooms grand miscellaneous concert followed by a Ball.

oOoOo

Mon Nov 9th 1st Dress Ball

Thur Nov 12th 1st Fancy Ball

Mon 16th Nov 2nd Dress Ball

Tues November 17th Death of Queen Charlotte

Balls cancelled

Wed 2nd December Funeral of Queen Charlotte

Thur 10th Dec Balls resumed with 2nd Fancy Ball

Mon 14th Dec 3rd Dress Ball

Thur 17th Dec. 3rd Fancy Ball

Mon 21st Dec 4th Dress Ball

1819

Fri Feb 19th Children's Ball, the second public assembly of the scholars of the Misses Giroux' dancing classes. Tickets 5/-

oOoOo

Thur Nov 18th First Fancy Ball

Wed Dec. 22nd,
An announcement in the newspaper that the Dress Ball at these Rooms was discontinued by the renter, in consequence of it having failed to receive sufficient support; a meeting to be held to decide what to do for Monday night balls.

Wed Dec 29th 1st Concert

1820

Wed Jan 5th 2nd Concert

Wed Jan 12th 3rd Concert

Wed Jan 19th 4th Concert with 'Il Fanatico Per La Musica' act 1

Wed Jan 26th Postponed, the 5th concert owing to clash with theatre's charity play. with Cosi Fan Tutti

Sat Jan 29th 5th Subscription concert; 1st act of 'Il Fanatico Per la Musica' and 1st act of 'Cosi Fan Tutte' with Signor Begrez from London for one night CANCELLED owing to the death of King George

Mon Jan 31st MC's Ball POSTPONED owing to the observance of the fast of the martyrdom of King Charles beginning Thur Jan 30th, the ecclesiast is ordering that it be kept with solemnity.

Mon Feb 7th MC's Ball Suspended due to death of George III.

Tue Feb 8th Funeral George III
Wed Apr 5th Mrs. Ashe's Annual Benefit Concert POSTPONED

Wed Apr 19th Mrs. Ashe's Benefit Concert tickets 7/-

August a 1/65th Part, one share in the rooms to be sold on the demise of a lady shareholder; annual dividend is £21

oOoOo

Fri Sept 29th The celebrated Miss Stephens in a Grand Concert

Thur Nov 16th First Fancy Ball

Wed Dec 6th 1st Concert

Wed Dec 13th 2nd Concert, Mrs. Salmon and Mr. Begriez to sing. Mr. Mori to perform grand concerto on Violin

Mon Dec 18th First Monday Ball, no more in December as last Monday is Christmas Day

Wed Dec 20th 3rd Concert with Mrs. Salmon

Wed Dec 27th 4th Concert

Chapter Eight: Theatre-Royal Bath

The first Theatre-Royal was in Orchard Street, but in October 1805, it was moved to the new building in Beaufort Square [now given the address of SawClose, which is where the current entrance is, added 1863]. The inaugural play on Saturday 12th October was Shakespeare's 'Richard the Third.'

The theatre took up most of the south side of Beaufort Square, and was 120 feet long, 60 feet wide and 70 feet high. "The walls are covered with a stamped cloth, stuffed [flocked] of a crimson colour; and are papered above, to the height of the boxes a paper of the same colour, an Egyptian pattern, fringed with a gold stripe. The seats and edges of the boxes are also covered with cloth. The front is painted in the same colour [crimson]with four broad stripes of gold and the centre ornamented with tasteful scrolls of gold. Four private boxes are taken from the first tier, on each side next the stage, handsomely fitted up with curtains, gild rails and chairs. The ceiling is divided into four compartments, in each one of which is a fine painting by Cassali, which once occupied a similar situation in a fine mansion on Font Hill.' [Phillips 'Watering and Sea Bathing places.']

Here I have presented every play I could find – and a few from 1810 are missing – advertised in the 'Bath Chronicle and Weekly Gazette'.

No performances on Ash Wednesday or Good Friday.

A number of Royal Deaths occurred in this decade; it was customary to eschew theatre performances and entertainments until after the funeral, when mourning would be worn.

1810

January

Thur 4th melo-dramatic opera *The Exile* with farce *No Farce, No Supper*
Fri 5th *The Foundling of the Forest* with the serious ballet pantomime *Raymond and Agnes*
Sat 6th *The English Fleet in 1342* with entertainments.

February

Thur 8th comic opera *The Cabinet* with *Ella Rosenberg*
Fri 9th *Romeo and Juliet* with *Peeping Tom of Coventry*
Sat 10th *The Siege of Belgrade* with entertainments
Thur 15th comic opera *The Duenna* with *The Deuce is in him*
Fri 16th *Nenoni,* or, 'the Novice of St Mark's' with *Ways and Means*
Sat 17th *The Castle of Andalusia*

March

Fri 2nd *King Henry VIII* with *Forty Thieves*
Sat 3rd comedy *Sudden Arrivals* with serious pantomime *Raymond and Agnes*
Tues 6th *The Wonder* with *Three and the Deuce*
Thur 14th *The Iron Chest* with *Of Age Tomorrow*
Sat 16th *Beaux Stratagem* with farce *The Lyar*
Tues 20th comedy *Town and Country* with comic songs and dancing; the interlude *Personation* and finishing with fairy tale *Edgar and Emmeline* with a fairy dance
Thurs 22nd comedy *A Cure for the Heart-Ache* with *A day after the Wedding* or, 'A Wife's First Lesson' with burletts *Tom Thumb the Great*
Sat 24th comedy *The Blind Bargain* with comic sketch of *Silvester Daggerwood* and to conclude the farce *Killing no Murder*
Tues 27th *Richard Coeur de Lion* with *The Voice of Nature* and concluding with burletta *Poor Vulcan*
Thurs 29th *Henry IV* with farce *The Mayor of Garrat*; Mr. Evans will sing the song of Romeo and Juliet, and to conclude, the pantomime *Don Juan*
Sat 31st Reynold's comedy *How to get Rich* with interlude *The day after the wedding* and concluding with *The Vale of Terror*

April

Tues 3rd *The Stranger* dancing by six of Miss Egerton's pupils, with a grand, serious, heroic pantomime *Oscar and Malvina*
Easter Tues 24th historical play *Pizarro* with pantomime *Raymond and Agnes*
Wed 25th *The Tempest* with melo-drama *The Blind Boy*
Thur 26th comedy *The School of*

Reform with a broadsword hornpipe, nautical hornpipe and sundry singing and dancing, after which *Valentine and Orson*
Sat 27th *The Hero of the North* with entertainments
Tue 30th *Jane Shore* with entertainments

May
Thur 31st comedy *Chapter of Accidents* with farce *Love in a camp*

June
Sat 2nd comedy *Clandestine Marriage* with farce *No Song, No Supper*
Sat 16th comedy *The West Indian* with *Ella Rosenburg*
Sat 30th comedy *Wild Oats* with *Love Laughs at Locksmiths*

July
Sat 14th *the Beggars' Opera* with farce *A Budget of Blunders*
Sat 21st historical opera *The English Fleet in 1342* with songs and musical entertainment *The Waterman*

oOoOo

October
Sat 6th the comedy *The West Indian* with farce *The Irishman in London*
Sat 13th as above
Sat 20th *Othello* with the melo-drama *A Tale fo Mystery*
Sat 27th comedy *The Provoked Husband* with farce *The Budget of Blunders*

November
Sat 2nd, Death of Princess Amelia, Tues 13th funeral
Sat 3rd comedy *The Rivals* with new musical entertainment *Hit and Miss* Cancelled
Sat 17th comedy *The Jew* followed by ballet dance *Dermot and Kathleen*, and musical farce *The Children in the Wood*
Thur 22nd comedy *The Heir at Law* with grand historical pantomime, never before performed here, *Perouse* or, 'The Desolate Island'
Sat 24th *A Bold Stroke for a Wife* with *Peeping Tom of Coventry*
Thur 29th historical musical drama *The Battle of Hexham* with pantomime *Perouse* or, 'The Desolate Island'

December
Sat 1st comedy *The Way to keep him* with *Ella Rosenberg*
Thur 6th melo-dramatic opera *The Exile* with musical farce *Rosina*
Sat 8th *Foundling of the Forest* with *Perouse*
Thur 27th tragedy *George Barnwell* with pantomime *Perouse*
Fri 28th *The Castle Spectre* with *Perouse*
Sat 29th *Clandestine Marriage* with ballet dance *Dermot and Kathleen etc*

1811

January

Thur 3rd *The Doubtful Son* with melo-drama *Valentine and Orson*
Fri 4th *Lovers' Vows* with *The Black Forest*
Sat 5th *The School for Scandal* with *Paul and Virginia*
Thur 10th tragedy *Pizarro* with pantomime *Don Juan*
Fri 11th *The Curfew* with *The Forty Thieves*
Sat 12th *The Foundling of the Forest* with entertainments.
Thur 17th Grand Miscellaneous Concert after which, the musical farce *The Romp*; song 'the mail coach' and concluding with melo-drama *The Blind Boy*
Sat 19th *The Doubtful Son* with pantomime *Perouse*
Thur 24th comedy *Country Girl* Peggy by Mrs. Jordan in her farewell visit to Bath before retiring from the stage. With melo drama *A Tale of Mystery*
Sat 26th *The Soldier's Daughter* and *The Sultan*; Widow Cheerly and Roxalana by Mrs. Jordan
Thur 31st comedy *The Belle's Stratagem*, Letitia Hardy by Mrs. Jordan. With operatic romance *The Forty Thieves*

February

Sat 2nd *All in the Wrong*, Belinda by Mrs. Jordan
Tues 5th *Man and Wife* and *Three Weeks After Marriage*; Helen Worrit and Lady Racket by Mrs. Jordan.
Thur 7th, Last night of Mrs. Jordan! *Much Ado About Nothing* and a farce *The Devil to Pay* Beatrice and Nell, Mrs. Jordan
Sat 9th *The Trip to Scarborough*
Thur 14th comedy *Inconstant* with *The Devil to Pay*
Sat 16th *The Curfew* and after a hornpipe, after which grand romantic melo-drama *Valentine and Orson*
Tues 19th *Pizarro* with *A Budget of Blunders*
Thur 21st *The Mountaineers* with *The Critic*
Sat 23rd *The West Indian* with *The Hunter of the Alps*
Thur 28th comedy *The Chances* with *The Doctor and Apothecary*

March

Sat 2nd *Speed the Plough*
Tues 5th comedy *The Way to get Married* with *Love Laughs at Locksmiths*
Thur 7th *The Maniac,* or, 'The Swiss Banditti'with *Forty Thieves*
Sat 9th *The Maniac* with entertainments.
Tues 12th drama *The Foundling of the Forest* with pantomime *Perouse*
Thur 14th tragedy in 3 acts *Oroonoko,* or, 'The Royal Slave' with comic songs. Then O'Keefe's farce *The Prisoner AtLarge* and *Incle and Yarico*

Sat 16th Murphy's comedy *Know your own Mind* with divertissement to be danced by Mr. Saunders and Mr. Webster's pupils. To conclude, the farce *The Farmer*, or, 'The Country Girl turned into a Fine Lady.'

Tues 19th new play *The Family Legend,* or 'The Lady of the Rock' with musical interlude and musical entertainment *The Young Hussar*

Thur 21st tragedy *The Orphan* with *Whittington and his Cat* after which the interlude *The Rival Soldiers* and comic farce *Tom Thumb*

Sat 23rd *Zorinski,* or, 'King and Country Preserved' then interlude *The Blue Devils* with musical farce *The Lake of Lausanne* or, 'Out of Place'

Tues 26th comedy *Jealous Wife* followed by songs, then melo drama *Tekeli,* or, 'The Siege of Montgatz'

Thur 28th play in 3 acts *Point of Honour* with musical farce *The Poor Soldier*; a comic song, and to conclude the melo-drama *The Blind Boy.*

Sat 30th historical play *Columbus,* or, 'A World Discovered'; end of play an allemande de trois and pas de trois by Mr. Saunders and Mr. Webster's pupils. With serious pantomime *Oscar and Malvina*

April

Tues 2nd comedy *The World in a Village,* or, 'A peep at them all'comic songs and dance of the Jolly Millers, and farce *Out of Place,* or, 'Lake of Lausenne'

Thurs 4th comedy *Every One Has His Fault* at end of play a dramatic sketch called 'The Wrangling Lovers, or like Master like Man.' To conclude a musical entertainment, *The Highland Reel*

Sat 6th comic opera *Love in a Village* with *Lock and Key* and during Easter week save the weekend

Easter Holidays Good Fri 12th, Easter Sunday 14th

Easter Tues 16th *The Beggars' Opera* to conclude with the pantomime *Perouse.*

Thur 18th comic opera *Castle of Andalusia* with musical drama *Paul and Virginia*

Fri 19th *Columbus* with *Perouse*

Sat 20th *The Quaker* with *The Child of Nature* and farce *The Waterman*

Thur 25th comic opera *The Castle of Andalusia* with *The Farmer*

Sat 27th *Adrian and Orrila* with a variety of dancing and comic songs, after which comic opera *Incle[sic] and Yarico]*

Tues 30th comedy *Such Things Are* with musical interlude *The Virgin Unmasked* and *The Agreeable Surprize*

May

Thur 2nd *The Maniac* or, 'The Swiss Banditti' with *Oscar and Malvina*

Sat 4th new comedy *Ourselves* and *Lake of Lausanne* [*Ourselves* Postponed owing to indisposition of Miss Jameson]

Wed 8th *The Doubtful Son* with new farce *The Bee Hive*

Sat 11th *The Foundling of the Forest* with entertainments

Tues 14th comedy *Laugh When You Can* with entertainments and the grand melo-dramatic romance *Valentine and Orson*

Fri 17th comedy *A Bold Stroke for a Husband* dancing at end of play, and serious ballet *Raymond and Agnes*

Sat 18th comedy *The Wheel of Fortune* followed by dances and a petit piece called *Personation* to which added the musical farce *The Deserter*

Tues 21st *The Stranger* with a farce and other entertainments.

Thur 30th *Castle Spectre* with dances including a Strathspey fling; with musical Drama *Paul and Virginia*

June

Sat 1st comedy *Chapter of Accidents* with farce, *The Budget of Blunders*

Sat 8th comedy *School for Scandal* with musical farce *Killing no Murder*

Sat 15th Murphy's comedy *Know your own mind* with musical farce *Love Laughs at Locksmiths*

Sat 22nd comedy *The Suspicious Husband*; between play and farce a hornpipe. Farce with music *Trial by Jury*

The Theatre will be open during race week

July

Tues 2nd comedy *Gazette Exraordinare* with musical farce *Love Laughs at Locksmiths*

Wed 3rd *Speed the Plough* with *Forty Thieves*

Thur 4th play *The Foundling of the Forest* and pantomime, *Perouse*

Friday 5th *Pizzaro* with new musical farce *Hit or Miss*, or 'Prime Bang-Up'

Sat 6th a favourite comedy with melo-drama *The Princess and No Princess*, or 'the forest of Hermanstadt'

Sat 20th new comedy *The Gazette Exraordinary*; end of play a variety of elegant and surprising manoeuvres on the tight rope. Particularly the Tambourine Dance; last night of Mr. Richer's performance on the rope. To conclude, musical entertainment, *Hit and Miss,* or, 'Prime Bang-up'

oOoOo

October

Sat 5th the comic opera *The Cabinet* with *The Prize*

Sat 19th serious opera *Artaxerxes* then comic interlude *Tag in Tribulation* and Musical Farce, *The Prize*

Sat 26th new historical play *The Royal Oak*

November

Sat 9th a comedy *The Will* with musical piece in 3 acts *Three and the Deuce* with Mr. Elliston playing Peregrine Single, Pertinax Single and Percival Single

Sat 16th comedy *Suspicious Husband* with farce *Of Age Tomorrow*

Tues 19th *The Iron Chest* and *Spoiled Child*

Fri 22nd, with Mr. Elliston, comedy *The Dramatist* then *The Critic*, or 'a tragedy relieved'

Sat 23rd *The West Indian* and *Doctor and Apothecary*

Tues 26th benefit Mr. Elliston, play in 3 acts *The Venetian Outlaw* then comic 1-act piece *Blue Devils* to which added musical drama *Hunter of the Alps*

Thur 28th the comedy *The Dramatist* to which added *The Critic*

Sat 30th *The West Indian* with *Doctor and Apothecary.*

December

Tue 3rd a play in three acts *The Venetian Outlaw* after which a comic piece *Blue Devils* concluding in *Hunter of the Alps*

Thur 5th Mr. Elliston for one more night; comedy *Honeymoon* to which added the celebrated entertainment *Three and the Duce*, Mr. Elliston to play all three singles!

Sat 7th new opera *The Peasant Boy* and the dancing of the 3 Misses Giroux with Mr. de Flesmoure

Thur 19th comedy *The Inconstant.* After, a ballet produced by Mr. Giroux called *Rendezvous or Little Mischief Maker* to be added the pantomime *Perouse,* or, 'The Desolate Island'

Sat 21st ballet dance *The Royal Oak* and for the last time *The Forty Thieves*

1812

January

Thur 9th Theatre Closed
Fri 10th *The Castle Spectre* followed by Mr. Richer's performance on the tight-rope then *Blue Beard*
Sat 11th new comedy never performed here before *The Kiss* with *Blue Beard*
Tue 14th comic opera *The Haunted Tower*
Thur 16th comic opera *The Castle of Andalusia* with pantomime *Perouse*
Fr 17th *The School for Scandal* and *Blue Beard*
Sat 18th comic opera *The Cabinet* with *Edgar and Emmeline*
Thur 23rd new operatic drama *The Maniac* with many airs including the much admired ballad 'Robin Adair' and 'last words of Marmion'. To which added the farce *Wedding Day.*
Fri 24th *Recruiting Officer* and *Blue Beard*
Sat 25th the opera of *Fontainbleau* with *The Tale of Mystery*
Fri 31st Farquhar's comedy *The Recruiting Officer* to which added *Blue Beard* the whole to conclude with the *Phantasmagoria* or grand display of optical illusions by the celebrated Signor Belzoni

February

Sat 1st comic opera *Abroad and at Home* with [not acted for 20 years] Mrs. Inchbald's farce *Widow's Vows*
Fri 7th *Pizarro* with *Blue Beard,* or, 'Female Curiosity' and to conclude *The Phantasmagoria* or optical illusions
Sat 8th *Richard Coeur de Lion* and *The Follies of a day*
Thur 13th comedy *The Heiress* with pantomime *Obi* or, 'Three fingered Jack'
Sat 15th historical play *The Earl of Essex* with musical entertainment *Rosina*
Tues 18th *Barbarossa*
Thur 20th *Hamlet Prince of Denmark* to which added the pantomime *Obi* or, 'Three Finger'd Jack'
Sat 22nd *Douglas*
Tues 25th *Tancred and Sigismunda*
Thur 27th tragedy *Alexander the Great* with pantomime *Perouse*
Sat 29th *The Earl of Warwick* with *Blue Beard*

March

Tues 3rd comedy in 3 acts *Duplicity* followed by *The Boarding House* or, 'Five Hours at Brighton', never before acted here. Comic singing and concluding with the farce *Ella Rosenberg*
Thur 5th Mr. Diamond's play *The Doubtful Son.* Interlude *A trip to Scotland or Cupid turns*

Postillion and a new farce *Darkness Visible*
Sat 7th Holcroft's comedy *The Road To Ruin* with *Lethe* or, 'The waters of Oblivion' and a new melo-drama *The False Friend,* or, 'The Assassin of the Rocks'
Tues 10th *The Founding of the Forest* with *Bombastes Furioso* and *The Boarding-House*
Thur 12th Colman's comedy *Who Wants a Guinea?* After which singing and dancing including a new Turkish dwarf dance with whimsical transformation into a woman by Mr. Coombs. Then [not acted these 10 years] *The Spanish Barber*
Sat 14th, not acted for 7 years here, the comedy *Which is the Man?* With interlude *The Day After the Wedding* to conclude the melo-drama *The Blind Boy.*
Tues 17th comedy *More Ways than One.* Comic songs, and grand melo-dramatic romance *Rugantino,* or, 'The Bravo's Bride'
Thur 19th *The Merchant of Venice* song 'Bucks have at ye all', dancing by Miss Egerton's pupils, the whole to conclude with the historical pantomime *Captain Cook,* or, 'The Island of O-why-ee'
Sat 21st *The Lady of the Lake* from the celebrated poem of that name by W. Scott. Then a new piece in 2 acts *Quadrupeds of Quedlinburgh,* or, 'The Rovers of Weimar'

April

Thur 2nd the dramatic melange *The Lady of the Lake* with *Cinderella*
Fri 3rd *Royal Oak* with *Cinderella*
Sat 4th comedy, *The Hypocrite,* with *Blue Beard*
Tues 8th *Alexander the Great* with *Barnaby Brittle*
Thur 10th tragedy *The Siege of Damascus* with *The Follies of a Day*
Fri 11th *The Lady of the Lake* with *Cinderella*
Sat 12th *Barbarossa* with musical farce *The Boarding-House*
Tue 14th tragedy *Zara* with farce *Miss in her Teens*
Thur 16th tragedy *Zara* with musical farce *Turn Out*
Fri 17th *Lady of the Lake* and *Cinderella*
Sat 18th *Siege of Damascas*
Tues 21st *Romeo and Juliet*
Thur 23rd *Macbeth*
Sat 25th *The Distressed Mother*

May

Fri 1st *Lady of the Lake* with *Cinderella*
Sat 2nd *The Birthday* with *The Agreeable Surprize*, and *The Review,* or 'the Wags of Windsor'
Tue 5th A concerto on violin, by Mr. Loder, before comedy *The Four Gentlemen* after which the interlude, *The Blue Devils* concluding with musical farce *Lock and Key*

Wed 6th *Cinderella,* or, 'The Little Glass Slipper'; following a dramatic fairy tale *Edgar and Emmeline* the whole to conclude with the pantomime *Perouse,* or, 'the desolate Island'

Fri 8th *Cato* with interlude *Personation* to end, musical farce *The Boarding-House*

Sat 9th comedy *The Pilgrim* with musical farce *Twenty Years Ago*

Tues 12th *The Lady of the Lake* and *Blue Beard.*

Thur 14th *Richard the Third* concluding with melo-drama *Tekeli*

Fri 15th comedy *The School of Reform* plus pantomime *Captain Cook*

Sat 16th *The English Fleet [of 1342]* with *Cinderella*

Thur 21st opera *Inkle and Yarico* with *Cinderella* and concluding with the musical farce, *The Deserter*

Sat 23rd Cumberland's comedy *The Brothers* with an interlude *Tag in Tribulation* and a variety of entertainments to conclude with one-act Pantomime, *Robinson Crusoe and His Man Friday*

Thur 28th drama *The Castle of Montval,* or, 'The Haunted Chamber'. With *The Hunter of the Alps*

Sat 30th tragedy *Venice Preserved* with *The Poor Soldier*

June

Sat 6th comedy *A Bold Stroke for a Husband* with dancing between the play and the melo-drama *The Blind Boy.*

Noted that John Perry, 40 years in the orchestra, is permitted to issue tickets as a paralytic affliction has robbed him of his career. He has 12 children, 7 of them under the age of 11.

Wed 17th comedy *The Belle's Stratagem* with farce *Turn Out*

Thur 18th *The Beaux Stratagem* with *Robin Hood*

Fri 19th *The Kind Impostor* and *Devil to Pay*

Sat 27th Sheridan's comedy *The School for Scandal* with farce *Turn Out*

July

Sat 4th Murphy's comedy *Know your own mind* with farce *Of Age Tomorrow*

Sat 11th comedy *Country Girl* with a comic piece *Lovers' Quarrels* with the pantomime *William Tell*

Sat 25th *A Bold Stroke for a Wife* with *Peeping Tom of Coventry* after which the theatre will close for the season.

oOoOo

September

Tues 29th by Mrs. Lefanu, *The Sons of Erin* with *Turn Out*

October

Sat 3rd comedy *Country Girl* with musical farce *No Song No Supper*

Tues 6th *The Sons of Erin* with the *Sultan*

Sat 17th the comic opera *The Cabinet* with *How to Die For Love*

Sat 24th melo-dramatic opera *Devil's Bridge* to which added the farce *The Irish Widow*

Sat 31st comic opera *The Castel of Andalusia* to which added farce *Follies of a Day.*

November

Sat 7th *The Pilgrim* with dancing and comic ballet 'The Wooden Leg, or the Sailor's Return' to which the musical farce *The Rival Soldiers*

Thurs 12th *Merchant of Venice.* End of act 2, new ballet called *The Swiss Lovers* by M. Diderot performed by Mr. Vestris and Mme Diderot, then 3rd act. After play, new grand Ballet *Fairy of the Enchanted Grotto* pas de deux by Charles Diderot, son of M. and Mme, and Miss More, followed by new musical play *Anything New*

Sat 14th *Adrian and Orrila*

Thur 19th *The Foundling of the Forest* in act 1 a ballet called 'Zelis or the Prince and the shepherd' in act 2 more dance. End of the play the divertisment of the *Seraglio* including the 'shawl dance' and the 'Russian dance'. To conclude with the farce *Rival Soldiers*

Sat 21st Cibber's *The Double Gallant,*or 'the Sick Lady's Cure'. End of act 1 divertisement *The Spanish Evening.* End of the play the ballet *Telemachus,* after which the farce *Lovers' Quarrels* and concluding with the divertissement *Seraglio*

Thurs 26th the historical play *Pizarro* to which added the Pantomime *Perouse,* or, 'The Desolate Island'

Tues 24th *Macbeth*

Sat 28th *The Stranger* with *Marian*

December

Thur 3rd *Hamlet* with the musical farce *The Padlock*

Sat 5th *The Wheel of Fortune* with *Coriolanus* and the musical romance of *Richard Coeur de Lion*

Thur 10th the dramatic melange *The Lady of the Lake* with which *Cinderella*

Sat 26th *Coriolanus* with the allegorical spectacle of *Cinderella*

Thurs 31st *Coriolanus* with musical farce, *Marian*

1813

January

Fri 1st M.G. Lewis's musical comedy *Rich and Poor,* or, 'The East Indian'; with a pantomime in one act, *Robinson Crusoe* with *Love, Law and Physic*
Thurs 21st comedy *Soldier's Daughter* Mrs. Jordan as Widow Cheerly farce *Three Weeks After Marriage* Lady Racket, Mrs. Jordan
Fri 22nd *The Knight and the Wood Daemon*
Sat 23rd *Love for Love*; Miss Prue by Mrs. Jordan, the last night of her engagement.

February

Thurs 11th the tragedy *Barbarossa* with the comic ballet dance the *Jolly Millers* to which added a musical drama *Peter the Great.*
Fri 12th the grand romantic musical spectacle *The Knight and the Wood-Daemon*
Sat 13th *The Earl of Essex*
Thur 18th *The Peasant Boy* with *The Day after the Wedding* concluding with *Bombastes Furioso*
Fri 19th Congreve's comedy *Love for Love* with an historical and operatic drama in 3 acts *Peter the Great,* or, 'Russian Laurels'
Sat 20th *Devil's Bridge*
Tue 22nd *Alexander the Great*

March

Thur 4th a grand concert of vocal and instrumental music; after which the comic burletta *Midas* to conclude the comedy *Animal Magnetism*
Sat 6th comic opera *Duenna*
Thurs 18th *The Foundling of the Forest* with a dance *Love in Spain* and the musical farce *The Bee-Hive*
Sat 20th comedy *The Students of Salamanca*; after the play the farce *Youth, Love and Folly* to conclude *Bombastes Furioso*

April

Thurs 1st comedy *The Wise Indian* after, the musical entertainment *The Adopted Child* to conclude the whimsical burlesque drama in one act, not acted in 18 years, *Lilliput* [taken from Gulliver's Travels.] All characters but one to be performed by children.
Sat 3rd opera *M.P.* or, 'The Blue Stocking'; Mr. Gattie to sing 'the Russian Bear', the whole to conclude with *Timour the Tartar*
Tues 6th drama in three acts based on Dryden's 'Don Sebastian' called *The Renegade* to be added *The Hunter of the Alps* the all to conclude with the burlesque tragedy *The Tailors*
Tues 20th, Easter Tuesday, *Measure for Measure* with the melo-dramatic spectacle of

Timour the Tartar
Thur 22nd comedy *The Wonder* with the pantomime *Harlequin and Mother Goose*
Fri 23rd *The Knight and the Wood-Daemon* with *Timour the Tartar*
Sat 24th *Every One Has his Fault*

May

Mon 24th Mr. Morton's new comedy *Education* and the Shawl Dance
Thur 27th repeated Mr. Morton's new comedy *Education* with the shawl dance and a new ballet, the whole to conclude with the musical farce *Paul and Virginia*
Sat 29th *The Merry Wives of Windsor* to which added a variety of entertainments

June

Thursday 3rd Cibber's comedy *The Double Gallant* with a new Indian Ballet of action *Koah and Zoah* to which added the musical farce *Rosina*
Sat 5th *The Virgin of the Sun* with *Sleeping Beauty of the wood*
Sat 12th Dramatic interlude in one ace, *Blue Devils;* then,revived after 30 years, Lillo's domestic tale in 3 acts *Cornish Shipwreck.*To conclude, Mrs. Inchbald's farce *Mogul Tale*

July

Sat 3rd comedy *Love Makes a Man* or, 'The Fop's Fortune' to which added Mrs. Inchbald's farce *The Mogul Tale*
Wed 7th comedy in 3 acts *Five Miles Off!* After the musical farce *The Poor Soldier* to conclude in the burlesque tragedy of *Tom Thumb the Great*
Thur 8th *Education* with *Agreeable Surprize*
Fri 9th *John Bull* with the *Wags of Windsor.*
Sat 10th comic opera *Privateer*
Sat July 17th for one night only Mrs. Kemble in comedy *Deaf and Dumb* and musical farce *The Prize*

oOoOo

October

Sat 2nd Opening the Season. Moore's tragedy *The Gamester*
Sat 9th *Coriolanus* with the farce *The Devil to Pay*
Sat 23rd *the Castle Spectre* with melo-drama *Llewellyn Prince of Wales* and the dog Gelert

November

Thur 4th Gay's *Beggars' Opera* with musical farce *The Prize*
Sat 6th *The Siege of Belgrade*
Sat 20th Gay's *Beggars' Opera* with farce *Deuce is In Him*

December

Company of Equestrians, 4 nights in each week.

Thur 2nd comedy *Life's Last Shift* then *Timour the Tartar*; With the company of equestrians and a grand procession of real horses escorting the Princess of Mingrelia on her Arabian Charger. In first act, a grand combat between Kerim and Sanballet on horseback. Concluding with view of the fortress by moonlight and grand attack with cavalry and infantry. On account of the expense nothing under full price can be taken; no free admissions of any description except subscribers' tickets.

Tues 7th *Timour the Tartar* with the equestrian troop

Thurs 9th comedy *Love Makes a Man* with the last performance of *Timor the Tartar* with the equestrian troop

Fri 10th *The Kind Imposter* with, for the first time, the equestrian spectacle of *Blue Beard*

Sat 11th revival comedy *The Lady's Last Stake* with *Blue Beard*

Thur 16th opera *Maid of the Mill* and grand spectacle *Lodoiska* and with concluding engagement of the equestrians

Fri 17th and Sat 18th repeat of *Lodoiska*

Mon 27th *Artaxerxes*

Wed 29th opera *The Duenna* to which added the farce *The Sultan*

Thur 30th opera *Love in a Village* with *The Wedding Day*

Fri 31st *The Knight and the Wood-Daemon* with ballet *The Orange Boven*

1814

January

Mon 3rd *George Barnwell*
Sat 6th opera *Artaxerxes*
Fri 7th Lille's tragedy *George Barwell* and grand romantic spectacle last night of *The Knight and the Wood Daemon*
Sat 8th *A Winter's Tale* with *No Song No Supper*
Mon 10th tragedy *Douglas*
Tues 11th *The Suspicious Husband* Clarinda by Mrs. Jordan. Then *The Children of the Wood.*
Thur 13th comedy *Inconstant*, or, 'The Way To Win Him' with Mrs. Jordan; with the historical pantomime *Perouse* or 'The desolate island'
Fri 14th *The Knight and the Wood Daemon*
Thurs 20th comedy *A Trip to Scarborough* Miss Hoyden by Mrs. Jordan; farce *The Pannel*
Thurs 27th comedy *A Trip to Scarborough* Miss Hoyden by Mrs. Jordan after which the ballet dance *Orange Boven* with the farce of the *The Pannel* with Beatrice by Mrs. Jordan
Sat 29th comedy *Man and Wife* the part of Helen by Mrs. Jordan. Also the farce *Lilliput*

February

Thurs 10th Mr. Morton's comedy *Education,* the ballet dance, *The Jovial Millers* and the farce *Killing no Murder!*
Fri 11th comedy *Which is the man?* And *The Hunter of the Alps* to conclude with burlesque deama by David Garrick *Lilliput*
Sat 12th *The Pilgrim* with entertainment
Thurs 17th comedy *The Honeymoon* with *A Day After the Wedding* to which added for the last time the Pantomime *Mother Goose*
Fri 18th comedy *The Chapter of Accidents* at end of third act double hornpipe. End of play interlude *Watkin and Winney.* Fancy dances by the Misses Perry. To conclude with a farce.
Sat 19th *King Henry the Fourth* concluding with comic farce *The Follies of a Day*
Thurs 24th *Pizarro*; end of play ballet dance, *the Gretna Blacksmith.* To conclude farce *Who's To Have Her?*
Sat 26th not acted for 8 years, *The School for Wives*; singing and dancing then *Forty Thieves*

March

Tues 1st Reynolds operatic melo-drama *The Exile,* or, 'The eventful trip North' after which O'Keefe's farce *Prisoner at Large* with various entertainments. The whole to conclude the burlesque tragedy of *Chrononononothologos, Queen of Queerumania.*
Thur 3rd comedy *Wild Oats,* or,

'The Strolling Gentleman' to which added the comic pantomime *Harlequin and Miser,* or, 'The benevolent cottager' with a pas de deux with Mr. Comer and Miss Perry.

Sat 5th *The Rivals* or 'A Trip to Bath' at end a ballet dance and to conclude with the melo-dramatic romance *Wandering Boys* or, 'The Castle of Otival.'

Tues 8th *The Merchant of Venice* with Sheridan's *St Patrick's day*

Thur 10th *King Henry V* songs by Mr. Ley and a hornpipe by Master Ewington. To which added the musical farce *Who's To Have Her?*

Sat 12th musical drama in 3 acts never before performed on any stage, *Zulieman* or, 'Love and Penitence' with melo-drama *For England Ho!* By Pocock.

Thur 17th grand melo-dramatic romance in 3 acts with dialogue, music. Spectacle, action and dancing *Orphan of the Castle,* or, 'The Black Banner' which has been in preparation all winter, with new and splendid scenes, machinery, dresses and decoration. With the melo-drama *The Miller and his Men*

Thur 31st Cumberland's comedy *The Jew* with the melo-drama *For England Ho!*

April

Sat 2nd *The Orphan of the Castle* After which the EASTER HOLIDAYS

Thurs 28th *Julius Caesar* Brutus by Mr. Kemble. Melo-drama *The Miller and His Men*

Fri 29th opera *The Farmer's Wife* with *Blind Boy*

Sat 30th *King Henry VIII* Cardinal Wolsey by Kemble

May

Tues 3rd Mr. Kemble will act Penruddock in *The Wheel of Fortune*

Thurs 5th *Merchant of Venice* with Mr. Kemble. Then the melo-drama of *The Miller and his Men.*

Fri 6th dramatic melange *The Lady of the Lake* to conclude with the romance *Forty Thieves*

Sat 7th *The Mountaineers* Octavius by Mr. Kemble, with *High life below Stairs* and *Bombastes Furioso*

Tues 10th *Cato* title role Mr. Kemble

Thur 19th Bickerstaffe's comedy *The Hypocrite* with *Killing no Murder* and comic songs like 'the Mail Coach' and 'Bartholomew Fair'

Sat 21st *The Good-Natured Man* with *The Sleep-Walker*

Thurs 26th the new comic opera *The Farmer's Wife* with Garrick's farce *The Lying Valet*

Fri 27th comedy *A Bold Stroke For A Husband* with interlude singing and dancing by various artists. The whole to conclude for the first time these 7 years the

pantomime *The Magic of Hope,* or, 'Columbine Captive'
Sat 28th Coleman's comedy *Who Wants a Guinea?* With *Love A-La-Mode* and *Killing no Murder*

June

Thur 9th June the tragedy *Jane Shore* with interlude of *The Jovial Millers* and the farce *How to Die for Love.*
Sat 11th comedy *The School of Reforms* with *The Bath Road* and *The Hunter of the Alps.*
Tues 14th comedy *Wild Oats* with a farce
Thurs 23rd comedy *The Rivals,* or, 'A Trip to Bath' with interlude *The Day After the Wedding* the whole to conclude with *The Devil to Pay*
Sat 25th *Belle's Strategem* with *Forty Thieves*
Thurs 30th the opera *Love in a Village* with the farce *The Wedding Day*

July

Fri 1st the *Orphan of the Castle*
Sat 2nd *The Cabinet* with *Matrimony*
Sat 23rd new Comedy *Debtor and Creditor* by James Kenny. An interlude with occasional and patriotic songs, called *Britain's Glory,* or, 'a trip to Portsmouth'; to conclude with the farce *How to Die for Love*

oOoOo

October

Sat 22nd a new opera by J.S. Arnold *Frederick the Great* founded on an historical anecdote. End of opera a divertissement by the 3 Misses Giroux, to which will be added the musical farce of the *Agreeable Surprize*
Sat 29th opera *The Devil's Bridge.* End act 1 an allemande by the Three Misses Giroux. End of opera double broadsword hornpipe. To which added the melo-drama *The Miller and his Men*

November

Sat 5th, first night of Mr. Grimaldi, the famous clown. Reynold's comedy *The Will.* End of play, Dancing by Mr. Ellar from the theatre of Sadler's Wells; and the Misses Giroux. To which added the pantomime *Don Juan,* or, 'The Libertine destroyed'
Thursday 24th comedy *The Blind Boy* with *The Flitch of Bacon* to conclude with *Harlequin and Padmanaba,* or, 'The Golden Fish'. Mr. Grimaldi the famous clown as Rondilbellyane and the clown
Sat 26th *Orphan of the Castle* with *Harlequin and Padmanaba*

December

Thurs 8th Comic one act piece *The Bath Road* or, 'Intrigue'. Entertainments of recitations, songs, imitations, ventriloquoy etc called *Mail Coach Adventures*; the whole to conclude with the farce *The Wedding Day*

Sat 10th comedy *Policy* or 'Thus runs the world' with *John of Paris*

Thurs 15th a comedy in 3 acts *Policy* and comic opera *John of Paris* to conclude with serio-comic burlesque tragedy *Bombastes Furioso*

Sat 17th Melo-drama in 3 acts *Forest of Bondy,* or, 'The Dog of Montargis' with *Shipwreck.*

1815

January

Thur 5th *Romeo and Juliet* after which the grand Chinese Spectacle *Aladdin* or, 'The Wonderful Lamp'

Fri 6th *John of Paris* and *The King and the Duke* with a pantomime of *Raymond and Agnes*

Sat *The Distressed Mother* with *Aladdin*

Thur 12th *King Henry IV* with *Aladdin*

Sat 14th *The Exile* with *Aladdin*

Fri 15th *The Curfew* with a Ballet by Mr. Giroux *Henry and Emma* or, 'The rival villagers' the whole to conclude with the comic opera *John of Paris*

Tue 17th *The siege of Belgrade* with *The King and the Duke*

Thur 19th Cobb's serio-comic opera *The Siege of Belgrade* after which a new comic ballet called *Leander and Leonor* produced by Mr. Giroux. To conclude the farce, *The King and the Duke.*

Fri 20th *The Haunted Tower* with *The Merry Mourners*

Sat 21st *Alexander the Great* with *Midas*

Thurs 26th *Richard II* with *John of Paris*

Fri 27th opera *The Castle of Andalusia* with *The Forest of Bondy,* or, The Dog of Montargis

Sat 28th The Misses Giroux present a new ballet called *Le Faux Magicien,* ou 'L'amour fixe'. In the ballet will be a skipping-rope hornpipe, new allemande and double tambourine dance. After, the tragedy *The Gamester* then a comic ballet of action entitled *Albert and Rosalie* or, 'The Guardian Duped' to which added the burlesque piece *Bombastes Furioso*

Mon 30th a grand selection of vocal and instrumental music from the works of Handel, Haydn, Mozart and Beethoven's sacred oratorio 'The Mount of Olives' and other songs and music

February

Thurs 2nd tragedy *George Barnwell* to which added the burletta *Midas*

Fri 3rd *The West Indian* with *The Merry Mourners*

Sat 4th *Artaxerxes* with *Aladdin*

Tues 7th grand historical opera *The Hero of the North*

Thurs 9th *Richard the Second* which has not been performed here for nearly a century, after which the opera in 2 acts *The Cabinet*

Sat 11th *The Hero of the North* with *John of Paris*

Tues 14th comedy *Riches,* or 'the Wife and Brother' after which a musical farce ...

Thur 16th O'Keefe's comic opera *Fountainbleau*, or, 'Our Way In France'. After the play 'the shawl dance' by Miss Giroux, and recitation 'Poor Mary, the Maid of the Inn'. To conclude with the musical entertainment of *Lock and Key*

Sat 18th for positively the last time, *Riches*. Comic songs, the whole to conclude with the musical *Hunter of the Alps*

Tue 21st comic opera *English Fleet in 1342* including popular songs and the concertante for two violins, Mr. Loder and Mr. T. Cooke. At the end of the opera the celebrated Mr. Ferdinand Panormo will play Stiebeltz' 'Storm' on the grand piano-forte. To which added the musical farce *No Song, no Supper*

Thur 23rd a dramatic tale *The Mysteries of the Castle* after which dancing by Master and Miss Stanley; then, compressed into one act, *The Jew and the Doctor* the whole to conclude with *Aladdin* or, 'The wonderful lamp'

Sat 25th the melo-drama *Devil's Bridge* with [not acted for several years] the musical farce *The Son-in-Law*

Tues 28th Colman's play in 3 acts *The Surrender of Calais*. An interlude burletta in one act *Quarter Day*, or, 'How to Pay Rent Without Money' to conclude with a comic Extravaganza in one act *Large Loaf*, or, 'Better Times in 1822'

March

Thur 2nd Mrs. Inchbald's comedy in 5 acts not performed in 20 years *I'll Tell You What* after which in one act *Blue Devils* with the grand allegorical spectacle of *Cinderella,* or, 'The Little Glass Slipper'

Sat 4th serio-comic opera *Swiss Banditi* or, 'Love and Constancy'. Recitation, 'For Mary, the Maid of the Inn', with the entertainment *John of Paris*

Tues 7th the comedy *Clandestine Marriage* after which the interlude *Little Hunchback,* or, 'A Frolic in Bagdad' to conclude with the musical farce *Paragraph,* or, 'The Plough the best Doctor'.

Thur 9th melo-drama *The Travellers Benighted,* or, 'The Woodman's Hut' after which the melo-dramatic *For England Ho!* The whole to conclude with *The Grand Alliance*

Sat 11th Grand Historical Opera, *The Hero of the North* and for one night only the Grand Allegorical Spectacle *Cinderella,* or, 'The Little Glass Slipper'. Then a pas seul by Miss Giroux.

Thur 16th *The Iron Chest* after the play, dancing. After Mrs. Opie's tale *The Orphan Boy* to be recited. A comic song. To conclude with *The Shipwreck*

Sat 18th, last night performing until Easter. Play, *Foundling of the Forest* to which added *Aladdin*

Thur 30th *Othello* with the grand Chinese spectacle of *Aladdin* or, 'the wonderful lamp'

April

Sat 1st a dramatic melangd *The Lady of the Lake* and a new dance called *The Magic Statue or Love in the Highlands* and to conclude a serio-comic opera called *Narensky*, or, 'The Road to Yaroslaf' in which will be performed a rural ballet

Tues 4th tragedy *Zenobia* with farce *Past Ten o'Clock and a Rainy Night*

Thur 6th the historical play *Edward the Black Prince* with *The Forest of Bondy*

Sat 8th *The Iron Chest* with the new farce *Past Ten o'Clock and a Rainy Night*

Thurs 13th Aaron Hill's tragedy *Zara* to which added opera *John of Paris*

Sat 15th *Tancred and Sigismunda* and *Weathercock*

Thur 20th Sheridan's *School for Scandal* and the farce *The Citizen*

Sat 22nd *Much Ado About Nothing* and *Turn Out*

Thur 27th the comedy *The Soldier's Daughter* with which the farce *No Song no Supper* with songs.

May

Thur 4th *Romeo and Juliet* and in act 1 a masquerade with a dance by Miss Perry [Juliet]. Following the farce, *The Wedding Day*

Sat 6th *The Will* and *The Romp*

Thur 11th Southern's tragedy *Oroonoko,* or, 'The Royal Slave' with the new farce *Past Ten o'Clock and a Rainy Night* and the comic opera *John of Paris.* The whole to conclude with a representation of the grand Chinese pagoda in real fire works as displayed at the fête in St James' Park

Sat 13th *Point of Honour* a play in 3 acts; then *A West Wind;* to conclude with the grand historical pantomime of *Perouse,* or, 'the desolate island'

Thur 18th *The Mountaineers* with an interlude *The Englishman returned from Paris* and the recitation of 'The African's Appeal to Britons' for the abolition of the slave trade. Celebrated comic songs. To conclude with the melo-drama *The Tale of Mystery*

Sat 20th Morton's comedy *A Cure for the Heart-Ache*. Between the play and the farce an interlude, a hornpipe by Mary Saunders a child of 3 years old. To conclude, farce *A West Wind,* or, 'Off to London'

Thur 25th Beaumont and Fletcher's comedy *Rule a wife, have a wife* after which *John of Paris*

Sat 27th Otway's tragedy *Venice Preserved* and a new farce *Past Ten o'Clock and a Rainy Night*

June

Thurs 1st a tragedy *Merope* or 'The Royal Shepherd' after which the interlude *Lovers' Quarrels* to which the favourite opera *Rosina.*

Sat 3rd the comedy *The Provoked Husband* with the musical farce *The Waterman*

Sat 10th Rowe's tragedy *Jane Shore.* To which to be added the celebrated old ballad fared of *Flora*, or, 'Hob in the Wheel'

Sat 17th a farce in two acts *The Fortunes of War* to which added Milton's masque *Comus* or, 'The Enchanted Wood'. To conclude with melo-drama *The Miller and his Men*

July

Saturday 1st the celebrated comedy by FG Reynolds *Laugh When You Can* with the opera *John of Paris* in act 2 rural ballet

Saturday 8th *Merchant of Venice* with Mr. Kean; to which added *The Waterman*

Thur 13th *Othello the Moor of Venice* with Mr. Kean. After which Milton's masque *Comus* or, 'The Enchanted Wood' and to conclude with *Doldrum,* or, 'the year 1822'

oOoOo

September

The performances for the season will commence 30th September

Sat 30th the tragedy *Alexander the Great* after which a grand divertissement which will consist of a grand pas de trois by M. Bourdin, Miss Giroux and Miss F. Giroux and a grand pas de deux by M and Mme Leon. The whole to conclude with the comic opera *John of Paris*

October

Sat 7th *King Henry V* with comic ballet *The Swiss Village* to conclude with the musical farce *The Romp*

Tues 10th the opera *The Duenna* with the musical farce *Rosina*

Sat 14th *The Maid and the Magpie* with which *Aladdin*

Sat 21st the new melo-drama *The Maid and the Magpie* or, 'which is the thief?' with new scened, and in act 1 a rustic ballet. After which the comic ballet of *The Jovial Millers* to which added a new musical farce *My Aunt.*

Sat 28th a new comedy *Love and Gout* or, 'arrivals from Bath'. To which added grand Chinese spectacle *Aladdin* or, 'The wonderful Lamp'

November

Sat 4th new melo-drama *The Maid and the Magpie* or, 'Which is the thief?' Act 1 a rural ballet with the Misses Giroux; after a comic ballet dance, after which a new farce *The Farce Writer*

Sat 18th new comedy *Living in*

London with *Valentine and Orson* with Mr. Grimaldi the celebrated clown as Orson
Thur 23rd Banks' historical tragedy *Albion Queens* after which the comic pantomime *Harlequin and Doctor Fostus* [sic] in which the clown is performed by the celebrated Mr. Grimaldi who will also sing the comic song 'Betty Brill'
Sat 25th *Love in a Village* with *Harlequin and Doctor Faustus* the last night of Mr. Grimaldi

December

Thur 7th tragedy *The Distressed Mother* with nautical spectacle *Black Beard, the Pirate of Africa*
Sat 9th *Much Ado About Nothing*, Beatrice played by A Lady [amateur performance.] With *John of Paris*
Thur 14th the tragedy *Jane Shore* after which a new ballet dance called 'drive love out of the door and he gets in at the window'. In the course of the evening Mr. Ellar will dance the hornpipe blindfold over 12 eggs, in wooden shoes, and demonstrate his flight from the gallery to the stage. In the course of the pantomime *Harlequin Mariner* the hornpipe will be danced by Master Saunders, a child of 4 years old. During the pantomime Mr. Ellar will perform surprising leaps – through a tambourine; a hogshead of real fire; the window of a post-chaise and will perform the laughable [in modern parlance' hilarious'] scene of 'Death and the Fiddle'
Sat 16th opera *The Woodman* and the burletta *Midas*
Thur 28th for the first time these 12 years the oper *The Woodman*. After which the grand nautical spectacle *Black Beard*
Fri 29th [Mr. Sinclair's Benefit]
Sat 30th *Fontainbleau* with *Aladdin*.

1816

January

Thur 11th *The Village Lawyer* after which *The Sleep Walker* to conclude with the grand Chinese Spectacle *Aladdin*
Fri 12th *The Young Quaker* with *The Critic*
Sat 13th *Ways and Means* with *Who's Who*
Tues 16th *The Country Girl* debut of Mrs. Alsop, a daughter of Mrs. Jordan, as Miss Peggy
Thur 25th the comedy *Belle's Stratagem* after the grand Nautical spectacle, *Black Beard*
Fri 26th *Hamlet*
Sat 27th *Trip to Scarborough* with *The Castle of Sorrento*
Tues 30th Benefit Mr. Loder a Grand Selection of Sacred Music

February

Thur 1st the comedy *Rule a Wife and Have a Wife* with *The Castle of Sorrento*
Fri 2nd *Romeo and Juliet* with *The Castle of Sorrento*
Sat 3rd *The Wonder* to which added the farce *Matrimony*
Thur 8th in Otway's tragedy *Venice Preserved* after which a musical Romance, *The Castle of Sorrento*
Tues 6th *Provencal Lovers* in which will be introduced La Provencal Minuet and Gavotte by the Misses Giroux; after which *Adrian and Orrila,* or, 'a Mother's Vengeance' with a waltz. To which added *Florio and Lucinda* the whole to conclude with *Intrigue* or, 'The Bath Road'
Fri 9th *The Wood Demon* with *The Maid and the Magpie*
Sat 10th *Every Man In His Humour* with *Black Beard*
Thur 15th Sheridan's *Pizarro* with the after-piece of *The Farce Writer*
Fri 16th Reynold's comedy *The Will* with a new Ballet Dance. To conclude with *The Young Hussar* or, 'Love and Mercy'
Sat 17th, *A Winter's Tale* with dancing by Misses Giroux. Then Murphy's petit comedy in one act *Three Weeks After Marriage*
Thurs 22nd *Merchant of Bruges* and melo-drama *Ella Rosenberg*
Thur 29th *The Foundling of the Forest* with a rural fête with dancing in act 2. Mrs. Ashe singing favourite airs like 'Sweet Bird' to which added the grand serious pantomime *Oscar and Malvina*

March

Sat 2nd new comedy *Where to find a Friend* by Mr. Leigh, author of 'Griving's Folly'. To which added Bickerstaff's opera of *The Padlock.* To conclude with a dramatic Fairy Tale *Edgar and Emmeline* with a fairy dance with the Misses Giroux.
Tues 5th *A Favourite Play*, with a musical afterpiece, and a variety

of other entertainments

Thur 7th play *The Busy Body* with *Hunter of the Alps*

Sat 9th *Every One Has His Fault* with the comic song 'Tippitiwitchit' by Master Bedford, a child of 4 years old. To conclude with the grand operatic romance of *The Forty Thieves*

Tues, comedy *Fortune's Fool* after which Garrick's burlesque *Lilliput* to conclude a grand serious pantomime *The Hermit of the Rock*

Thur 14th Sheridan's *St Patrick's Day,* or. 'The Scheming Lieutenant' after which *John of Paris*; then the celebrated Mr. Duchow exhibits his unrivalled performance on the tight rope. The whole to conclude with the pantomime *Harlequin Aesop,* or, 'Hymen's Gift'

Sat 16th the singing of the celebrated Miss Hughes as Urganda in *Cymon.* Ballet from the Misses Giroux, then the melo-drama *Blind Boy* and to conclude the musical entertainment *Inkle and Yarico*

Tues 19th Reynolds Comedy *The Dramatist* then burlesque interlude *Bombastes Furioso* to conclude *Tekeli* with a representation of a mill at work in act 2, a rural ballet, and the storming of Montgatz with broad sword combat.

Thur 21st A historical play in 3 acts *The Wanderer* with a dance by the Misses Giroux after which a musical farce, *Rosina* and to conclude the musical spectacle *Blue Beard*

Sat 23rd a melo-dramatic romance in 3 acts *The Orphan of the Castle* including a ballet; end of play, select concert and then the farce *What Next?*

Tues 26th comedy *Town and Country* and melo-drama *Rugantino*

Thurs 28th Garrick's musical romance *Cymon* after which a new serious pantomime *The Great Devil* with performances by the celebrated singer Miss Hughes

Sat 30th *Artaxerxes*

April

Easter Tues, 16th *King Lear*[1] with grand serious nautical spectacle *Black Beard the Pirate of Africa.* Lear was banned in London because of the King's own illness, and most provinces honoured it; as the Queen was residing in Bath this seems tactless.

Thur 18th *The Wheel of Fortune* with *First Floor*

Fri 19th *Accusation* with *For England Ho!*

[1] King Lear was generally banned during the later life of King George III because it was a little close to the knuckle, though there was a version with a happy ending, which we must assume this was. It was most tactless to perform this while Queen Charlotte was in Bath as it upset her.

Sat 20th *Iron Chest*
Thur 25th *The Stranger* with new melo-dramatic musical farce *Bobinet the Bandit*, or 'the Forest of Montescarpini'
Fri 26th *Accusation* with entertainments
Sat 27th *The Mountaineers*

May

Sat 4th *Deaf and Dumb,* or, 'The Orphan Protected' then musical farce *The Prize*
Tues 7th *The Inconstant* with *Of Age Tomorrow*
Thurs 9th Murphy's *Way to Keep Him* with the farce *The Devil to Pay*
Sat 11th comedy *The Jealous Wife* with entertainments
Thurs 16th Tobin's comedy *The Honey Moon* and *The Rival Soldiers* a tambourine pas de deux, then *The Wedding Day*
Sat 18th *Smiles and Tears* and *An Amateur*
Thurs 30th *The Castle Spectre* end of play the Misses Giroux dance the Spanish bolero, then the farce *The Farce Writer*

June

Mr. Kean of Drury Lane to visit Bath for Race Week and act his principle characters
Sat 1st *The Foundling of the Forest* in act 2, a rural fête with dancing; after, *Blue Devils* and epilogue *Young Actresses* and to conclude a farce *The Fortune of War*
Sat 8th comedy *The Poor Gentleman* followed by comic songs, and then the farce *The Sleep-Walker*
Sat 15th June comedy *Suspicious Husband* with the veil dance at the end of the play, and then the melo-dramatic opera *For England Ho!*
Sat 22nd the comedy *Education* to which added comic entertainment *'Tis All a Farce*
Sat 29th *Richard III* with Mr. Kean

July

Thurs 4th *Othello* title role Mr. Kean. To which added *Rosina*
Fri 5th *Duke of Milan* with *The Rival Soldiers* and *High Life Below Stairs*
Sat 6th *Riches* with *For England Ho!*

oOoOo

October

Sat 12th Tobin's comedy *Honey Moon* to which added the comic opera of *The Cabinet*
Sat 19th, last performance of Mr. Incledon before his departure for America. Presenting the comic opera *Love in a Village* to which will be added the musical farce *The Quaker*
Sat 26th O'Keefe's opera *The Castle of Andalusia* with the farce *Bon Ton,* or, 'High Life above Stairs'

November

Sat 2nd Bickerstaff's comic Opers *Maid of the Mill* with O'Keefe's musical farce *Poor Soldier*

Sat 9th opera *Lord of the Manor* to which will be added the musical farce the *Turnpike Gate*

Sat 16th the tragedy *Bertram* or, 'the Castle of St Aldobrand' followed by *The Conquest of Algiers*

Thurs 21st tragedy *Bertram* or, 'The Castle of St Aldobrand' after which the pantomime *Mother Goose*

Sat 23rd *The Clandestine Marriage* with *The Conquest of Algiers*

Thurs 28th *Guy Mannering* or, 'The Gypsy's Prophecy' to conclude with *What's Next?*

Sat 30th Mr. Tobin's new comedy *The Faro Table* or, 'The Guardians' with *The Conquest of Algiers*. A new operetta called *Is He Jealous?*

December

At some point in the first week, *Tamerlane* or, 'the Fall of Bajazet' with Mr. Kemble playing Bajazet.

Missing data

Thurs 12th the melo-drama *The Maid and the Magpie* dance incidental to act 1. Then operetta *Is He Jealous?* To which added the last and only night, the pantomime *Mother Goose* or, 'The golden Egg'

Sat 15th *The West Indian*

1817

January

Thurs 9th the comedy *Wheel of Fortune* to be added to the oriental fairy tale *Selima and Azor*; or. 'Beauty and the Beast'
Wed 22nd Lillor's moral tragedy of *George Barnwell* with *Whittington and his Cat*
Thur 23rd *Guy Mannering* with the pantomime *Whittington and his cat,* or, 'Harlequin, Lord Mayor of London'.
Sat 25th new melo-drama *The Watch Word* with the new comic opera *Brother and Sister*; to conclude, *Selima and Azur*
Thur 30th Grand Miscellaneous Concert benefit Mr. Loder [leader of the band and owner of the Musical Warehouse in Milsom Street.]

February

Thur 13th *The Doubtful Son* then new ballet dance, to which added musical farce *The Farmer*
Sat 15th General Burgoyne's elegant comedy *The Heiress* with dances by the four Misses Giroux to which added the musical farce *The Bee Hive*
Tues 17th *Guy Mannering* with the comic opera *John of Paris*
Thurs 20th a new drama called *The Ravens* or, 'the home of Conscience' with the comic opera *Brother and Sister* with *Whittington and his cat*
Tues 25th opera *Devil's Bridge* after which the interlude of *Romlastes Furioso* the whole to conclude with the musical farce of the *Young Huzzar*

March

Thurs 6th operatic play *The Exile* or, 'events of the north' to which added the melo-drama of *The Forest of Bondy*
Sat 8th *Blind Bargain* or'Love in a basket' followed by a comic song, and a musical interlude called *A Chip off the Old Block* and other songs, to conclude with the melo-drama *The Brazen Bust*
Tues 11th *Heir at Law* with the interlude *Is He Jealous?* And the farce *The Guardian*
Thurs 13th *The Slave*. In the course of the play, an Indian dance by Mr. Ellis and a pas de deux by two of the Misses Giroux. At the end of the play a new comic dance called *The Miller and his Men*. To conclude, a comic pantomime *Harlequin and the Sylph of the Oak* or, 'the blind beggar of Bethnal Green.' The pantomime is replete with Machinery, Tricks &c
Sat 15th *Rich and Poor* with a variety of entertainments and concluding with the whimsical farce *Plot and Counter-Plot* or, 'The portrait of Cervantes'
Tues 18th musical play in 3 acts *The Africans* or, 'War, Love and Duty'. After which a comic piece *The Invisible Girl*. To conclude

The Lady of the Lake
Thur 20th Sheridan's *Pizarro*. After Master Saunders will dance a Spanish Fandango. End of play, a new comic dance called *Jack and Jill*. To conclude a new comic pantomime called *Harlequin and the Sylph of the Oak*.
Sat 22nd the operatic play *The Peasant Boy*. Incidental to the opera a balley with skipping-rope dance by the Misses Gireux and a child 4 years old. To which added musical spectacle in 2 acts *The Conquest of Algiers*
Thurs 27th the tragedy of *Bertram*, or, 'The Castel of St Aldobrand' with Mr. Conway of Covent Garden. Followed by Ballet *Drive Love out of Doors* and farce *Catherine and Petruchio*
Sat 29th *The School for Scandal* with *Brother and Sister*

April

Tues 8th the tragedy of *Mahomet the Impostor* with Mr. Howard Payne, the American Roscius; to which added the musical drama *Selima and Azor*
Thurs 10th, G.M..Lewis's play *Adelgitha* with the comic opera *Brother and Sister*
Sat 12th *Lover's Vows* after which *Wandering Boys*
Thurs 17th *Hamlet* with a musical fairy tale, *Selima and Azor*
Sat 19th comic opera *Guy Mannering* with *Wandering Boys*
Thurs 24th with the celebrated Italian Musician Signor Rivolta. Presented the musical play *The Slave*. After the play, Signor Rivolta will play. After the burletta *Midas*
Tues 29th Bickerstaff's comic opera *Love in a Village* with musical farce

May

Thurs 1st Morton's comedy *Speed of the Plough* with the *Conquest of Algiers*
Sat 3rd an opera *Sherwood Forest* with *Tale of Mystery* to conclude with the burletta *Midas*
Thurs 8th with favourite opera *The Peasant Boy* with *Plot and Counterplot*
Sat 10th the comedy *The Poor Gentleman*. After the comedy a comic song, then the serio-comic burlesque tragedy *Bombastes Furioso*. A Spanish pas seul dance the whole to conclude with the melo-drama in two acts *Tekeli*
Thurs 15th Massinger's play *A New Way to Pay Old Debts*
Sat 17th *The Iron Chest* with *The Mayor of Garratt*
Tues 20th the grand historical opera *The Hero of the North* with the comic opera *Brother and Sister*
Thurs 22nd Reynold's play *The Exile* to which added the farce *Turn Out*
Sat 24th *A Cure for the Heart-Ache* with *Inkle and Yarico*

June

Sat 28th *Richard the Third* with Mr. Booth from Covent-Garden

oOoOo

November

Thur 6th the death of Princess Charlotte of Wales, Wed 19th funeral

December

Fri 26th *Macbeth* with *The Inkeeper's daughter*

Sat 27th *The knight and the wood daemon* with farce of *The Lyar*

Mon 29th *The foundling of the forest* with pantomime *Dick Whittington and his cat*

Tue 30th *She stoops to conquer* with *Comus*

1818

January

Tue 6th the new tragedy *Fazio*
Fri 9th musical romance *The Lady of the Lake* with *Don Giovanni*
Sat 10th tragedy *Fazio* with farce *Husbands and Wives*
Mon 12th Dryden's tragedy *All for Love* with pantomime *Whittington and his cat*
Fri 16th Mr. Millman's tragedy *Fazio* with a new farce *Husbands and Wives*
Sat 17th *Merchant of Venice* with the comic opera *Brother and Sister*
Thurs 29th musical drama *The Lady of the Lake* to which added the farce *Husbands and Wives*
Fri 30th A Grand Miscellaneous Concert
Sat 31st Sheridan's play *Pizarro* followed by the farce *Love-A-La-Mode*

February

Mon 2nd Grand opera *The Travellers* with *The Innkeeper's Daughter*
Thur 12th comedy *All in the Wrong* with comic interlude *Sylvester Daggerwood* and melodrama *The Maid and the Magpie*
Sat 14th the musical play, *The Slave* with the musical farce *The Escapes* or, 'The water carrier'
Mon 16th comedy *Speed the Plough* with musical farce *The Bee-hive*
Tue 17th play in 3 acts *Point of Honour* interlude *Is He Jealous* and farce *The Follies of a day,* or, 'The Marriage of Figaro'
Thur 19th the comedy *The Will* with the musical romance of *Bluebeard*
Sat 21st comedy *Wives as they were and Maids as they are* with a new dance; and to conclude with the musical entertainment *John of Paris*
Mon 23rd *The Rivals* after which a variety of entertainments, concluding with a favourite farce to be decided
Thur 26th Lillo's moral tragedy of *George Barnwell* to which added the melo-drama *The Maid and the Magpie*
Sat 28th Mr. Sheridan's comedy *School for Scandal* to which added grand musical romance *Forty Thieves*

March

Mon 2nd the popular tragedy *Fazio* after which the interlude *A Day After The Wedding* the whole to conclude with the Musical farce of the *Agreeable Surprize*
Tue 3rd opera *The Haunted Tower* with songs 'taste o taste this spicy wine', 'The soldier tir'd' and 'Trump of Fame' to which added musical farce *No Song, No Supper*
Friday 6th, Wed 11th and Fri 13th are *Three Oratorios* on a similar plan to those in Theatre-Royal Covent Garden and DruryLane

oOoOo

October

Sat 31st Opening for the season with comedy *Wonder! A Woman keeps a Secret* to which added musical farce *The Quaker*
Days of performing will be Monday, Wednesday, Friday, Saturday

November

Wed 4th Bickerstaff's comic opera *Love in a Village* to which added Murphy's comedy *Three weeks after Marriage*
Fri 6th *The Honeymoon* with *Of Age Tomorrow*
Sat 7th *Orphan of the Castle* with *Matrimony*
Wed 11th first time this season *Rob Roy* with musical farce *No Song, No Supper*
Fri 13th *Beggar's Opera*; after the romp *Priscilla Tomboy*
Sat 14th *The way of the World* with *The Cabinet*
Tue 17th death of Queen Charlotte; funeral 2nd December

December

Thur 17th For One Night Only, Mr. Matthews presents *Mail Coach Adventures* with comic songs, imitations, ventriliquoy, recitations and eccentricities. His imitations include how Messrs Kemble, Pope, Young, Kean, Fawcett, Banister, Braham, Incledon, Blanchard, Betty and Munden will give their ideas how Hamlet's 'advice to the players' should be spoken. Box 5/- Pit 3/- Gallery 1/6d

1819

January

Fri 15th *Coriolanus* to which is to be added the *Forty Thieves*
Sat 16th *Maid of the Mill* with *Rendezvous*
Mon 18th [sixth time] opera *The Barber of Seville*
Wed 20th *Cinderella* or, 'The Little Glass Slipper'
Fri 22nd *Rob Roy* or, 'Auld Lang Syne' and a pas de deux by the Misses Giroux. With a farce to be expressed in the bills. It is announced that the celebrated Actress Miss Kelly whas been engaged for 6 nights.
Sat 23rd grand historical opera *The Hero of the North* after which will be Milton's celebrated music of *Comus*
Fri 29th the musical play *Rich and Poor* to which will be added the comedy *Midnight Hour*
Sat 30th benefit Mr. Loder, leader of the band, a Grand Selection of Vocal and Instrumental Music including an entire act of Mozart's *Zauberflotte* for the first and only time in Bath. Boxes 5/- pit 3/- gallery 1/6d

February

Mon 1st *Know Your Own Mind* with *The Blind Boy*
Wed 3rd *The Kind Impostor*
Fri 5th Mrs. Cowley's comedy *Belle's Stratagem* to which added the melo-drama *Deserter*
Sat 6th *Rich and Poor* with *Wanted: a Governess*
Mon 8th *The Knight and the Wood Demon*
Wed 10th *The Peasant Boy*, the peasant boy by Miss Kelly in a breeches role
Thur 25th the grand romantic play, *The Aethiop* or, 'The Child of the Desert' as performed at the Theatre-Royal Covent Garden. After, the Misses Giroux will dance the waltz and sauteuse the whole to conclude the comic piece *A Day After The Wedding*
Lent commencing with the present week, the nights of performances at the theatre must be arranged upon Monday, Tuesday, Thursday and Saturday until the Passion Week after which their previous regulation will be resumed.
Sat 27th *A Grand Romantic Play* after which *Mother Goose*, or, 'The Golden Egg'

March

Tues 2nd the popular new farce *The Rendezvous*
Thurs 4th the grand romantic play, *The Aethiop*, or, 'The Child of the Desert' after which the new farce *The Rendezvous*
Sat 6th grand musical spectacle of *The Knight And The Wood Demon*, or, 'The Clock Strikes One!' followed by the *Ballet of the Seasons* to conclude with *Brother and Sister*

Mon 8th grand melo-dramatic romance in 3 acts *The Orphan of the Castle*, or, 'The Black Banner' to which is added *Budget of Blunders*

Thur 18th comedy *Every One has His Fault,* and then the grand melo-drama *The Castle of Paluzzi*

Sat 20th *Rob Roy* or, 'Auld Lang Syne' after which the musical farce called *High Notions,* or, 'a Trip to Exmouth'

Mon 22nd *A Winter's Tale* in act 4 an arcadian ballet in which the 'bergere pas de trois' will be performed by the Misses Giroux. After a new Ballet dance called *The Sisters* or, 'Village Gambols' when the Misses Giroux will dance their admired Allemand, 'Skipping Garland pas de Trois' and a new pas de quatre. The whole to conclude with the comic piece of the *Bath Road.*

Tues 23rd musical drama *Zorinski* with *John of Paris*

Thur 25th play *Town and Country* or, 'Which is Best?' with melo-drama *The Castle of Paluzzi* incidental to this piece a fête champêtre in which Miss Giroux dances the 'bugle hornpipe'

Sat 27th *Guy Mannering;* at the end of the play a new ballet dance called *Village Gambols*

Mon 29th a favourite comedy *Clandestine Marriage;* songs to follow and then the farce of the *Deaf Lover*

April

Fri 16th Cumberland's comedy *Wheel of Fortune* with comic opera *Don Giovanni*

Sat 17th *King John*

Mon 19th *The Iron Chest* with new farce *High Notions*

Fri 23rd *King Lear*[2] after which the opera *Don Giovanni*

Sat 24th *Macbeth* with *Midnight Hour*

Mon 26th for the 9th time *Barber of Seville* for the last time

Wed 28th *Rob Roy*

Fri 30th, *Castle Spectre* with the musical farce *Love Laughs at Locksmiths*

May

Sat 1st Sheridan's comedy *School for Scandal* with the musical farce *Adopted Child*

Mon 3rd *The Clandestine Marriage*

Wed 5th *A Bold Stroke for a Husband*

Fri 14th Cobbe's opera *Siege of Belgrade* with a new comic piece, in one act *Where Shall I Dine?*

Mon 17th *Rob Roy* plus the new extravaganza *The Actress of All Work* in which Mr. Edwin plays 6 different characters. To conclude with the Melo-drama *The Maid And The Magpie*

June

[2] See previous note re Lear, but Queen Charlotte had died by this time so was not there to be offended.

Thurs 10th tragedy *The Gamester* to follow, the farce *Two Strings to your Bow*
Fri 11th tragedy *Evadne*, or 'the statue' with *Rosina*
Sat 12th *Isabella*
Mon 14th *Fazio*
Tue 15th tragedy *The Apostate*
Wed 16th tragedy *The Orphan*
Thur 17th tragedy *Bellamira* with farce *Devil to Pay*

oOoOo

October

Opening for the Season with entirely new interior with decorations and embellishments which have been accomplished over the summer

Sat 30th Vanburgh's comedy *The Provoked Husband* or, 'a Journey to London'. After, the musical farce *No Song, No Supper*

November

Mon 1st *Guy Mannering*
Wed 3rd *The Will*
Fri 6th the popular musical play *Rob Roy* or, 'Auld Lang Syne' for the Last Time this season. Plus a farce
Fri 19th, Burgoyne's opera *Lord of the Manor*
Sat 20th Mr. Phillips' Night
Mon 22nd *She Stoops to Conquer*

December

Fri 3rd for the first time a new drama *The Heart of Midlothian* or, 'The Lily of St Leonards' with entirely new and picturesque scenery considting chiefly of real Scottish Views, accurately taken on the spot. Music Scotch Melodies selected and arranged by Mr. Bishop. To which added a farce *The Day After The Wedding*
Sat 4th *The Maid of the Mill* with *Love Laughs at Locksmiths*
Fri 10th *The Heart of Midlothian* to which added the farce *The Ghost* or, 'the dead man alive'
Sat 11th *Heart of Midlothian* with *Rendezvous*
Mon 12th – Wed 14th second play *Artaxerxes*
Fri 17th grand melo-dramatic romance in 3 acts *The Orphan of the Castle* to which added a new farce called *A Roland for an Oliver*
Sat 18th Dr. Arne's opera *Artaxerxes* after which new comedy *A Short Reign And A Merry One*

1820

January

Thurs Jan 6th, the tenth night of Mr. Kean's engagement, the tragedy of *Brutus* or, the 'Fall of the Tarquins' to which will be added *The Devil to pay*

Fri 7th, Mr. Kean's Benefit, *The Merchant of Venice*

Sat 8th, ditto

Monday 10th popular play *Rob Roy,* after which the grand romance *Forty Thieves* will be repeated

Wed 12th *Heart of Midlothian* to be repeated weekly until further notice

Fri 14th the melo dramatic play *The Orphan of the Castle* to which added the opera *John of Paris*. In act 2 a pas de deux by the Misses Giroux

Sat 15th *Artaxerxes* followed by *Tekeli*

Wed 19th *Heart of Midlothian*

Wed 26th *Heart of Midlothian*

The Charity Play

Sat Jan 29th death of King George III

February

No Performances from Friday 2nd owing to the death of George the Third

Funeral Tue 8th

Fri 25th *Comedy of Errors* plus the new pantomime *Harlequin Gulliver* or, 'the flying island'

Sat 26th Sheridan's comedy *School for Scandal* after which 'the skipping garland pas de trois' to which added a melo drama *The Falls of the Clyde*

March

Fri 3rd the new musical play *Antiquary* with a farce, expressed in the bills

Sat 4th the play *Royal Oak* or, 'the perils of King Charles II'. After the play Mr. Meadows will recite a comic address 'riding on an ass'. In the course of the evening Mr. Woulds will sing a comic song, the Misses Giroux will dance an allemande, and then the new comedy called *A Short Reign and a Merry One.*

Mon 6th operatic play *The Peasant Boy*. Incidental dance by the Misses Giroux after act 1 then burlesque interlude called *Amoroso, King of Little Britain.* The evening to conclude with J. Pocock's Melo-drama *Zembuca* or, the net-maker's wife with broad sword combat between Mr. Baker and Rowbotham and dancing.

Fri 10th a new musical play *Antiquary* with farce

Sat 11th the grand romantic play *St Clara's Eve*, or 'the conquest of Toronto'. Between play and farce, Miss Green will sing 'the soldier tir'd' and the Misses Giroux will dance the 'bergere pas de trois'; to conclude, the farce *Too Late for Dinner.*

Mon 14th *As You Like it;* in the

course of the evening a variety of entertainments, to conclude the melo-dramatic romance *The Blind Boy*

Fri 17th the dramatic romance *The Orphan of the Castle* after which the dance of *the jovial millars* concluding with the grand musical romance of *The Forty Thieves*
Sat 18th Mrs. Centlivre's comedy *The Wonder, a Woman Keeps A Secret!* With songs. To conclude *Zembuca*, or 'the netmaker and his wife'. A ballet incidental to this piece in which the Misses Giroux will dance a new pas de trios
Mon 20th *Lady of the Lake;* presented Mr. Simon Paap, the celebrated Dutch dwarf only 37" tall and 28lb in weight who will demonstrate exercises. The whole to conclude with *Cymon, Prince of Arcadia*

Fri 24th a melo-drama will be performed, *Ella Rosenberg* with the farce *The Man in the Moon*, a hornpipe by Master T Saunders and the Burletta of *Tom Thumb*

Sat 25th *The Heart of Midlothian* the Misses Giroux to dance, followed by the farce *The Wags of Windsor*

April
Easter Monday, Mon 3rd *King Lear* with the new farce *The Man in the Moon*

Tues 4th *The Antiquary* and *The Forest of Bondy*

Wed 5th *The Iron Chest*
Fri 7th *Coriolanus*

Sat 8th *the Wheel of Fortune*

oOoOo

October
Sat 28th, the theatre opens for the season with the play *Adrian and Orrila*. In act 3 the three Misses Giroux will make their appearance in the celebrated 'Bergere Dance'. After, the comic opera *No Song, No Supper*
Mon 30th *Every One Has His Fault*

November
Fri 3rd new historical tragedy adapted from Schiller, *Mary Stuart, Queen of Scotland.* With *Raising the Wind*
Sat 4th *The Jealous Wife*
Fri 10th for fourth time and positively the last for at least 7 weeks, the tragedy *Mary Stuart, Queen of Scotland.*
Sat 11th Murphy's comedy *All in the Wrong.* After the place Mrs. Bartley to recite 'Collins's Ode on the Passions' followed by *The Adopted Child*
Mon 13th opera *Guy Mannering*
Fri 17th an opera; with melo-drama *The Maid and the Magpie*

Saturday 18th play *The Antiquary*
Mon 20th opera *Guy Mannering*
Fri 24th Coleman's opera *Inkle and Yarico* after which the melo-drama *The Maid and the Magpie* to conclude with the favourite farce *Rendezvous*
Sat 25th *The Antiquary* after which concert of vocal music consisting of songs, duets, glees etc

December

Fri 8th The grand musical romance *Henri Quatre* or 'France in the 'Olden Times' with the burletta of *Midas*

Fri 15th for third time the grand musical romance *Henri Quatre*, or 'France in the olden times' after it a musical extravaganza *Giovanni in London.*
Sat 16th the melo-dram of *The Inkeeper's Daughter*
Mon 18th *Julius Caesar*
Tue 19th an extra performance at request of Marquis of Lansdown. The most popular performances will be selected for this occasion

Fri 22nd new tragedy *Virginius* or, 'the Liberation of Rome' with *Hunter of the Alps*
Sat 23rd *The Wheel of Fortune* with *Giovanni in London*

During the Holiday week the doors will be opened at half past 5 and the curtain will rise at half past 6 o'clock
Tue 26th, Christmas Tuesday *Macbeth* with *The Forty Thieves*
Thur Dec 28th a new tragedy called *Virginius,* or, 'The Liberation of Rome' with the musical drama *Hunter of the Alps*
Fri 29th *The Iron Chest* with *Midas*
Sat 30th the new tragedy *Wallace* with *Ways and Means*

The new musical drama of *The Lady and the Devil* will be produced on Monday; the grand melo-dramatic spectacle called *The Vampyre* is in a state of active preparation with new and splendid scenes, machinery, dresses and decorations

Chapter Nine: At the Races

The Bath Racetrack has been in its present position since 1811. It is set on Lansdown about three and a half miles out of the town of the period, to the North-West. The track is a sharp left-handed track. This is supposed to favour horses which are able to gain good early position. The finish is uphill and quite stiff, and because it is set high on the downs, the swirling wind can be a factor. It is reckoned to be a quite challenging track.

The land belonged to the Blathwayte family, and the Eastern end of the track is close to the 'Blathwayte Arms' on the Lansdown road. Opposite it may be found a site to delight those who would rather sketch picturesque views than watch horse-racing. This is Chapel Farm and its annexe of a former hospital for pilgrims on their way to or from Glastonbury. The chapel has scanty remains, but the east end remains, partially hidden in ivy, with the tracery of old windows. A mile and a half further along the Lansdown road may be found a monument erected to Sir Bevil Grenville in 1720, by his grandson, Lord Lansdown.

From a drawing by Samuel Grimm, 1738

It is a conspicuous object at the extreme end of the down, and marks where he fell during the civil war, in 1643. Sir Bevil was a Parliamentarian under Sir William Waller. His monument is of ashlar stone, 25 feet high and surmounted by the family griffin and with the escutcheon of the Grenville family. [aka Granville or Greville]. His eldest son assisted with the Restoration of the Monarchy and was enobled as the 1st Earl of Bath.

The races usually take place around the end of June or beginning of July, with races on two or three days, and the whole city in a holiday mood. The Lower Rooms had balls most race days, and often concerts as well, as may be seen in the chapter concerning them. There were public breakfasts in Sydney Garden Vauxhall during Race Week and there was at least one gala with music and fire works. The races begin at one o'clock sharp.

The lady who attends the races should beware of pickpockets at all times! Though many of these villains may be apprehended, and their misdeeds published in the newspaper 'The Bath Chronicle and Weekly Gazette,' many more get away with their thefts than are captured. It should also be remembered that straying onto the track is forbidden, and one might be roughly manhandled off it. The stewards expressly warn that dogs will be destroyed. However, one need not be uncomfortable since there are plenty of booths selling a variety of goods, not least refreshments.

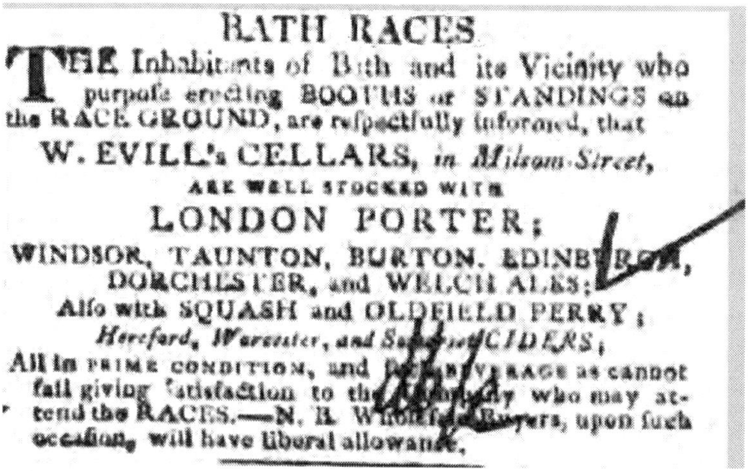
BATH RACES

THE Inhabitants of Bath and its Vicinity who purpose erecting BOOTHS or STANDINGS on the RACE GROUND, are respectfully informed, that

W. EVILL's CELLARS, *in Milsom-Street*,

ARE WELL STOCKED WITH

LONDON PORTER;

WINDSOR, TAUNTON, BURTON, EDINB[illegible], DORCHESTER, and WELCH ALES;

Also with SQUASH and OLDFIELD PERRY;

Hereford, Worcester, and S[illegible] CIDERS;

All in PRIME CONDITION, and [illegible] BEVERAGE as cannot fail giving satisfaction to the [illegible] who may attend the RACES.—N. B. Wh[illegible] Buyers, upon such occasion, will have liberal allowance.

Advertisement from Bath Chronicle and Weekly

Beware also of the swindlers who generally frequent the race course to defraud the unwary with such games as 'pricking in the garter'. [also known as Fast and Loose.]

Those who subscribe 10/6d [half a guinea] will be entitled to a ticket for admission for the three days of the races, and a non-subscriber pays 5/- per day. These subscriptions may be given at principle Inns and libraries in Bath.

In the second year of the races, 1812, a portable room was invented, a prefabricated pavilion, with balcony, veranda and windows in all directions.

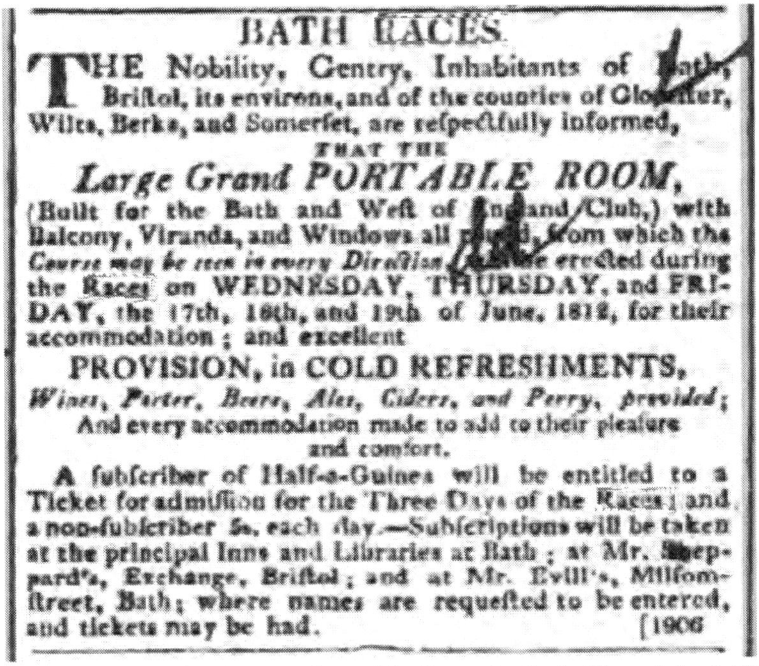
BATH RACES.

THE Nobility, Gentry, Inhabitants of Bath, Briſtol, its environs, and of the counties of Glo[illegible]ter, Wilts, Berks, and Somerſet, are reſpectfully informed,

THAT THE

Large Grand PORTABLE ROOM,

(Built for the Bath and Weſt of En[illegible]land Club,) with Balcony, Viranda, and Windows all [illegible], from which the *Course may be seen in every Direction,* [illegible] erected during the Races on WEDNESDAY, THURSDAY, and FRIDAY, the 17th, 18th, and 19th of June, 1812, for their accommodation; and excellent

PROVISION, in COLD REFRESHMENTS,

Wines, Porter, Beers, Ales, Ciders, and Perry, provided;
And every accommodation made to add to their pleaſure and comfort.

A ſubſcriber of Half-a-Guinea will be entitled to a Ticket for admiſſion for the Three Days of the Races; and a non-ſubſcriber 5s. each day.—Subſcriptions will be taken at the principal Inns and Libraries at Bath; at Mr. Sheppard's, Exchange, Briſtol; and at Mr. Evill's, Milſom-ſtreet, Bath; where names are requeſted to be entered, and tickets may be had. [1906

Advertisement for the new Portable Room in Bath Chronicle & Weekly

Every accommodation made to add to pleasure means that there will be rooms for ladies and gentlemen to make themselves comfortable with screens and closed stools. Anyone selling drinks and wanting people to buy, make sensible provision for the removal of the natural course of such liquids.

Note: horses come into their adult strength at 6 years old, and continue to gain strength hence the handicaps.

And now, on to the races!

1811

Pony races were also held this year.

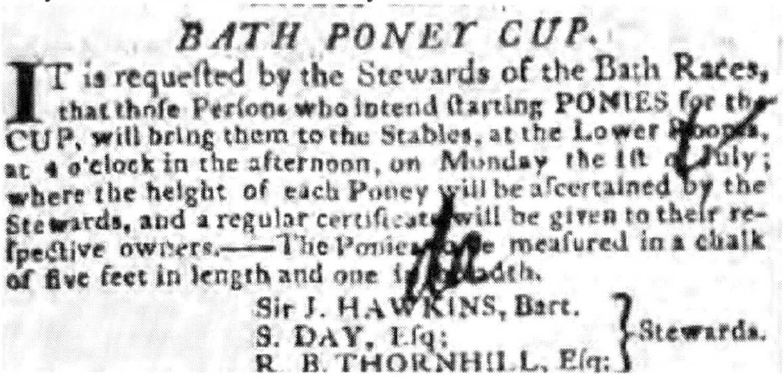

BATH PONEY CUP.

IT is requeſted by the Stewards of the Bath Races, that thoſe Perſons who intend ſtarting PONIES for the CUP, will bring them to the Stables, at the Lower Rooms, at 4 o'clock in the afternoon, on Monday the 1ſt of July; where the height of each Poney will be aſcertained by the Stewards, and a regular certificate will be given to their reſpective owners.——The Ponies to be meaſured in a chalk of five feet in length and one in breadth.

Sir J. HAWKINS, Bart.
S. DAY, Eſq;
R. B. THORNHILL, Eſq; } Stewards.

Announcement of the Pony race in the Bath Chronicle and Weekly

All subscribers to the races were asked in the last week of June to pay their subscriptions.
Admissions to the Grand Stand; to subscribers of £1 and upwards to the Racing Fund, 5/6d; to non subscribers 10/6d.

Wednesday July 3rd, Thursday July 4th and Friday July 5th

Sir J. Hawkins, bart.
S. Day, esq.
R.B. Thornhill, esq. Stewards

Mr. Langley, Clerk of the Course.

Wednesday July 3rd

Sweepstake of 10g each with 25g added for three & four year olds.
3-year-olds to carry 7st 5lb [103 lb; 46.8kg]
4-year-olds to carry 8st 9lb
Fillies and geldings allowed 3lb
One 2-mile heat. Names to be given to Mr. Weatherby Oxedon St, four subscribers minimum or no race.

Note: I stone [st] = 14lb. 1kg = 2.2 lb therefore 1lb =0.4545kg

Same day, A Maiden plate of sixty pounds for all ages.
2-mile heats.
3-year-olds 7st
4-year-olds 8st 4lb
5-year-olds 9st
6-year-olds and aged 9st. 4lb
Mares and geldings allowed 3lb.

Same day, a Fifty Pound Plate given by the Members for the City for all ages, 2 mile heats.
3-year-olds 6st 6lb
4-year-olds 8st 2lb
5-year-olds 8st 12lb
6-year-olds 9st 3lb
Aged 9st 4lb
Mares and geldings allowed 3lb. The winner to be sold for 300g if demanded within a quarter of an hour after the race, the owner of the second horse being the first entitled.

Thursday July 4th

A sweepstake of ten guineas each, with 25g added
4-year-olds to carry 8st 2lb
5-year-olds 8st 12lb
6-year-olds 9st 3lb
Aged 9st 5lb
The winner of a plate or sweepstake [handicaps excepted] in 1811 to carry 3lb extra, of two, 5lb extra one 2-mile heat. Four subscribers or no race. Mares and geldings allowed 3lb.

Same day, a Plate of One Hundred Pounds, 4 mile heats.
4-year-olds 7st 7lb
5-year-olds 8st 4 lb
6-year-olds 8st 12 lb
Aged 9st 5lb.
The winner of the 25g sweepstakes, 5g sweepstakes or 100g plate at Bilbury in 1811 to carry 7lb extra. Mares and geldings allowed 3lb

Friday July 5th

A Sixty Pound Plate given by the Bath and West of England Club, for all ages.
3-year-olds to carry 6st 9lb
4-year-olds 8st 2lb
5-year-olds 8st 13lb
6-year-olds and aged 9st 3lb
The winner to be sold for 250g if demanded within a quarter of an hour after the race, the owner of the second horse to be the first entitled. The winner of a plate or sweepstakes in 1811 [handicaps excepted] to carry 3lb extra, of two, 5lb and three or more 7lb extra.

Same day, a handicap sweepstake of Five Guineas each, with 30g added; one-mile heat

Same day, a Silver Cup and Cover, value 55 g, given by the Bath and West of England Club, for ponies of 13 hands, the best of mile heats. Name to Clerk of the Course before 8 o'clock of the evening before running. The weights to be fixed by the stewards or whom they may appoint.

Horses for the plates to be entered with the clerk of the course before 6 o'clock on the 1st of July; 1g entrance or 5g at the post and 10/6d to the Clerk of the Course. A winner of every plate, match or sweepstakes except the £50 plate to pay one guinea for weighing.

Every horseman not a subscriber of one guinea to pay half a crown for admission to the course; and every carriage belonging to any person who is not a subscriber of one guineas to pay 5/-. The course is walled round.

NB the Bath and West of England Club admits members of the Bibury, Maddington and Kingscote Clubs as honourary members to it during the races.

The newspaper advertised a public breakfast daily in Sydney Gardens, and a ball every evening at the Lower Rooms and positively NO cockfighting at the races.

1812

Wednesday 17th June, Thursday 18th June, Friday 19th June

Sir H. Lippincott, bart.
Thos. Calley esq. stewards

Runners
Sir J. Hawkins's *Matilda*, by *Ambrosio*, aged
Sir H Lippincott's *Rail,* 4 years' old
Mr. Northey's bay colt *Angelo*, by *Sancho*, out of *Lady Brough*, 4 years old.
Mr. Goddard names Mr. Hallett's *Coelebs*, 4 years' old
Mr. Langton names *Waltzers*, 6 years' old.
Mr. Biggs's *Demetrius*, 4 years' old
Mr. J Calley names *Mantidamun*, 5 years' old
Mr. Mills names *Beresford*, 4 years' old
Mr. Cope names *Julian*, 5 years' old
Mr. J Maddocks names *Eliza*, sister to *Trimbusa*, 4 years' old
Mr. Elton names *Dorisa*, 4 years' old
Mr. Sadler's brown horse *Carmelite* [late *Fourth of June*] 5 years' old
Mr. Jenner's *OP* by *Hambleton*, 5 years' old.
Mr. West's bay mare *Tulip*, 5 years' old.
Col. Williams [bi-colour? Bc] colt *Worcester,* by *Sir Oliver*; 4 years' old.
Mr. Terrett's bay colt by *Orlando*, 4 years' old
Mr. Terrett's brown filly by *Orlando,* dam, by *Moorcock*, 4 years' old
Col. Draper's horse *Topsyturvy*, by *St George*, aged [over 6].
Mr. Calley, Mr. Day, Mr. Evered, Mr. Pinis, Mr. Surtees, Mr. Bissett, Mr. Thornhill, Mr. Peach, Mr. Wodehouse, Mr. Clutterbuck and Mr. Holder all subscribers, but did not name.
28 subscribers

Wednesday 17th June

The sweepstakes of 5g each with £50 added from the Racing Fund, for horses which have never won £100 except at Maddington, Bibury or Kingscote

Won by Mr. J. Calley's *Mantidanum*, beating Mr. Sadler's *Carmellite*, Mr. Biggs's *Demetrius*, Sir Henry Lipincott's *Rail* and Mr. Terrret's bay colt by *Orlando*

The Maiden Plate of £50 for all ages was won, at two heats by Sir H. Lippincott's *Rail*, beating Mr. Terrett's brown filly by *Orlando*, and Mr. Dilly's bay colt *Rodrigo*.

Thursday 18th June

The Stapleton Stakes of 100g each, two miles and a distance, were won by Mr. Biggs's *Beresford* beating Mr. Mills's *Wood Daemon*; an excellent heat, contested every inch of the ground and won by half a head only.

The City Members' Plate of £50 for all ages was won by Major Pigott's *Morgiana*, beating Sir H. Lippincott's *Kangaroo* and Mr. Sadler's *Carmelite*; the two latter were drawn after the first heat.

Friday, 19th June

The Bristol Plate of 50g or upwards, two mile heats was won by Sir H. Lippincott's 'Kangaroo' beating Mr. J. Calley's 'Matilda' and Mr. Calley's 'Morgiana'[presumably sold to Mr. Calley under the conditions sometimes imposed over the sale of the winner]

The Ladies' Plate of £50 handicap, was won in two heats by Sir H. Lippincott's *Kangaroo* beating Mr. Calley's *Morgiana* and Mr. Starling's *Maid of the Mill*.

The County Members' Plate of £50 was won, at two heats, by Mr. Biggs' *Beresford*, beating Sir H. Lippincott's *Araxes*.

1813

Wednesday 7th July, Thursday 8th July, Friday 9th July
W. Gore Langton esq. MP
A Moffatt Mills esq. Stewards

Wednesday 7th July

Runners
Sir H.C. Lippincott names Mr. Eades's *Accident*, 4 years' old
Mr. Calley's *Barbara*, 6 years' old
Mr. Biggs's *Demetrius*, 5 years' old
Sir J.C. Hawkins names *Dorina* 5 years' old
Mr. Mills's *Jesse* by *Totteridge*, 4 years' old
Mr. Pigot names *Tinker* ...... 4 years' old
Mr. Terrett's *Bluster* by *Orlando*, dam by *Pegasus* 5 years old.
Mr. Hallett's *Coelebs*, 5 years' old
Mr. Langton names *Mountebank,* 5 years' old
Mr. Napier names *Lamia*, 4 years' old
Mr. C Fisher's chestnut filly *Perhaps*, by *Haphazard*, 4 years
Mr. Tate's bay colt *Venom* by *Vermin*
Mr. Langton jun., Mr. Day, Mr. E.J. Bury, Mr. Taylor, Mr. Dunn, Mr. G. Hawkins, Mr. Lynn, Mr. Howden, Mr. Cope, Mr. Erskine, Mr. Farquharson, Mr. Elton and Mr. Tate are subscribers but did not name.

<u>A sweepstake of five guineas</u> each with fifty pounds added from the Racing Fund, for horses which have never won except at Maddington, Bibury or Kingscote.
4-year-olds to carry 8st 7lb
5-year-olds 9st 5lb
6-year-olds 9st 12lb
Aged 10st. The winner of the 5g stakes at Maddington or Bibury to carry 5lb extra; mares and geldings allowed 3lb; 2 miles

Same day a Fifty Pound Plate given by the Members for the County for three and four year olds.
3-year-olds 7st 7lb
4-year-olds 8st 12lb
Two mile heats/ Mares and geldings allowed 3lb

[one of the races was won by Lamia, who is bought by Mr. Biggs]

Thursday 8th July

Runners
Mr. Biggs's *Lamia*, 4 years' old
Sir H. C. Lippincott's *Beverley*, 5 years' old
Mr. Calley's *Barbara*, 6 years' old
Mr. Biggs's *Demetrius*, 5 years' old
Sir J Hawkins names *Cambric,* 6 years' old
Mr. Langton Jun. names *Wood Daemon*, aged
Mr. Elton names Mr. Mills's *Jesse*, 4 years' old
Mr. J Smyth names *Crossbow*, 5 years' old
Col. G Langton names *Romeo*, aged
Mr. Day names *Busac* by *Whiskey*, 3 years' old
Col. Courtney names *Scorpion*, aged
Sir H. Smyth names Mr. Farquharson's filly by *Gameller* out of *Cracker*, 3 years' old.
Mr. George's black filly *Algarsise*, 3 years' old
Mr. Colt's brown colt *Coker* by *Totteridge* out of *Thrasher*'s dam, 4 years' old.

A Fifty Pound Plate given by the Members of the County for all ages. Two mile heats.
3-year-olds 6st 9lb
4-year-olds 8st 2lb
5-year-olds 8st 12lb
6-year-olds 9st 3lb
Aged 9st 5lb
Mares and geldings allowed 3lb. The winner shall be sold for 250 g if demanded within a quarter of an hour after the race; the owner of the second horse being first entitled.
Won by Mr. Mills's *Jesse*, beating Mr. Biggs's Beresford

Same day, the Bristol Gold Cup with Fifty Guineas added. The winner to be sold for 400g if demanded within a quarter of an hour. The winner of the 5g, 25g, or 100g at Bibury to carry 5lb extra; if of two of them 7lb extra. Three miles.
3-year-olds 6st
4-year-olds 7st 7lb
5-year-olds 8st 7lb
6 and aged 9st 2lb
Won by Mr. Biggs's *Demetrius* beating Mr. J Smith's *Crossbow* and Sir H. Lippincott's *Beverley*.

Friday 9th July

The Handicap Sweepstakes of £50 was won at 3 heats by Mr. Smith's *Crossbow*, beating Mr. Biggs's *Beresford.*

Same day, a Fifty Pound Plate, given by Members for the City, was won by Mr. Mills's *Jesse*, beating Mr. Biggs's *Beresford.*

The Earl of Cork and Col. Horner have accepted stewardship for next year's races.

1814

Wednesday 29th June, Thursday 30th June and Friday 1st July

Earl of Cork and Orrery
Col. T Strangeways Horner, Stewards
Mr. Langley, Clerk of the Course

Horses for the Plates and Purses to be entered with the Clerk of the Course before six o'clock on the day preceding; one guinea beforehand or 5 guineas at the post and one guinea to the Clerk of the Course.
The Steward's Ordinary will be the first day at the York Hotel, and on the second day at the White Hart.
Public breakfasts, Balls, &c as usual.

Wednesday 29th June

Runners
Mr. G Langton names Mr. Dundas' *Clwyd* by *Cesario* out of *Adela*, 4 years' old
Mr. Mills names Mr. Whitmore's chestnut filly *St Anne*, by *Alexander*, out of *Lampedosa*
Major Wilson's bay gelding *Fineshade* 4 years' old
Mr. Mugley's bay colt by *Meteor* dam by *Highflyer*, 3 years' old
Mr. F Langton's *Roses* by *Selim,* 4 years' old
Mr. Calley names Mr. Ruth's *Crestless* by *Walton* 4 years' old
Sir J. C. Hawkins's filly by *Smuggle*r out of *Martha* 3 years' old
Mr. Elton's *Christina* by *Eaglt....* of *Stapleton'*s dam 3 years
Mr. W G Langton names Sir .... *Illusion*, 4 years
Mr. Taylor's *Zuleika* by *Garth* out of *Trinedada* 4 years
Mr. T. S. Horner names Mr. Winton's chestnut colt by *Whiskey* out of *Agnes,* 3 years' old
Mr. Hart's bay *Surprise* by *Stamford* out of *Gawkey*, 6 years
Mr. Terrett's *Bluster*, 6 years' old
Mr. Wentworth's brown colt *Lustre* by *Mirror*, 4 years' old
Col. Thornton's brown/bay colt by *Kite* out of *St Anne*, 4 years' old.
Mr. Dove, Mr. Core, Mr. Farquharson, Mr. Browne, Lord Cook, Mr. Happitly, Mr. Shute and Mr. Thornhill are subscribers but did not name.
23 subscribers
A beautiful day.

A sweepstake of 5g each with £50 added from the Racing Fund for horses that never won £100 at any time before the day of nominations
3-year-olds 7st 3lb
4-year-olds 8st 7lb
5-year-olds 9st 5lb
6-year-olds 9st 12lb
Aged 10st
2 miles. The winner of £100 in any race after the day of nomination and previous to the day of starting to carry 5lb extra, mares and geldings allowed 3lb
Won by Mr. Terrett's *Bluster* beating 5 others

Same day a Fifty Pound Plate given by the Members for the County for 3 and 4 year olds.
3-year-olds to carry 7st 7lb
4-year-olds 8st 12lb
Two mile heats, mares and geldings allowed 3lb
Won by *Barsac* [entered at the post] beating Mr. Weatherall's *Fairy* and Mr. Lucas's filly by *Walton.*

Thursday 30th June

Mr. Langton names Mr. Dundas's *Mountebank* 6 years' old
Mr. Collins names Mr. Lucas's horse *Rodham* 5 years' old
Mr. Day names Sir H. Lippincott's gelding *Crossbow* 6 years' old
Col. Thornton's grey by *Camilla* dam by *Ruler* 4 years' old
Mr. Calley's *Dinarzade* 3 years' old
Mr. T.S. Horner names *Worcester* by *Sir Oliver* 6 years' old
Mr. Elton's *Janet* 5 years' old
Mr. W.G. Langton names Sir H Lippincott's *Illusion* 4 years
Mr. Kneller's *Barsac* 4 years
Lord Leberter names *Jannette* aged
Mr. R. B. Thornhill names *Demetrius* 6 years' old
Mr. Manley's bay mare *Meteorina* 6 years' old
Gen. Cower's bay filly *Lama* 4 years' old
___________ *Aquarius* 5 years' old
Sir J. Hawkins and Lord Cork are subscribers but did not name

The Gold Cup of One Hundred Guineas by subscription of ten guineas each, ten subscribers or no race. If more than ten subscribers, the surplus in specie.
3-year-olds 6st
4-year-olds 7st 7lb
5-year-olds 8st 7lb
6 and aged 9st 2lb
Winners of races at Bibury this year to carry 5lb extra, if two wins, 8lb more

Private race Sir John Hawkins's bay filly *Avora* by *Smuggler* out of *Martha* against Mr. Calley's brown filly *Dinerazade* by *Selim* out of *Princess* 8st 7lb each, one race, 100g. One mile; a dead heat, a good race.

A Fifty Pound Plate given by the Members for the City, for all ages. 2 mile heats
3-year-olds, 6st 9lb
4-year-olds 8st 2lb
5-year-olds 8st 12lb
6-year-old 9st 3lb
Aged 9st 5lb
Mares and geldings allowed 3lb
The winner to be sold for 250g if demanded within a quarter hour after race, the owner of the second horse being first entitled.

Friday 1st July

A sweepstake of 25g each, 15 feet one mile
3-year-old colts 8st 3lb
3-year-old fillies 8st

3-year-olds in this race:
Mr. Calley's brown filly *Dinarzade* by *Selim*
Sir J.C. Hawkin's bay filly *Avora* by *Smuggler* out of *Martha*
Mr. Farquharson's brown filly by *Witchcraft* out of *Margaretta's* dam
Mr. Pryce's chestnut *Magpie* colt by *B.....* out of *Laura*

<u>A City Purse of Fifty Guineas</u>, two mile heats
3-year-olds 7st
4-year-olds 8st 1lb
5-year-olds 9st
6-year-olds 9st 6lb
Aged 9st 9lb
Mares and geldings allowed 3lb

1815

Wednesday 28th June, Thursday 29th June, Friday 30th June beginning at 1 o'clock.

22 subscribers for the 5g stake, almost as many as for the Gold Cup.

Sir C.W. Bamfylde, bart.
Wm Dickenson esq. MP stewards

Mr. Langley, clerk of the course

Horses for the Plates to be entered with the Clerk of the Course before eight o'clock the Tuesday preceding. One guinea entrance, or 5 g at the post and one guinea to the Clerk of the Course. The entrance money of each horse to go to the general fund.

Wednesday 28th June

A sweepstake, 5 guineas each with Fifty Pounds added from the Racing Fund for horses that never won £100 at any one time before the day of nomination.
3-year-olds 7st 3lb
4-year-olds 8st 7lb
5-year-olds 9st 5lb
6-year-olds 9st 12lb
Aged 10st
2 miles. The winner of £100 at any time after the day of nomination, and previous to the day of starting, to carry 5lb extra. Mares and Geldings allowed 3lb.

Runners
Mr. Terrett's brother to *Bluster*, 4 years' old
Mr. Calley's *Yellow Slipper* 3 years' old
Sir J. Hawkins names *Zuleika,* 5 years' old
Mr. J Browne names Mr. Calley's bay *Buccaneer,* by *Mountaineer*, 3 years' old
Mr. Elton names Mr. Rawlinson's bay filly by Williamson's *Ditto* out of *Agnes,* by *Shuttle* 3 years' old
Mr. G. Hawkins names *Illusion* 3 years' old
Mr. J. Taylor names a bay filly *Caroline* by *Barbarossa* out of *Biddy*

Tipkin 3 years' old
Mr. Guyenette names *Ippogrifo* [late *Henley*] by *Sorcerer* 4 years
Sir C. Bampfylde names *Hecate* 3 years' old
Mr. C.F. Bampfylde names a gelding *Falconer* by *Whiskey* dam by *Hawk* 4 years' old.
Col. Thornton's bay mare by *Esher,* dam by *Chance* out of *Rofoletts* 5 years' old.
Mr. Wills's bay colt *King Charles* 4 years' old
Mr. Hamyold names a bay filly *Prototype* by *Ditto* 3 years' old
Mr. Hart's bay horse *Surprize* by *Scamford* aged
Lord Cork, Mr. G. Langton, Mr. Reilly, Mr. Erskine, Mr. Horner, Mr. Mortimer and Mr. Dickinson are subscribers but did not name.

A Fifty Pound Plate given by the Members for the County, for 3 and 4 year olds.
3-year-olds to carry 7st 5lb
4-year-olds 8st 12lb
Two mile heats. Mares and geldings allowed 3lb

Thursday 29th June

The Gold Cup of One Hundred Guineas by subscription of 10g each. Ten subscribers or no race. If more than ten subscribers, the surplus in specie.
3-year-olds 6st
4-year-olds 6st 7lb
5-year-olds 8st 7lb
6 and aged 9st 2lb.
The winner of a King's Plate, Gold Cup of £qoo in this year to carry 5lb extra if two 7lb. Three miles.

Runners

Mr. Elton names a bay filly, *Caroline* by *Barbarussa* out of *Biddy Tipkin* 3 years' old
Lord Cork names Mr. Walker's chestnut colt *Ippogriffo* by *Sorcerer* 3 years' old
Mr. G. Langton names *Pyramus* 5 years' old
Mr. Horner names *Midnight* 4 years' old
Mr. Calley's *Miss Plasoff* 5 years' old

Mr. S Day names *Foxglove* 3 years' old
Sir J.C. Hawkins names *Zuleika* 5 years old
Mr. W.G. Langton names *Bijou* by *Orville*, 4 years' old
Sir C. Bampfylde names *Touley* 6 years' old
Mr. Collins names *Topsy Turvey* aged
Mr. Dickinson names *Illusion* 5 years' old
Col. Thornton's bay mare by *Esher* dam by *Chance*, 5 years' old
Sir W. Roberts' bay horse *Venture* 6 years' old
Mr. Wilks's bay colt *King Charles* 4 years' old
Mr. Parkin's bay horse *Industry* [late *Scout*] 6 years' old
Mr. J. Perren's grey colt, brother to *Quizzer* 4 years' old

A Fifty Pound Plate given by the Members for the City for all ages. Two mile heats.
3-year-olds, 6st 9lb
4-year-olds, 8st 2lb
5-year-olds 8st 12lb
6-year-olds 9st 3lb
Aged 9st 7lb
Mares and geldings allowed 3lb. The winner to be sold for 250g if demanded &c.

Friday 30th June

No information

1816

Wednesday 3rd July and Thursday 4th July

Wm Gore Langton jun., esq.
G.M.B. Napier, esq. Stewards

Wednesday 3rd July

The Sweepstakes of 5g each [29 subscribers] with £50 added from the racing fund
Won by Mr. Jones's *Fatima* beating Mr. Smith's *Sweetheart*, Mr. George's grey gelding and Mr. West's *Coquelicot*
For the sweepstakes of 50g each, for 3-year-old colts, *Pythoness*, named by Mr. Calley walked over.

The County Members' £50 plate for 3 and 4 year olds was won by Mr. Hassenden's colt by *Stavely*, beating Mr. George's *Eugene,* Mr. Day's cream gelding and Mr. Lipton's *Cleopatra.* Great odds on *Cleopatra* against the field; but owing to a loose horse crossing the course, she threw her rider and was distanced.

Thursday 4th July

The weather was most unfavourable, but plenty of people came anyway.

The Gold Cup of 100g value was won by Mr. Jones's *King of Diamonds*, beating *Grey Marquis*, named by Mr. Strode; Mr. West's *Charles Surface; Casanet*, named by Mr. Dickenson; and *Offa's Dyke*, named by Mr. Langton jun.

The City Members' £50 Plate for all ages was won by Mr. Farquharson's *Grey Marquis*, beating Mr. Smith's *Sweetheart* and Mr. Scott's *Offa's Dyke.*

A Handicap Plate of £50 two mile heats was won by Mr. Goddard's *Castanet,* beating Mr. West's *Coquelicot,* Mr. Robert's *Wellesley* and Mr. Calley's *Yellow Slipper.*

Some very fine heats were seen; those between *Grey Marquis* and *Offa's Dyke* will long stand conspicuous in the annals of sporting endeavour.

1817

Wednesday 2nd July and Thursday 3rd July

J. Payne Tudway esq. MP
G. Hawkins esq. Stewards.

Wednesday 2nd July

Private race: Mr. Dundas; *Original*, 5 years' old, 9st 7lb against Mr. Calley's bay gelding *Shrog* by *Hedley* 3 years' old, 7st, one mile, h ft 100g; walked over by *Original.*

Sweepstakes of 25g each, for 3-year-olds
Colts 8st 7lb
Fillies 8st 4lb
the last mile. Stakes to be paid to the Clerk of the Course before 12 o'clock the day of running, or not entitled, though a winner
runners
Mr. Calley's bay gelding *Shrog* by *Hedley* out of *Augusta* by*Buzzard*
Mr. Dundas' grey filly *Mermaid* by *Canopus* out of *The Witch of Endor*
Mr. Hassenden's bay colt by *Sorcerer* out of *Slipper*
Mr. West's *Brother to Trout*
Mr. Jones's *Algernon Sidney*
___________ *Clearwell Lass*
six subscribers.
Won by Mr. Tomes' *Duplicate*, beating Mr. Jones's *Clearwell Lass* and Mr. Hassenden's *Sorcerer.* An excellent race.

Private Race: Mr. Jones's *Fatima* 5 years' old, 8st, against Mr. Dundas; *Pyramus,* aged, 8st 7lb. 2 miles, 200g h ft won by *Fatima.*

Sweepstakes of 5g each, with £50 added from the Racing Fund for horses that never won £100 at any time before the day of nomination
3-year-olds 7st
4-year-olds 8st 7lb
5-year-olds 9st 5lb

6-year-olds 9st 12lb
Aged 10st
Two miles and a distance. The winner of £100 at any time after the day of nomination, and previous to the day of starting to carry 5lb extra. Mares and Geldings allowed 3lb.

Runners
Mr. W.G. Langton senr names Mr. Pierce's filly by *Sorcerer* out of sister to *Rosette* 3 years' old
Mr. W. Langton jun names chestnut filly by *Rubens* out of *Nymphina* 4 years' old
Mr. Napier names *Grey Marquis* 6 years' old
Sir J.C. Hawkins names *Snowball* 4 years' old
Sir C. Bampfylde names Mr. Hallett's bay colt by *Hedley* out of *December* 3 years' old
Mr. Bampfyld names brown mare *Bullrush* 5 years' old
Mr. Calley's *Shrog* by *Hedley* 3 years' old
Mr. Elton names Mr. Sadler's chestnut filly *Venus* 4 years' old.
Mr. Price's chestnut gelding by Williamson's *Ditto* out of *Brandy Nan* 4 years' old.
Mr. Lindow names Mr. Tomas's filly *Diana* 4 years' old
Mr. West's bay cold *Bulgarian* 4 years' old
________________*Coquelicot* 4 years' old
Mr. G. Hawkins names Mr. ....*The Rat* 3 years' old
Mr. Dundas. Grey filly *Mermaid* by*Canopus* out of the *Witch of Endor* 3 years' old
Mr. Hassenden's bay colt by *Sorcerer* out of *Slipper* 3 years' old
Mr. Erskine names chestnut colt *Dot-and-go-one* by *Rubens* bought at General Gower's sale
Mr. Williams names Mr. Jenkins's *Cuirassier* 4 years' old
Sir J Cope's *Buffalo* 4 years' old
Mr. Morgan names chestnut filly by *Junius*, dam by *Young Eclipse* 4 years' old.
Mr. Bacon's bay colt by *Election,* dam by *Delphini* out of *Zenobia* by *Sir Peter* 3 years' old
Mr. King's chestnut colt by *Clinker* out of *Fulford'*s dam, 4 years.
Mr. George's *Non Conductor* 4 years' old
Mr. Pryce's *Meg Murdoch* 4 years' old
_________ *Duplicate* 3 years' old
Sir W. Robers's brown colt by *Rubens* 4 years' old
Mr. Clark's chestnut filly *The Lovely Maid* by *Walton*, dam *Capella* 4

years' old
Mr. Radclyffe's *Sir Christopher* 5 years old.

.

27 subscribers.
Won by Mr. West's *Bulgarian*, beating Sir J.C. Hawkins's *Snowball,* Mr. Bampfylde's *Bullrush* and eight others. *Bullrush* came in first, but having run on the wrong side of a post, the stakes were given to *Bulgarian.*

The County Members' £50 Plate for 3 and 4 year olds
3-year-olds to carry 7st 7lb
4-year olds to carry 8st 12lb
Two mile heats, mares and geldings allowed 3lb

Won at 3 heats by Sir T. Cope's *Buffalo,* beating Mr. Whalley's *Lovely Maid* and Mr. Day's *Snowball.*

Thursday 3rd July

The City Members' £50 Plate weights as usual. The winner to be sold for 300g if demanded &c. Heats, 2 miles and a distance.

Won at 3 heats by Mr. Farquharson's *Grey Marquis*, beating Mr. Pryce's *Meg Murdock*, Mr. Tomes's *Diana,* and Mr. Whalley's *Dot-and-go-one.*

The Gold Cup of 100g by subscribers of 10g each. 10 subscribers or no race. If more than 10 subscribers, the surplus in specie.
3-year-olds 6 st
4-year-olds 7st 7lb
5-year-olds 8st 7lb
6 and aged 9st 2lb.
The winner of a King's Plate, Gold Cup or £100 in this year to carry 5lb extra; if two, 7lb. Three miles. Stakes to be paid to the Clerk of the Course before 12 o'clock on the day of running, or not entitled, though a

winner.

Runners
Mr. Langton sen'r, names *Robin Adair* 6 years' old
Mr. Langton jun. names *Sir Christopher* 5 years' old
Sir J.C. Hawkins names *Clearwell Lass*, 3 years' old
Mr. Napier names *Garus* 5 years' old.
Mr. Calley names a colt by *Election* out of *Vixen*, 3 years' old
Mr. Dundas's *Pyramus* aged
Mr. Jones's *Fatima* 5 years
Mr. King's brown colt *Gainsborough* 4 years
Mr. West's *Bulgarian,* 4 years' old
Mr. Hassenden's *Pythoness* 4 years
Mr. Tomes's bay colt *Duplicate* 3 years' old
Col. Whaley's *Robinson Crusoe* 6 years' old
_____________ chestnut colt by *Rubens* bought at Gen. Gower's sale. 3 years' old
Sir C. Bampfylde did not name
13 subscribers, 10g each, 3 miles.
Won by Mr. King's *Gainsborough,* beating *Bulgarian, Duplicate* and Col. Whalley's *Robinson Crusoe.*

The races this year greatly increased in celebrity, as there were double the number of running horses that have been seen here for several years. The company was very numerous; the ordinaries and balls were well attended, and considerable subscriptions were raised for next year's sport for which Col. Tynte was appointed steward.

1818

Wednesday July 8th, Thursday July 9th

Col C.K.K Tynte, steward [deputed by Sir John Hawkins]

Mr. Langley, Clerk of the Course

Wednesday July 8th

Sweepstakes of 5guineas each with Fifty Pounds added from the Racing Fund for horses that never won £100 at any one time before the day of nomination.
3-year-olds 7st
4-year-olds 8st 7lb
5-year-olds 9st 5lb
6-year-olds 9st 12lb
Aged 10st
2 miles and a distance. The winner of £100 after nomination day to carry 3lb extra. Mares and geldings allowed 3lb. Stakes to be paid to the Clerk of the Course by 12 o'clock on the day of running or to the stewards before starting, or not entitled, though a winner.

Runners
Mr. Langton names bay filly *Fanny* sister to *Original* 3 years' old
Mr. Langton jun names bay gelding by *Vespasian,* dam by *Hambletonian* 3 years' old
Mr. Elton names bay colt *Soothsayer* out of *Flighty* 3 years' old
Mr. Terrett's brown filly by *Doctor* out of *Bauble*'s dam, 4 years
Mr. Bampfylde names bay gelding by *Vespasian* out of *Rumbo*'s dam, 3 years' old
Mr. Hassenden's *Collier* 3 years' old
Mr. Lawrence's chestnut colt, *Overthrow* by *Marmion* dam by *Dragon* 3 years' old*
Mr. Jones's *Charming Molly* by *Rubens* 5 years
Mr. King's chestnut horse *Traveller* by *Clinker* 5 years' old
Sir J.C. Hawkins names bay filly by *Camerton* out of *Snowdrop,* 3 years' old
Mr. Pryce's bay colt by *Cambric* dam by *Fortunio* 3 years' old
Mr. Thornhill names chestnut gelding *Skeleton* by *Rubens* 5 years
Mr. Fielder's *Edwin* by *Sir Oliver* 4 years' old

Mr. Morgan's bay mare *Mrs. Fudge* by Williamson's *Ditto* out of *All-Dickey'*s dam 5 years' old
Sir R. Williams names *Hugh Lupus* by *Hambletonian* 6 years' old
Mr. Tomes's grey gelding *Aljerine* 4 years' old
Mr. J. Walker's *Sidrophel* 4 years' old
Colonel Leslie names *Brother to Trout* 4 years' old
Mr. Kneller's bay colt *Silverlegs* by *Camerton* 3 years' old
Mr. Fellowes's *Birmingham Countess* by *Rubens,* dam by *Sir Peter* 5 years' old
Sir C. Bampfylde, Mr. Morgan, Mr. Erskine, Mr. Napier, Mr. Tynte, Mr. Hawkins, Mr. Farquharson and Mr. R. Hammond are subscribers but did not name.
*Late entrance Mr. Lawrence's colt *Minstrel* [Late *Secundus*] 3 years' old [Substitition for *Overthrow*?]

1st Mr. Tomes's *Aljerine*
2nd Mr. Lawrence's colt *Minstrel*
3rd Mr. Pryce;s *Cambric*
Placed: *Hugh Lupus, Mrs. Fudge, Collier, Charming Molly*

A Sweepstake of 25 guineas each for 3-year-olds
Colts 8st 7lb
Fillies 8st 4lb, the last mile

Runners
Mr. Hassenden's blac colt *Collier* by *Sorcerer*
Mr. Dundas's bay filly by *Rubens* out of *Philadelphia*
Mr. Jones's *Fanny* by *Poulton*
Mr. Hill's brown filly *Emma* sister to *Crusader*
Mr. C. Day's bay filly by *Camerton* out of *Snowdrop*
Mr. R.C. Hammond did not name.

1st Mr. Jones's *Fanny*
2nd Mr. Hassingden's *Collier*
3rd Mr. Hill's *Emma*

Private race Mr. Jones's *Fatima* carrying 8st 8lb against Mr. Charlton's *Indus* carrying 8st 4lb. Two miles, 50g, h, ft; won by *Indus*

A Fifty Pound Plate given by the Members for the County for 3 and 4 year olds
3-year-olds to carry 7st 7lb
4-year-olds to carry 8st 12 lb
Two mile heats; mares and geldings allowed 3lb

Mr. Lawrence's *Minstrel* [Late *Secundus*]	0 – 1 – 1
Mr. West's chestnut filly *Leah* 4 years' old	0 – 3 – 2
Mr. Pryce's *Duplicate* 4 years' old	3 – 2 – dr

Thursday July 9th

A Gold Cup of 100 guineas by subscribers of 10g each on dislplay in Mr. Evill's in the Market-Place.
3-year-olds 6st
4-year-olds 7st 7lb
5-year-olds 8st 7lb
6-year-olds and aged, 9st 2 lb
The winner of the King's Plate, Gold cup of £100 this year to carry 5lb extra, any two 7lb extra. Three miles. The stakes for this cup and the 2g stakes to be made to the Clerk of the Course by 12 o'clock in the day of running.

Runners
Mr. Tynte names Mr. Page's *Doctor Busby* 4 years' old
Mr. Hawkins names *Garus* 6 years' old
Mr. Wests *Bulgarian* 5 years' old.
Mr. W.G. Langton names *Fascinator* 4 years' old
Mr. W.G. Langton jun. names bay colt *Cartoon* 4 years' old
Sir J. C. Hawkins named *Zuleika* aged
Mr. Charlton's *Indus* 4 years' old
Mr. Hill's *Emma* 3 years' old
Mr. King's bay colt *Sober Robin* by *Orville* 4 years' old
Sir C.W. Bampfylde is a subscriber but did not name.

1st Mr. Charlton's *Indus*
2nd Mr. West's *Bulgarian*
3rd Mr. Hill's *Emma* - A capital race

Private Race Mr. Charlton's bay colt *Cartoon*, brother to *Raphael* carrying 8st 2lb against Mr. Hill's bay jare *Mrs. Fudge* by Williamson's *Ditto* 7st 9lb one mile, 50 Guineas h. Ft/
Won by *Mrs. Fudge*

A Fifty Poung Plate given by the Members for the City
3-year-olds to carry 6st 9lb
4-year-olds 8st 2lb
5-year-olds 8st 12lb
6 year-olds 9st 3lb
Aged 9st 5lb.
The winner to be sold for 300g if demanded &c; heats two miles and a distance.
Horses for the plated to be entered with the Clerk of the Course on the Tuesday evening preceding. One g entrance and one more to the Clerk of the Course, or 5gs at the post. The entrance money to go to the Racing Fund.

Two Heats
1st Mr. Steven's *Charming Molly* [sold by Mr. Jones]
2nd Mr. West's *Bulgarian*
3rd Mr. C. Day's chestnut mare by *Wazy*
Each beast placed by only half a neck.

The North Somerset Yeomanry Plate of 70g by horses, *bona fide* property of non-commissioned officers or privates of the Corps that have been regularly used and worked as troop-horses in their respective troops at least 6 days previously to the days of starting, to be certified by the Captains or the Troops and that have never started for plate, cup or purse
4-year-olds 10st
5-year-olds 11st
Six year olds 12 st
Aged 12st 2lb
The best of the heats of two miles and a distance. To be rode by members of the corps who are to declare the colour of the jackets and caps they intend riding in at the time of entrance, which cannot be altered afterwards. To pay 1g entrance, to go to the second horse, and half a guinea to the Clerk of the Course for weights and scales and to enter the Saturday before the races.
Two Heats

Mr. Dualy's grey mare *Gypsy* 4 years ....1 – 1
Mr. Jones's chestnut mare *Dame Durban* 7 years ....2 – 3
Mr. W. Reynold's brown gelding *Cricket,* aged ...... 3 – 2
Mr. Adam's *Chance* 5 years.....................................4 – 4
Mr. J Walker's *Matilda*..5 – 5
Mr. W. Harris's *Jack* ....dis
Mr. J. Loder's [jun] chestnut mare *Little Margery*....dis

This race excited considerable interest but was won easily. Some doubts, however, have arisen as to the qualification of the winning mare, which are not yet decided.

The Down was numerously attended, particularly on the second day, notwithstanding so many leading characters engaged in the General Election. Col. Tynte was unavoidably absent through a domestic affliction, and Sir John Hawkins officiated in his stead as steward.

Ordinaries as usual
The first Race Dinner will be at the White Hart Inn

The Ordinaries of the White Hart and York House were not so well frequented as usual, or as the excellent fare deserved.

A numerous company attended the Gala at Sydney Gardens on Wednesday with Fire-works; and the Race Ball at the Kingston Rooms

1819

Wednesday 7th July and Thursday 8th July

K Lechmere Charlton esq., Steward
Mr. Langley, Clerk of the Course.

Wednesday July 7th

Sweepstakes 5 guineas each with £50 added from the Racing Fund, for horses that have never won £100 at any one time before the day of nomination.
3-year-olds 7st
4-year-old 8st 7lb
5-year-olds 9st 3lb
6-year-olds 9st 12lb
Aged 10st
The winner of £100, at any date after the day of nomination and previously to the day of starting to carry 5lb extra. Mares and geldings allowed 3lb. Two miles and a distance.

Runners
Mr. W.G. Langton jun. names Mr. Charlton's chestnut colt by *Ditto*, out of the dam of *Democles*. 3 years' old
Sir J.C. Hawkins names *Calendula* 4 years old.
____________ brown colt *Elastic* by *Whalebone*, dam by *Driver* out of *Nightshade*, 3 years' old
Mr. Napier names brown filly by *Smuggler* out of *Sorceress,* 3 years' old
Mr. L. Charlton's bay colt by *Haphazard* dam by *Sancho* 3 years
Mr. G. Hawkins names bay colt *Agabas* by *Soothsayer* dam by *Guildford* out of *Vixen*
Mr. Tomes names *Leah* 5 years' old
Mr. D.J. Long names bay colt *Douro* [late *Yarmouth*] 4 years' old
Mr. Morgan names bay colt by *Truffle* out of *Maria*
Mr. Tadway's chestnut colt by *Mountaineer* out of *Hernia*
Mr. West's bay colt by *Selim* dam by *Giles* out of *Monymusk* 4 years' old
Mr. Sadler's chestnut filly *Defiance* by *Rubens* out of *Polly* 3 years
Mr. Hill's filly, sister to *The Rat* by *Poulton* 3 years' old.
Sir T.B. Lethbridge's brown colt by *Orville* out of *Gramarie* 4 years' old
Mr. Roger's *Thunderstorm* 4 years' old

Mr. Brunswick names bay filly *Tambourine* by *Cervantes,* dam by *Sir David* 3 years' old
Mr. Jones is a subscriber but did not name.

1st Mr. Sadler's *Defiance*
2nd Mr. West's brown colt
3rd Mr. Morgan's bay colt

A sweepstake of 25 guineas each, for three-years-old
Colts 8st 7lb
Fillies 8st 4lb
Stakes to be paid to the Clerk of the Course before 12 o'clock the day of running, or not entitled though a winner. The last mile.

1st Mr. Jones's *Ethelinda*
2nd Mr. Biggs's brown colt *Elastic* by *Whalebone*, dam by *Driver*
3rd Mr. Calley's *Champignon*
A well-contested heat with Ethelinda the favourite

A Fifty Pound Plate given by the Members for the County for 3 and 4 year olds.
3-year-olds 7st 7lb
4-year-olds 8st 12lb
Two mile heats. Mares and geldings allowed 3lb

1st Mr. L. Charlton's *Effie Deans*
2nd Mr. Jones's *Ethelinda*
3rd Mr. Clark's *Red Rose*

Private race Mr. Moggridge's chestnut mare beat Mr. Rigby's brown gelding over two miles carrying 11st each for 50 guineas. An easily won race.

Thursday July 8th

Private Race Mr. Calley's *Imposter* beat Mr. Biggs's *Thomas* for 50g. Last half mile.

Sweepstakes of 10 guineas [in lieu of the Cup]

3-year-olds 6st
4-year-olds 7st 7lb
5-year-olds 8st 7lb
6-year-olds and aged 9st 2lb
The winner of a King's Plate, Gold Cup or £100 in this year to carry 5lb; of two to carry 7lb extra. Stakes to be paid to the clerk of the Course by 12 o'clock the day of running.

Runners
Mr. G. Langton names *Indus* 5 years' old
Mr. W. G. Langton jun names brown filly by *Smuggler,* out of *Sorceress*, 3 years' old
Mr. L. Charlton's *David* 5 years' old
Mr. R. Jones's *Ethelinda* 3 years' old
Mr. Hill's filly, sister to *The Rat* 3 years' old
Mr. King's *The Student* 5 years' old
Mr. Napier did not name.

1st Mr. Jones's *Ethelinda*
2nd Mr. Hill's filly sister to *The Rat*

<u>A Fifty Pound Plate given by the Members for the City</u>
3-year-olds to carry 6lb 9st
4-year-olds 8st 2lb
5-year-olds 8st 12lb
6-year-olds 9st 3lb
Aged 9st 5lb
The winner to be sold for 300g if demanded &c, heats 2 miles and a distance.
Two heats
1st Mr. L. Charlton's *Effie Deans*
2nd Mr. West's brown colt by *Selim*
3rd Mr. Farquharson's*? Garm*

The weather was delightful and many people turned out including the notorious 'Captain' Groves, pickpocket and his men. The police arrested 14 pickpockets including one Jos. Caines, one of the Cockroad tribe, who assaulted a Mr. Baker, knocking him down, rifling his pockets and cutting off the silver buttons on his coat and waistcoat.
As the Ordinaries of the York Hotel and White Hart were not as well attended as the sumptuous fare might have caused one to expect.

1820
Wednesday June 28th and Thursday June 29th

Wednesday June 28th

No information

Thursday June 29th

The Kelston Stakes of 25 Guineas each for 3 year colts, one mile

1st Mr. H Jones's bay colt by *Rubens*
2nd Mr. Jones's *Sophia*
3rd Mr. Hill's chestnut filly *Jenny Sutton*
4th Mr. Biggs's bay colt *Bay Camerton*

The Gold Cup of 100 guineas 3 miles

1st Lord Aylesbury's bay colt by *Golumpus*
2nd Mr. King's *Gainsborough*
3rd Mr. Sadler's *Defiance*
This race excited much interest. The Golumpus colt kept in the rear at a respectful but recoverable space until within a few lengths of the distance, when the rider made grand play, passed by the Dons and came in handsomely to the great surprise and no small discomfiture of the knowing ones!

The City Members' £50 Plate

Won easily in two heats
1st Mr. Dilly's *Effie Deans*
2nd Gov. Bailey's *Lady Jane*

The Dyrham Stakes of 10g with 30 g added

1st Mr. Bartley's *Swindon*
2nd Mr. Ockenden's *Strephon*

Chapter Ten: Sydney Garden Vauxhall and other gardens

The addition of 'Vauxhall' to the name of a garden indicated it was a pleasure garden.

Laura Place, looking towards Sydney Gardens

The 'Bath Chronicle and Weekly Gazette' held a notice on Thursday 19th September, 1793:

> *Monday last* [16th September 1793] *the first tree, a young oak, was planted on the elevated site of the new-intended gardens, at the end of Pulteney Street, to be called Sydney Gardens; on this occasion the cannons from Spring Gardens were fired, and a barrel of strong beer was given to the attending spectators.*

Sydney Gardens was opened for public entertainment on 11th May 1795 under the management of J. Gale. It is at the culmination of Great Pulteney Street, on the other side of the river from the main city. It was designed by Mr. Harcourt Masters, architect.

The Prince of Wales made a visit for the public breakfast on Monday 29th of April 1799, where the banqueting room was open for the occasion and dancing continued until almost 4 in the afternoon. The public breakfasts in Sydney Gardens were suitable for ladies to attend.

Sydney gardens was owned by shareholders, and 77th part shares occasionally came up for auction, as on Friday 8th February 1811, when the two shares of the late John Goldwyer esq. were sold separately along with the rest of the deceased's property.

Terms of Subscriptions for walking in Sydney Gardens

	1 year	6 months	3 months	1 month
1 person	£1/1/-	13/6d	10/6d	5/-
2 persons, relatives in one house	15/- each	10/- each	7/6d each	3/6d each
3 or 4 persons relatives in one house	10/6d each	7/6d each	5/6d each	2/6d each
5 or more relations in one house	7/6d each	5/- each	3/6d each	2/- each

Non-subscribers were admitted for 6d, and tea 6d. The subscription also covered bowling.

Terms of subscription to ride on Sydney Ride; one person £1/1- per annum, 12/6d for 6 months, 7/- for 3 months, or 4/- for one month. Non-subscribers 6d each per ride.

There were two bowling greens and two swings, but no swinging was permitted on Sundays. There was also a labyrinth in which a Merlin's swing was constructed and should have opened in June 1795. Unfortunately, this was postponed until the third week in July. The Grotto in the labyrinth also opened at this time. Merlin's swing, said to be most conducive to good health, was available by subscription at 5/- for 3

months; non-subscribers 6d per use, and 3d for the Grotto and Labyrinth. Correct plans for the labyrinth are available at the bar for 6d.
Horns and clarionets[sic] every Thursday evening.

Large parties were asked to give timely notice for breakfasts to be provided.

Gravy and pea soup every day from noon until 3pm

Servants in livery were not admitted!

There was a subscription room attached to the gardens with London and Bath papers available, and from 1813 the subscribers set up a card assembly.
Refreshments were available.

In August 1795 an encomium was given by a correspondent who had been taken to the gardens against his will, and was impressed by how well the trees and shrubs had grown in so short a time. He describes how the principal pavilion on the brow of the hill is supported by Ionic columns of beautiful free-stone and is as fine as any you might find; and that the water is prettily managed and the ruin, though on a small scale, is proportional, and 'when the rough stones are grown mossy by time will have a very romantic and picturesque appearance.'
He even wrote a poem.

On Sydney Gardens

Would you enjoy fine views, and breathe pure air
To Sydney slopes each morn and eve repair:
Thither cool grots and falling streams invite
And every lends its various charms delight.

Whether you go to see, or to be seen,
At Sydney Gardens, you'll be pleas'd I ween.
Whate'er your taste, for prospects or good cheer,
Cascades, or rural walks, you'll find them here.
Whether you'd muse alone, be tete-a-tete
With some fair nymph, you'll find a snug retreat.

Ye gayer parties! Who'd have others see
How happy and how frolic you can be;
In open boxes brave the public eye,
And laugh and romp and saucy man defy!
But if to matrimony you aspire
Ascend the swings, some amorous youth you'll fire:
Shewn to advantage thus, your heighten'd charms
Will surely tempt some lover to your arms.

Ye Critics! If some faults you chance to find,
Pray point them out, we'll take it vastly kind.
But let these scenes your wives and daughters view,
Who, in this case, can judge as well as you.
And if they are not charm'd with Sydney Garden
We'll give them back their money – every far'din

Palaemon

P.S. The Labyrinth is a great curiosity – and the ladies need not be afraid of meeting any horned animal there as in the labyringh of Crete.

In April 1819 there is a notice that the Gardens are open for the season; the band will attend every day the weather is fine. So presumably either it closed over the winter, or one might walk there but there were no refreshments or entertainments.

Public Breakfasts

These took place twice a week through the summer as a general thing and every morning during race week, with a full band. Tea, coffee, Sydney rolls and Sally Lunns were served. Tickets 2/6d. It was quite acceptable for Ladies to attend.
Commencing first or second week in May.
Music will also be in the gardens in the afternoon from 5pm to 8pm.

There was no public breakfast on the 19th June 1812 as it was a grand gala

The first public breakfast of 1819 on 10th May was well attended. The first meeting of the card assembly will be on Monday 17th May and every Monday through the summer season at 7pm

1820 Monday 24th April a public breakfast in honour of his majesty's birth day. Accompanied by a full band. Doors to open at 11am, breakfast at 12 noon. Admission 3/- [April? Why April? George IV's birthday is 12th August. A mystery.]

Grand Galas

These were held yearly for the King's birthday; below see a sample.
From 1812 they were also held for the Regent's birthday.

Tuesday 4th June 1811
A Grand Gala, with full concert of vocal and instrumental music.
Principal vocal performers: Mr. Gattie, Mr. Benson, Mr. Evans, Mr. Chatterly, Mr. Parsons and Mrs. Cunningham.
Principal instrumental performers, Mr. J. Loder, Messrs Hershchell, Ashley, Philpot, Percival etc.

The illuminations and decorations will be the most magnificent feature with the exhibition of the cascade* &c.

On the evening will be displayed the transparencies of his Majesty's arms, the naval column and the new and beautiful transparency upon a large scale representing a perspective view of the town and harbour of Cadiz, being of particular interest at the moment, painted by Mr. Grieve.

With a grand display of Chinese Fire works under the direction of Signor Vincento de Mortram, engineer to his Royal Highess the Prince Regent, and artist in fire-works to Vauxhall Gardens,
Order of Firing;
First division: 1. Signal rocket with lights and maroons; 2. Battery of maroons; 3. Pyramid of Calcutta Light; 4. Rockets with comets and stars; 5. Wheel of Boreas, of various coloured fires, representing the gustful winds of the Heathen Deities; 6. A Metamorphose wheel with Prussian Cross, richly adorned with stars of knighthood; 7. Flight of rockets.
Second division: A discharge of Soissons 2. A grand horizontal wheel, with display of Egyptian spire fire, which will discharge a flight of rattle-

snakes; 3. A discharge of tail-star rockets; 4. A Saxon wheel, decorated with Chinese flyers; 5. A Girandole wheel, which will discharge five pump stars &c; 6. a flight of Soissons; 7 rockets
Third division: 1. A vertical wheel representing small cannon, with a rolling sun; 2. A spiral wheel illuminated in silver fire; 3. A flight of rockets; 4. A regulating piece with a wheel in the centre, of blue and gold fire; to conclude with 5. A mosaic cross; 6. Maroons 7. A flight of rockets.
Fourth division a magnificent mosaic temple, with Egyptian pyramids in gold and silver fire, with Chinese spiral fountains and a representation of throwing red hot; at the same time will discharge a flight of rockets, shells, chests of artillery etc, etc.
The doors will open at 5-30pm, the garden band will commence
At 6-30pm; the concert will begin at 8pm; the cascade to be exhibited after the second act of the concert, and the fire works to be played off at 11-00pm.
Tickets 2/6d to be had at the gate, Gye's stationer, principle libraries etc.
All parties requested to provide themselves with tickets ahead of time.
Cold refreshments, wines, spirits etc. Servants in Livery NOT admitted.

> * The Cascade was copied from Vauxhall Gardens in London, first appearing in 1752, which was an artificial waterfall. It was a central feature of a three-dimensional landscape and gave the illusion of water by means of a system of tin sheets on belts which moved as the mechanism was turned by a team of men. The lighting of it, and the sound of roaring water made it a grand spectacle.
> Erasmus Darwin wrote in 1756:
> *"The artificial water-fall at Vaux Hall I apprehend is done by pieces of tin, loosely fix'd on the circumferences of two wheels. It was the motion not being perform'd at bottom in a parabolic curve that made me first discover its not being natural."*
> It was generally hidden during the daytime. It operated for 10-15 minutes in the evening, and a bell was rung to announce the performance.

oOoOo

In 1812 the Grand Gala was on Thursday 4th June. The view of Cadiz was shown again as a transparency. In the evening the grand promenade to be illuminated in a style never before exhibited, representing the beautiful perspective of a grand Turkish tent, lighted with magnificent Chinese lanterns, each forming a succession of novel and curious transparencies. The Cascade, much improved since last season, to be shown after the second act of the concert. Open at 5pm, music commencing 6pm, the concert at 7pm, fire works at 10-30pm. Notice of exhibiting the cascade given by ringing a bell. Tickets 2/6d each, cold refreshments, wines, spirits etc.

1812 Friday June 19th a grand gala with illuminations and decorations on the same lines as those of the King's birthday, including the cascade. The band belonging to the garden will be stationed in the Chinese Orchestras. Also the full band of the Oxford Militia. Open 5pm, music from 6pm, cascade at 10pm, fire works at 10-30pm. 2/6d.

The grand gala for the Regent was on Wednesday August 12th with Chinese fire works. In the course of the evening will be given the grand, terrific representation of Mount Vesuvius at the time of its eruption in year 173.
The band of the Leitrim Militia with the much-admired battle-piece of Trafalfar and a variety of Irish melodies. The garden to be illuminated and decorated with transparencies of his highness's arms, the naval column, view of Cadiz, etc..

1812 Thursday Sept 24th a grand gala with the celebrated Band of Pandeans from Vauxhall who will perform in the Chinese Orchestra.
The town and harbour of Cadiz was shown again and various illuminated devices emblematic of the late victories in Spain by the Marquis of Wellington.
At 8-30pm a grand display of fire works, and following this the cascade. The doors open at 5pm, music at 6pm. Admission 2/-

oOoOo

1813, Friday 4th June celebrations had a new Grand Scene. Exhibited at the Ivy Tower in the ruins of the old castle in the Gardens, in sight of which is an open space of lawn sufficient to admit ten thousand spectators. Clouds will be brought down on the turrets and as they disperse, the heathen deities will commence their operations. In conformity with the mythology of the Ancient, Phaeton will descend in a fiery car, whose wheels in rapid rotaton will set the world on fire and the

whole garden will appear in one mighty blaze! On returning he is struck by a thunderbolt from Jupiter into the River Po, whilst a cascade is playing through its gothic battlements, producing a most impressive and wonderful effect.
Fire Works and concert, cold refreshments, bottled porter, cider, wines etc.

1813 Thursday 8th July a grand gala fête with fire works by Signor de Mortram for his own benefit. With illuminations. The Garden to open at 6pm, music from 7pm, the cascade at 10pm and the fire works at 10.30pm. Tickets 2/6d each, cold refreshments etc. To be exhibited the illumination of the Temple of the Sun. [much admired]. This was race week

1813 Thursday 12th August a grand gala fête with a display of fire works for the Prince Regent's birthday with Chinese fire works, appropriate military devices on transparencies, and the Temple of the Sun. A beautiful transparency of Field-Marshal Wellington on horseback, and the cascade will be exhibited.
Order of firing fire works:
Grand salute of maroons; planks of Madras signal lights; rockets with snakes; cannonading wheel, with rolling sun and fixed rays in gold fire, reporting; discharge of mines; double piece, consisting of 2 vertical wheels illuminated with 5 pointed stars and Chinese flyers of various colours, changing to 2 mosaic crosses; discharge of double rockets [never before attempted]; double working globe in silver and gold, supported by 2 Grecian spirals adorned with mosaic railing; small brilliant wheel, changing to a grand thunder wheel, embellished with the stars of knighthood and rolling suns, finishing with a gold glory marooned; flight of rockets with comet stars; discharge of rockets with rain stars; flight of rockets with tail stars; grand fountain wheel with numerous changes, accompanied by Mad Tom, to conclude with a discharge of mines; horizontal balloon wheel, discharging mines and flights of rockets, grand vertical working cutting-piece ornamented by 5 thunder wheels beautifully illuminated in gold, finishing with a grand representation of throwing red hot shot. Flight of Torbillions; Plank of Soissons; Flight of rockets with illuminated Maroon signals; grand Metamorphose piece with horizontal sun supported by a gold standard; flight of rockets; discharge of maroons; magnificent figure piece with white, blue, green, red and gold fires, finishing with 5 gold vertical suns; flight of rockets.
To conclude with a grand working temple which will be illuminated with

silver fire and gold rays marooned, discharging mortars, bombs, shells, volarts, Soissons, flight rockets, stars, battery sascines, and chests of artillery. During the Exhibition the whole of the Grand Walk will be illuminated with Calcutta lights. 3 bands.
Open 6pm, music 7pm, cascade 10pm, fire works 10-30pm, tickets 2/6d.

oOoOo

1814 Monday June 6th Gala Fête for his Majesty's birthday. The usual. Worcester Militia band; and the grotto in the labyrinth to be fitted up as a menagerie in transparencies, and exhibited every Monday, Wednesday and Friday, admittance as usual 3d, the labyrinth still open every day.

1814 Friday 12th August, the Regency Festival for the Regent's birthday. Magnificent fire works, concert of vocal and instrumental music. Magnificent transparencies, and the cascade. Much as usual.

oOoOo

1815 Monday 5th June the Gala Fête for the King's birthday. Fire works as usual, with an interesting piece called *Mad Tom, accompanied by a Wheel of Fury.* Concluding with a magnificent mosaic temple with Egyptian pyramids, in gold and silver fire, and representing the throwing of red hot shells etc. In addition, a signal night balloon, prepared for the occasion to let off in the course of the evening.
A grand full concert. Illuminations and transparencies, the cascade etc.
The weather was propitious, the concert excellent and the fire works brilliant. Upwards of 4,000 people attended.

1815 Thursday 29th June, middle day of the races, the grand gala fête for the King to be repeated.

1815 Monday 14th August Grand Gala fête for the Prince Regent's birthday. The illuminations will introduce the golden eagle, the emblem of France and the Rattle-Snake, the emblem of America, overpowered by the Royal Lion, emblem of Great Britain. The ship Bellerophon, brilliantly illuminated will heave in sight bringing Bonaparte into a British Port under royal salute, all concluding with a new piece, allusive to the Prince Regent, surmounted on a Grecian Column, exhibiting his crest, plume and initials with a grand discharge of rockets, maroons, mines, barrels of artillery etc. And a concert; a grand martial piece expressive of the Battle of Waterloo illustrated in Transparencies. NB At Sydney House, accommodations on the hotel or lodging house.

oOoOo

1816 Thursday July 4th, second day of the races, a Grand Military Gala in commemoration of the Battle of Waterloo. Fire works with the decorations displaying the field of battle. Military bands to play through the evening. Open at 6pm, music from 6-30pm. Cascade at 10pm, re-enacted engagement and fire works at 10-15pm. Tickets 2/6d. NB the gardens are strictly guarded, all persons trespassing will be prosecuted.
It was remarked that this delightful garden shone with more than usual brilliance at its illumination in Race Week than ever.

1816 Monday 12th August grand gala for the Prince Regent's birthday. Illuminations, decorations, transparencies, a full concert and fire works with the cascade.

oOoOo

1817 the grand gala for the king's birthday set for Thursday 5th June was rained off and took place instead on Tuesday 10th June

1817 Grand gala and public evening Wednesday 2nd July, concert, fire works. No mention of the cascade.
The produce of the evening was £15 which sum was divided between the penitentiary and infirmary. The expenses were defrayed by the former proprietor to the tune of £9. The new proprietor is Mr. Farnham.

1817 Tuesday 12th August a gala fête for the Prince Regent's birthday. Grand concert, fire works and Military and Pandean bands engaged. Concluding with the exhibition of the Cascade. Doors open at 5pm, music a 6pm, concert 7-30pm, fire works at 10-30 precisely. NO country bank notes taken at the gate of the Garden, except those of Bath and Bristol.

oOoOo

1818 Thursday 4th June Grand Gala Fête for His Majesty's birthday. Military and Pandean Bands, fire works and cascade, etc etc.

It was reported that it went off with peculiar *éclat.*

1818 Wednesday July 8th, being the first day of the races, a grand gala, including a brilliant display of fire-works in which will be introduced a representation of the eruption of Mt Vesuvius exhibiting in the most lively manner the vomiting of burning lava from the crater of the mountain. The cascade will be exhibited. 2/6d, refreshments.

1818 Wednesday 12th August for the birthday of the Prince Regent a grand gala, with concert, fire works in which Signor de Mortram is assisted by his son. Etc as usual

oOoOo

1819 Friday 4th June gala for his majesty's birthday with concert and fire works and the cascade etc etc; the cascade is thoroughly repaired and fitted with new scenery.

1819 Thursday August 12th the grand gala for the Prince Regent's birthday. Fire works, concert of military music, etc, and the cascade etc. The Elysian scene shown.

oOoOo

George III died in January so a Gala for his birthday would not be held this year; the new His Majesty is George IV, formerly the Prince Regent.

1820 superb gala fête Tuesday May 23rd with fire works, full military band, concert, and the cascade. Etc.

1820 Wednesday 28th June a Partial Gala with illuminations and fire works and full military band.
M. Il Diavolo Antonio will exhibit his astonishing feats of Agility on the rope. The gardens will be opened at 6pm, admittance 2/-

1820 Monday 14th August in honour of his Majesty's Birthday. Fire works, the Cascade, full band and Mr. Flemmington's Mail Coach Adventures and imitations of London and Bath actors. His performance at 8pm, the cascade at 9pm the fire works at 9-30pm.

Other events

6th July 1811 a most curious and interesting hopping and running race in Sydney Garden at 9-30am between Capts. Charrettee and Kelly and Mr. Stewart. Great bets are pending the event.

Thursday 9th July 1812 a public evening and promenade, with brilliant illuminations and the exhibition of The Cascade. The Leitrim Band will play as the principle orchestra. Admission 1/- the music to commence at 6pm.

In May each year the first Tuesday in the month, after their examinations the 200+ boys of the Bath and Bathforum Free School [established 1810] are regaled with a dinner of roast beef and plum pudding in the gardens whilst a select band of music performs appropriate national airs etc. In 1817 the lunch was postponed owing to the unfavourable weather.
In 1819 it was on Saturday 26th June, with girls of the Free School in Morford Street, having also been delayed by weather; indeed, the weather was still so miserable they had to dine in their respective schoolrooms.

In 1816 the proprietor took the concern again and promised that the public breakfasts would continue in the same way, as will galas and other amusements. The house, furnished to be let in separate apartments, the whole house available for a family. The tavern was taken by T.H. Parker, wine and brandy merchant, who stocked up on wines and spirits, bottled porter, prime Herefordshire and Somersetshire Cider, real squash perry, Noyeau, rich cordials and compounds. Tea, coffee and chocolate with Sally-luns, biscuits of every sort, tarts, cakes and confectionary; cold ham, beef, fowls, tongues etc etc.

1818 Thursday 19th March in the afternoon, John Wright, the Yorkshire pedestrian, aged 52, completed his arduous task of walking 600 miles in ten successive days in Sydney Gardens, half an hour within the prescribed time. He accomplished the feat with such spirit and vigour as decidedly prove him the first pedestrian of the day. Upwards of 2000 ladies and gentlemen attended to witness the accomplishment of the task when, independent of the full amount of the admission receipts at 6d each considerable sums were presented to the pedestrian.

The following is a correct statement of each day's walk

Day	Miles	Yards		Day	Miles	Yards
First	71	1370		Sixth	53	400
Second	65	400		Seventh	60	600
Third	57	1180		Eighth	60	380
Fourth	61	1280		Ninth	51	1260
Fifth	64	1720		Tenth	52	560

1818 John Wright the pedestrian, now described as 'of Bristol' wagered to walk 750 in 15 successive days at 13 hours each day, resting time included, to commence Thursday October 22nd.

Day	Miles	Hours	Mins		Day	Miles	Hours	Mins
1	60	10	52		9			
2	51	"	45		10			
3	51	"	52 ½		11			
4	50	"	21		12			
5	52	"	18		13			
6	50	"	26 ½		14			
7		"			15			
8								

Extra time was allowed on the 4th day, being Sunday, for attending Divine Service. Total time was around 2 hours more permitting rests.

I could not find the record of his success, but one may assume he was successful as he is described as having remarkable vigour and bottom. He went on to a wager of 400 miles in 8 days finishing Thursday 24th December 1818 in Blenheim Gardens, near Gloucester, and has engaged to walk 1200 miles in 20 successive days, Sundays excepted, in the same gardens.

Other Gardens

Spring Gardens or Spring Garden Vauxhall

This was to be found on the other side of the river from the main city, off Argyl Street. A road named Spring Garden Road remains, and I assume the modern recreation ground is on the site of the original garden. It was first built around 1735 in what had been the hamlet of Bathwick, the area around it developed by William Pulteney when he inherited the estate of Bathwick. There was no bridge before 1770 however when the Adam brothers were contracted to build it after a lot of previous shenanigans. Incongruously the gardens were right opposite the gaol ...

The earliest newspaper reference to this garden is in July 1761, when it appears to be well established, advertising a subscription to view fire works to be exhibited there for Thursday July 23rd. Tickets of 5/- would admit two gentlemen or a gentleman and two ladies into the rooms, tickets for the gardens 1/- each. The passage from the Grove [Orange Grove, part of St James' Garden qv] will be properly lighted and a band of music will attend.

Before the inauguration of Sydney Gardens, the Spring Gardens hosted the fire works and galas for the king's birthday, and public breakfasts every Wednesday and Saturday through the season; the breakfasts had moved to Sydney Garden by 1799, but were still being held in the Spring Gardens in 1796.

Breakfasts were being held Monday and Thursday in 1773 with cakes and rolls every morning from 9-30am to 10-30 am, except Sundays. Half a crown subscription for the season for ladies and gentlemen to walk, except public mornings. The distance from the pump-room to the gardens is 472 yards, being a 6d chair ride.

In 1781, the breakfasts were Tuesdays and Saturdays.

An advertisement of 'this much improved and admired spot' on 12th May 1785 advertising the coming fête 'after the manner of Vauxhall, London' with illuminations, concert and so on opening Friday 20th May. Presumably it had been somewhat improved and revamped.

In 1798 the notice was given that J. Townsend, the proprietor intended to quit the gardens, having a final grand gala night with illuminations and fire works on 30th August.

Thereafter it is only mentioned in context of location, eg an unfurnished house to let on the Spring Gardens side of Laura Place or Pulteney Street. Also reference to the street.

It may be assumed that the gardens just declined.
In 1810 the location was being used to auction lumber and timber, a load of Baltic and Pine Timber, and Swedish and Norway deal [fir or pine], the ground needing to be cleared being about to be sold.
Feb 1811 a large messuage [enclosed house and garden] being part of Spring Gardens being sold.

St. James'Gardens
Originally part of the Abbey orchard, this was laid out as a garden to accompany the Assembly Room in 1709. It was laid out with a walk lined with sycamores [Acer pseudoplatanus] known as Harrison's walk, and the rest was lawns. Entrance was by subscription only. A grove was added to the gardens, named Orange Grove in honour of the Prince of Orange when he visited. It is bounded by the river, North Parade and to the west Pierrepont Street and Grand Parade. One circular lawn was laid out as a bowling green. Nowadays known as Parade Gardens.

Parade Gardens from over the river, photo S. Waldock.

Grosvenor Gardens
This garden was opened on meadows which had long been a site of riding or walking out along the London Road, for an 'airing' to Bathwick and Bathampton.
It stood on nearly 14 acres, offering bowling, angling in the River Avon and the well-stocked pond. Subscriptions in 1801 for the season was 3/6d, 2/6d for bowling, and 3/6d for fishing. Admittance to non-subscribers, 6d each which covered wine, tea, coffee etc. Pleasure boats also to let capable of carrying a large party at 1/- per hour. The ferry at the bottom of the Garden was free. Later the subscription for walking in

the gardens was 7/6d for the season, 3/- for bowling and 3/- for angling. It opened in 1792, but there were already financial problems. Entrance was through a wide arch in the centre of what was supposed to be the hotel. On the east side was a maze or labyrinth. There were two bowling greens, a space for fire works, a greenhouse, hot house and archery green. By the river near the fishpond was an area with swings. On the southwest was a swimming bath, with dressing rooms and private plunge baths.

In 1792 it was advertised as having hot, green, succession, fruiting and ice houses serving the hotel, as well as conservatories, pinery, fruit, flower and kitchen gardesn, an aviary, a temple with chimes, Merlin's swings and cave, grotto, Labyrinth as well. Meadows for Alderny cows, Alcoves, Boxes, retreats, pleasant and rural walks with lamps for both summer and winter amusements.

Unfortunately, this pleasure garden was short lived. On the outskirts of the city to the North and East, it was laid out by the architect John Everleigh in 1791, when he was laying out Grosvenor Place. The river was deliberately included in the plan. There was to be a hotel but unfortunately Everleigh went bankrupt.

It was sold in 1793 by auction, and was still in fashionable use up to 1802.

Being so far out of town, and hampered by river mists and flooding, though it appears on maps up to 1819 and was in use, its popularity declined. After about 1812 it acquired an insalubrious reputation as the haunt of gamblers, prostitutes and thieves. Beware, any maiden offered an assignation in such a place of ill repute!

By 1820 it became a domestic garden for the buildings there.

Chapter Eleven: The Baths and The Pump Room

The baths [left] next to the pump room from the Abbey end of the square. The buildings behind the arcade replaced the White Hart Hotel.Photo S Waldock.

The legend of Bladud is known to all the inhabitants of Bath; Bladud, eldest son of King Lud Hudibras, King of Britain, and in descent of Brutus, who founded Britain, became a leper and was kept in close confinement at court. He decided to escape the royal court in disguise, and became a swineherd in the best tradition of fairy tale. Watching the pigs in the cold of winter, he saw them head for a hot spring and followed them, and wallowed with them in the hot mud, and on emerging found himself cured.

This legend was undermined by the Earl of Rochester at the end of the 17th Century, but the fact that there are such names as Bladud Buildings testifies to the affection the inhabitants have for it.
It is probable that the Ancient Britons knew of the benefits of the springs before they were claimed by the Romans in the name of Sulis Minerva. Roman artefacts have been preserved when found, many when the modern development of the baths took place from the time of its city charter under Queen Elizabeth.

The main growth of the city and the fashionable aspect of its waters came into being under Richard Nash, who took the position of Master of Ceremonies, after the first holder of that title, Captain Webster, was killed in a duel in 1703. Much is written about Nash elsewhere, so I will not repeat the many histories of his tenure. Nash wrote the original rules which were accepted in 1742.

Nash's memorial may be found in the Abbey Church where a subscription was set by Dr. Harrington.

Lord Manvers, owner of the Kingston Estate, on which the baths are situate, caused great improvement to them at personal expense, and rented them out to the ingenious Dr. Wilkinson, celebrated for philosophical researches, and author of a work on Galvanism. Dr. Wilkinson lectures regularly in the reading room at the Pump Room, see 'lectures' in Chapter 4, Other Entertainments.

The Nature and Qualities of the Bath Waters

It being supposed that the waters are heated by some underground volcano, which has not sufficient inflammable matter to explode, the waters duly heated become impregnated with the substances through which they pass, to paraphrase in précis John Feltham's book on the watering places of England and Wales. Several springs arise for the King's Bath, the Hot Bath and the Cross Bath.
The waters contain:
A small quantity of carbonic acid gas, and of azotic gas [carbonated water and nitrogen.]
Some sulphate and muriate of soda [Sulphate and sodium chloride aka salt.]
Selenite, carbonate of lime, siliceous earth and a very small portion of oxyd of iron. [crystalised gypsum, calcium carbonate, diatomaceous earth similar to Fuller's earth, and Iron Oxide.]

Feltham says:

> *This water, for delicacy, transparency and other agreeable qualities, appears equal or superior to any hot mineral waters hitherto known. In all chronic distempers, it is used with the most beneficial effects; and is never injurious, except in haemorrhages, inflamations or pulmonic complaints, or when it is taken in too large doses; or combined with too hot a regimen. Etc., etc.*

The water is said to be beneficial for many complaints and should if possible be drunk hot from the pump or as warm as possible if conveyed to the patient's lodgings. It should be drunk in the morning fasting, between 6am and 10am. The quantity should be between one and three pints, but a physician should be consulted.
A course of Bath water should seldom exceed a month or six weeks.

Bathing should not be undertaken if the blood-vessels are too full, ie high blood pressure, and should be in the morning, fasting or for the delicate, in the evening. Ten minutes to half an hour is generally long enough.

Dry-Pumping: this is when water is directed onto a portion of the body without having to be immersed in the bath as a whole.

The Public Baths are chiefly used by hospital invalids or by persons of the lower class of life since the erection of private baths.
The time at which most people bathe in the King's Bath and the Cross Bath is between 6am and 9am, when there is a fresh supply of water. That which rises one day is discharged the next by drains into the R. Avon, by which means the baths are kept sweet and wholesome.

Description of the Public Baths

The public baths are the King's and Queen's Baths, which are connected to each other; the Hot Bath and Cross Bath.

King's Bath
This lies behind the Great Pump-Room with the windows at the upper end of which it is visible. It is more than 65' long, 40' wide and contains 346 tons, 2 hogsheads and 36 gallons of water when filled. There is an octagonal brass handrail enclosing the centre where the main spring has its source. The sides are enclosed by a handsome colonnade of Doric order. The bath fills in 9 hours and is between 100 and 103 °F.
Two commodious rooms are connected to this bath, fitted with pumps and pipes to direct the hot water to any particular part of the body. There are also fire-places and other conveniences for the use of the bathers. This bath has a statue of Bladud erected in 1699.

The Queen's Bath

This is attached to the King's bath, and forms a square of 25' and is furnished with the same conveniences as the other. The temperature is somewhat lower than the King's Bath.

View of the King's Spring bath from the Pump Room. Photo S. Waldock.

The Cross Bath

This is located elsewhere, in Bath Street, south west of the King and Queen baths. The exterior is by Baldwin after the style of Adam.
This is so named because of a cross erected in the centre by the Earl of Melfort, secretary of state to James II. The cross has been removed. This bath is at the end of Bath Street. It is triangular in form, and has convenient slips [changing rooms] for the bathers. A small pump-room is attached to it. This bath fills in 16 hours and the temperature is 93-94 °F.

The Hot Bath

This stands about 40 yards south-west of the King's Bath and is named for the higher heat of its waters which rise to 117 °F. The structure was built under the direction of the late John Wood, esq. It is about 56' square, consisting of an open bath, private baths, dry pump-rooms and vapour baths, constantly kept warm by the fires of an adjoining dressing room, with which they communicate. The pump-room is a little to the westward and is rather a gloomy apartment. The hot bath fills in 8 hours.

Desciption of the Private Baths

The private baths were built in 1788 under the direction of Mr. Baldwin, belonging to the corporation in Stall Street. They adjoin the King's Bath, and contain dry pump rooms, sudatories [sweating rooms; the Romans called it a caldarium] and other suitable conveniences. There are also the neat and convenient private baths called the Duke of Kingston's Baths or the Abbey Baths, the property of Lord Newark.
There is no detail given on the warmth of these baths, or which spring fills them. One assumes the King's Bath and hence a temperature somewhere between 90-100 °F.

Rules of Baths and Prices for services

- A sergeant shall not demand more than 3d for each time of bathing [A sergeant took care of the bather's possessions while they bathed.]
- A guide shall not demand more than 1/- for each time of bathing [a guide enters the water with the bather in order to help them and if need be to duck them.]
- A cloth-woman shall not demand more than 3d for each time of bathing. [a cloth-woman provides a linen shift to wear if the bather has not brought her own, and is responsible for laundering them.]
- Pumping in the King and Queen's bath, 2d each 100 strokes: 4d at the dry pump. Pumping in the private baths, 3d per 100 strokes.

The above fees are to be understood so as not to affect people in low circumstances or servants, such being allowed to bathe for 6d only to the guide, linen and attendance.

- No sergeant, bath-guide, cloth-woman or chair-man shall demand anything of a bather for his or their entrance on bathing or pumping, in the name of footing-money [opportunistic fraud!]
- That sufficient fires at the expense of the Chamber of the City to be made in the slips, to be lighted at 6am in the winter or 5am in the summer, to be continued for the usual hours of bathing.
- Bathing to be allowed on all holidays except Christmas Day and Good Friday.
- Each person bathing in the open bath to pay 1/6d for each time of bathing. In the private bath, vapour bath or sweating-room, 3/-.

> Bathing in the private bath, and afterwards using the sweating-room or vapour bath, 4/-. Pumping in the bath, 3d for 100 strokes; and at the dry pump, 6d.

NB, any lady of gentleman having cause of complaint against the attendants belonging to any of the baths are desired to make such complaints known to the Magistrates at the Town Hall any Monday morning at 12 noon.

<u>The Pump Room</u>

This was build in 1797 under the direction of Mr. Baldwin, architect. The outer aspect of the Pump-Room is finished in a classical fashion with an architrave on which is the Greek inscription:

ΆΡΪΣΤΟΝ ΜΕΝ ΔΩΡ
Or
Bath Water is better than Bath Wine
Literally, 'Water is best'

The pediment of the pump room labeled in Greek with the epigram 'Water is better than wine', photo S. Waldock.

The pump-room is attended to drink the waters as well as to see and to be seen. One may attend from 6am until noon and perhaps again in the early evening after a stroll in Sydney Gardens, visiting shops or walking in the pleasant Crescents and Parades. The band is in attendance daily. At the south end of the pump room is a dais and above it a gallery for the band.

As one who has drunk the waters, I can testify that it has a metallic tang to the taste, and slight sulphurous overtones, but it is not truly unpleasant, especially at the warm temperature at which it comes out of the ever-flowing pump. It is mildly invigorating.

The pump sits in an alcove towards the back of the pumproom, in a window embrasure overlooking one of the Roman baths.

The pump in situ and as a close-up, photos S. Waldock.

The new Pump-Room is 60' long, 46' wide and 34' high. Each end has a semi-circular recess, making the length of the room in the centre part about 85'. The inside of the room is set around with ¾ columns of the Corinthian order, crowned with an entablature, above which rises a coving of 5'. In the recess at the west end is the music gallery, and in that at the east end a time-piece given by the late Mr. Tompion. Over this in a niche is a marble statue of the late Mr. Nash, by Hoare. In the centre of the south side is the pump and on each side a fireplace.

All persons who are decently dressed, without any regard to fashion, may freely perambulate the Pump Room. Those who drink the waters, however, are expected to pay about a guinea a month, besides a gratuity to the pumper.

<u>Subscriptions:</u>
1810
Kingston hot-baths and pump-room
Abbey Street and Kingston Buildings

<u>Drinking the Waters</u>
Per year £1/11/6d
Per Quarter 15/-
Month 7/-
Week 3/-

<u>Hot Baths for subscribers</u>
Private Bath 2/6d
Tepid Bath 1/6d
Shower bath, hot or cold water 1/6d

Chapter Twelve: Who's Who in Bath

Residents of Note or celebration

The Bishop of Bath and Wells, usually in Wells, but may be in Bath.
Rev. Archdeacon Phillott of the Abbey, Bath

Lord Lansdowne, and son, Lord Wycombe

Lord J. Thynne, Member of Parliament for the City of Bath 1796-1830, Tory.
John Palmer, esq, Member of Parliament [second member] 1801-1807, instigator of the mail coach and twice mayor of Bath [1796-7 & 1809-10]. Whig. D 16th August 1818. Inherited the Theatre and oversaw it, and his second theatre in Bristol.
Lieut.-Col. Palmer, Member of Parliament [second member] the City of Bath 1808-1826. Served with his regiment during the Peninsular war as Lieut.Col., May 1810-1814, ADC to the Prince Regent from 1811. Whig. Wine grower in the Gironde, and proprietor of Bath Theatre Royal after the death of his father, John Palmer.

Elections: 30 people qualified to vote: I have included earlier MPs to demonstrate the relations of people involved in Bath.
21st June 1790, John Jeffreys Pratt, viscount Bayham [Later 1st Marquess Camden; the Pratts were associated with Bath and his grandson was MP in the 1820s, his father was recorder for the corporation.] AND Thomas Thynne I, visct. Weymouth. [3rd contender, John Morris.]
3rd May 1794, by-election Sir Richard Pepper Arden, following Bayham. Called to the upper house 1802
7th July 1802, by-election, Lord John Thynne.
27th May 1796 Thomas Thynne I, AND Sir Richard Pepper Arden
1st June 1801 John Palmer replacing Arden, called to Upper House again; beating John Berkely Burland.
7th July 1802, Lord John Thynne AND John Palmer
20th July 1804 Thynne re-elected after appointment to office
29th March 1805 Thynne re-elected after vacating his seat
31st October 1806 Lord John Thynne AND John Palmer
7th May 1807 Lord John Thynne AND John Palmer
2nd February 1808 Charles Palmer takes over from John Palmer

7th October 1812 Lord John Thynne AND Charles Palmer
19th June 1818 Lord John Thynne AND Charles Palmer
10th March 1820 Lord John Thynne AND Charles Palmer

Earl Poulett, Lord Lieutenant of the County

Capt. J. Wiltshire, esq., and Col. Chas, Dumbleton, esq., commanders of the Bath Volunteer corps of cavalry and infantry.
Bath had a mayor, 9 aldermen, and 20 councilmen, who held their offices for life. Aldemanic vacancies were filled by common councilmen on seniority, and new common councilmen chosen from the freemen. Freedom of the city could be purchased for 250g.

<u>Mayor of the city of Bath</u>
John Palmer, Mayor of the City 1809- Sept. 1810
Abel Moysey esq., new mayor elected 1810-1811
Joseph Phillot, esq. 1811-1812
Charles Crook esq. 1812-1813
William Anderton esq. 1813-1814
Charles Phillot esq. 1814-1815
Morgan Nicols esq. 1815-1816
Edmund Anderton esq. 1816-1817
George Tugwell esq. 1817-1818
John Kitson esq. 1818-1819
George Edward Allen esq. 1819-1820
John Wiltshire esq. 1820-1821

<u>Other members of the corporation:</u>
Thomas Slater, Chamberlain 1810

<u>Justices of the Peace,</u>
<u>1810</u>
H. Parry, esq.
John Horton, esq.
John Palmer esq., [mayor 1809-10]
H. Harrington, M. D.
Thomas Slater, esq.
Harry Atwood, esq.
Chas. Phillot, esq.

Sir Wm. Watson
Joseph Phillott, esq. [mayor 1811-12]
Charles Crook, esq.

Sheriffs
1810
W.W. Dimond, esq.
W. Tudor, esq.

Constables 1810
J.F. Davis, M.D.
Geo. Lye, esq.

The Earl of Leven and Melville, president of the Harmonic Society
Walsh Porter esq., vice president of the Harmonic Society
Mrs. Langdon, embroideress to royalty
J.A. Sanders, landscape painter
Thos. & Ben. Parker, aka the Barkers of Bath, painters.
Dr. Wilkinson, renter of the Kingston Pump Room.
W. Gore Langton esq., MP [Race Steward 1813]
J. Payne Tudway, esq., MP [Race Steward 1817]

The race stewards oversaw the applications of the rules, and were arbiters of fair play, an unpaid but very responsible position.

Horsey and sporting Gentlemen

Mr. Bacon, Governor Bailey, *Sir C.W. Bampfylde, Bart [Race Steward 1815],* Mr. C. F. Bampfylde, Mr. Bartley, Mr. Biggs, Mr. Bissett, Mr. Browne, Mr. J. Browne, Mr. Brunswick, *Thos. Calley esq., [Race Steward 1812],* Mr. J. Calley, *K. Lechemere Charlton esq., [Race Steward 1819]* , Mr. L. Charlton, Mr. Clark, Mr. Collins, Mr. Colt, Lord Cook, Mr. Cope, Sir J. Cope, *The Earl of Cork and Orrery, [Race Steward 1814,]* Mr. Clutterbuck, *S. Day esq. [Race steward 1811]*, Mr. C. Day, Wm. Dickenson esq. [Race steward 1815], Mr. Dilly, Col. Draper, Mr. Dundas, Mr. Dunn, Mr. Elton, Mr. Erskine, Mr. Evered, Mr. Farquharson, Mr. Fielder, Mr. C. Fisher, Mr. George, Mr. Goddard, Gen.

Gower, Mr. Hallett, Mr. R.C. Hammond, Mr. Hamyold, Mr. Happitly, Mr. Hart, Mr. Hassenden, *Mr. G. Hawkins [Race Steward 1817], Sir J. Hawkins, Bart, [race steward 1811 deputy 1818],* Mr. Hill, Mr. Holder, Mr. Horner, Mr. T.S. Horner *Col.T. Strangeways Horner [Race Steward 1814],*Mr. Howden, Mr. King, Mr. Jenner, Mr. Jones, Col. G. Langton, Mr. William Gore Langton, *Mr. William Gore Langton jun. esq. [Race Steward 1816],* Mr. F. Langton, Mr. Langton, Mr. Lawrence, Lord Leberter, Sir T. B. Lethbridge, Mr. Lindow, *Sir Henry Lippincot, Bart,[Race Steward, 1812],* Mr. Lipton, Mr. D.J. Long, Mr. Lucas, Mr. Lynn, Mr. J. Maddocks, Mr. Manley, *A. Moffat Mills esq [Race Steward 1813]*, Mr. Moggridge, Mr. Morgan, Mr. Mortimer, G. M. B. Napier,esq, [Race Steward 1816], Mr. Northey, Mr. Ockenden, Mr. Page, Mr. Parkin, Mr. Peach, Mr. J. Perren, Mr. Pierce, Major Pigott, Mr. Pinis, Mr. Pryce, Mr. Radclyffe, Mr. Reilly, Mr. Rigby, Sir W. Roberts, Mr. Roberts, Mr. Rogers, Mr. Sadler, Mr. Scott, Mr. Shute, Mr. Smith, Sir H. Smyth, Mr. J. Smyth, Mr. Steven, Mr. Strode, Mr. Surtees, Mr. Tadway, Mr. Tate, Mr. Taylor, Mr. J. Taylor, Mr. Terrett, Captain Thornhill, *R. B. Thornhill esq. [Race Steward in 1811],* Col. Thornton, Mr. Tomes, *Col. C.K. K. Tynte [Race Steward in 1818],* Mr. Walker, Mr. Weatherall, Mr. Weatherby, Mr. Wentworth, Mr. West, Mr. Whalley, Col. Whalley, Mr. Whitmore, Mr. Wilks, Col. Williams, Sir R. Williams, Mr. Wills, Mr. Winton, Mr. Wodehouse.

Masters of Ceremonies

Mr. Francis John Guyette, Lower Rooms, 1811-1815
Mr. James Heaviside, Lower Rooms, 1815-1818
Charles H. Marshall, Lower Rooms, Feb 1818 – spring 1820

Mr. James King, Upper Rooms until his death in 1816
Captain Wyle 1816-beginning 1818
James Heaviside from Feb 1818

Musicians

Mr. and Mrs. Ashe and offspring; conductor and musician
Signor Anelli
Mr. T. Light
Mr. Loder violinist, leader of orchestra

Mme Catalani
Signora Bianchi [visiting celebrity]
Signor Tramezzani [visiting celebrity]

People came to Bath yearly, or for one season, for the social life or perhaps for the baths.

Visitors

I have limited this to those listed monthly in the newspaper with some kind of title, earned or inherited, for the simple expedient of space. I have cut off the precedence after generals and admirals. Theere are Colonel, Lieut.Colonel, majors, Rev. Dr. [with or without wife or offspring]; Rev. Mr., and family; then Captains. Following captains in precedence are lieutenants; Mr. & Mrs.; Mr. & Miss; Mrs. & Miss; Mr.; Mrs.; and finally Miss....

These are all the visitors who presented their names to the MC of the Upper Rooms, to be recognised. The spelling variations are copied from the newspaper, so eg General Rial/Riall/Ryall is the same person but a different editor ...

1810

4th **January**
Earl & Countess of Banbury, Earl Pomfret, Baron Monck, Lady Yarmouth, Lord Wallingford, *Ladies* Saxton, Hay, Napier; Hon. Lady Wood, Hon. Mr. Mackensie, Hon. G. Annesley, Sir John & Lady Anstruther, Sir J. Hawkins, Sir J. Oraham, Maj.Gen. Sherbett, Vice-Adm. Phillips
11th January
Earl, Countess & Lady Charlotte Nelson, Bishop of Norwich, Baron de Silverchoile, Lady Bayntun, Hon. Mrs. & Miss Gordon, Sir W. Ousley, Sir T. Knight, Sir C. & Lady Hartopp, Lieut.Gen. Wemys
18th January
Earl & Countess of Ormond, *Ladies* Peel, Douglas, Blundell; Hon. Mr. Lyons, Hon. Mr. & Mrs. Hare, Hon. Mr. Austyn, Sir Wm. Chalmers
25th January
Lady Harriett Ponsonby, Hon. Rev. Mr. Moore, Sir M. Colethurst, Sir C. Coate, Gen. Kerr, Maj.Gen. Constance

1st **February**
Lord & Lady Carhampton, *Ladies* Elford, Gardiner, Hon. Lady Bromhead, Sir G. Williams, Commordore Bortase
22nd February
Lord Somers, Lady S. O'Brien, Gen. Montgomerie.

8th **March**
Count Carlewitz, Lord W. Somerset, Lord Blayney, Lady Burke, Hon. Mrs. Gordon, Sir Charles Talbot, Gen. Poulett.
15th March
Lady Elford, Sir C. Whalley
22nd March
Earl & Countess of Dartmouth, Lord & Lady Vernon, Lord Wilton, Lady Cotton, Lady Packer, Lady M. Long.
29th March
Marquis of Hartington, Lord Wilton, Lord W. Somers, Lord Gwydir, Lady Suffolk, Lady Williams, Lady Gresley & family, Lady Broughton, Sir J. Fellowes.

5th **April**
Baron Often, Hon. Mrs. Ford, Sir T., Lady & Miss Sheppard, Sir G.

Pownell, Gen. Smith.

18th April

Earl of Malmesbury, Bishop of St David's, *Ladies* Lemon, Seaforth, Meredyth; 2 Hons. Miss Mackenzie, Sir L. Palk, Sir J. & Lady Smith, Sir R. & Lady Bedingfield, Maj.Gen. Archdale

26th April

Marchioness of Clanricarde, Lord Jocelyn, *Ladies* Willis, Dalrymple, Williams, Styles, Gen. Delancey.

3rd **May**

Lord & Lady Bridport, Lord Scarsdale, Lady O'Brien, Lady Gordon, Sir Wm. Call, Sir C. Halkett, Sir John Aubrey, *Generals* Campbell, Stuart, *Admirals* Wolseley, Luke, Graves & Mrs. and Miss.

10th May

Lady Nepean, *Ladies* Taylor, Smith, Stanley, Riddell, Sir W. Johnston

16th May

Lady Kingston, Lady Blackiston, Sir C. & Lady Watson, Gen. Stuart.

23rd May

Sir Wm. Johnson

30th May

Bishop of Cork, Baron Pimpercher, Lord F. Montague, Lady Gordon, Sir B. Wrey and family, Gen. Drummond, Adm. & Mrs. Countess

6th **June**

Duke of Liston, Countess of Lonsdale, Lady Colebrook, Sir C. Halkett, Gen. & Mrs. Leighton

13th June

Countess D'Alton, Lady E. Montagu, Sir W.W. Wynne, Sir F. Hartwell, Sir C. Grant, Adm. Bertie, Adm. & Mrs. Luke

20th June

Marquis of Salisbury, Lady Williams, Lady Brisbane, Adm. & Mrs. Kempe, Governor & Mrs. Field

27th June

Hon. Mr. Brown, Hon. Mrs. Hewitt, Sir B. Chinnery, Sir T. Styles.

11th **July**

Bishop of Winchester, Lady Styles, Sir H. Crosby.

18th July

Earl of Belmore, Lord & Lady Elliot, Lord and Lady John Townsend, Lord Bute, Sir C. Pegg, Adm. Wolseley, Dean of Wells.

1st **August**
Lord Bishop of Waterford, Lord G. Grenville, Lady Styles, Sir Wm. Rowley, Sir W. B. Hughes, Sir Montague & Lady Cholmely
8th August
Gen. Dunne, Adm. Mann, Vice-Adm. Grindall
15th August
Lord Wallscourt, Gen, Glenson.
22nd August
Countess Spencer, Adm. Wolseley, Col. Parker, Col. Brooke.
29th August
Marchioness Cornwallis, Lady Russel, Hon. Miss Flower, Sir C. & Lady Dumbarton, Sir Robert Baker.

12th **September**
Earl & Countess of Cavan, Countess of Beverley, Lord Carleton, Hon. Mrs. Shute, Lieut-Gen. Leighton.
19th September
Dowager Countess Spencer, Countess Dysart, Lady C. Long, Lady Morris, Hon. Mrs. Yorke, Sir Rich. Phillips, Sir James Crawford, Justice Hardinge.
26th September
Lord Craig, Lady Gambier, Lady Williams, Sir B. Chinnery

3rd **October**
Earl & Countess of Uxbridge, Earl & Countess of Dartmouth, Lady Call, Hon. Mrs. Vane, Sir O. Gordon, Sir F. Goolde, Chief Justice Mansfield, Gen. O'Ferral, *Adm*. Hargood, Christie.
25th October
Lady Emily Montague, Sir James & Lady Fitzgerald, Sir Harry Parker, Adm. & Mrs. Bowen & family, Adm., Mrs. and Miss McDonald, Maj.-Gen. & Mrs. Poyntz, Brigade-Major Montgomery.

1st **November**
Lady Clark, Hon. Mrs. Yorke, *Generals*. Tolson, Vereker & wife., *Admirals*. Stirling & family, Fayerman.
8th November
Earl & Countess of Uxbridge, Lord Vernon, Lord & Lady Mountjoy, Lady Briscoe, Hon. Mr. Barnwell, Sir J. Affleck, Sir Digby Mackworth, Gen. Horoker, Lieut.-Gen. McKenzie, Adm. Wella.

15th November
Lord & Lady Carteret, Lord Rodney, Lady Clarina, Lady Hardy, Sir John Trevelyan, Commodore Borlase.
21st November
Lord Harberton, Sir Hugh & Lady Bateman, Sir Ewen Baillie, Sir William James, Sir William Wynne, Maj.Gen. Dunn
28th November
Lord O'Brien, Lady Talbot, Lady Jane James, Hon. & Rev. Mr. Maude, Adm. & Mrs. Dickers.

5th **December**
Earl and Countess of Guildford, Earl of Malmesbury, Countess Hessell, Lady C. Deny, Lady M. Hay, Lady Bampfylde, Hon. Capt. Maude, Hon. Mrs. Taylor, Sir F. Vane, Gen. O'Ferrall, Maj.Gen. Sir E. Baillie.
12th December
Lady Lisle, Lady Charlotte Ram, Lady Ann Clifton, Lady M. Taylor, Sir Charles Talbot, Sir Wm. & Lady Watson.
19th December
Countess of Aldborough, Lord Glastonbury, Lady Scott, Lady Dalrymple, Sir Drummond & Lady Smith, Sir J. Stewart, Sir J. Rich, Sir J.C. Hippisley, *Generals* Ritchie, Grenville, Stuart, Lefevre.

1811

2nd **January**
Countess of Aldborough, Lord Newark, Lady Garnier, Hon. C. Pitt, Sir J. Dalrymple, Sir P. Taylor, Sir M. & Lady Blakiston, Maj.Gen. Tilson
9th January
Lord & Lady Riversdale, Lord Clive, Lady Napier, Lady Staines, Hon. Mr. Dillon, Hon. E. Plankett, Hon. Mr. & Mrs. G. Vanneck, Sir Charles & Lady Brisbane, Adm. Phillip, Vice-Adm., Mrs. & Miss B. Douglas.
17th January
Lord Henniker, Hon. Mrs. Rushworth, Sir J. Jervis, Sir P. Shuckborough.
30th January
Earl & Countess of Guilford, Hon. Mrs. Plunkett, Sir W. Hart, Sir N. Colthurst, Sir F. Baker, Generals O'Ferrall, Ambrose.

6th **February**
Lady Catharine Bourke, Sir E. O'Brien, Sir M. & Lady Lopes, Sir C. Smith.
14th February
Marquis of Worcester, Lady C. Dormer, Lady Barclay, Lady Williams, Sir John & Lady Pollen, Sir Chas. & Lady Blois & family, Gen, Orr, Adm. & Mrs. Dixon, Adm. Sutton.
21st February
Hon. Mrs. Wyndham, Sir Charles, Mr. & Miss Blicke, Rear-Adm. Ingram.

6th **March**
Earl & Countess of Rothes, Earl & Countess of Lyndsey, Lady Mary Lefine.
13th March
Countess of Westmoreland, Dowager Countess of Rothes, Lady Coghill, Lady James, Lady Vaughan, Lady Smith, Hon. R. Plunket, Hon. Mr. Hare, Sir Wm. Elford, Sir Stapleton Cotton, Adm. & Mrs. Bertie
20th March
Earl & Countess of Wilton, Earl of Pembroke, Countess of Lucan, Lord Miford, Lady A. Jeffery, Lady Rumbold, Lady Williams, Lady E. Hepenitak, Lady M. Cathcart, Dowager Lady Abdy, Sir G. Wombwell, Maj.Gen. & Mrs. Dickson.
27th March
Earl & Countess of Northcote, Lord Chief Justice & Lady Mansfield,

Lord & Lady Glenbervie, Lady Day, Lady Ann Carnegie, Lady E. Garnier, Hon. Mrs. Talbot, Hon. Col. Knollis, Sir Wm. & Lady Pole, Sir Edw. Littleton, Gen. Stuart, Lieut.Gen. Paulett, Brig.Gen. Veacy & family, Maj.Gen. Cameron.

3rd **April**

Lord Gwydir, Lady Vyon, Hon. Mrs. Vane, Sir Capel Molineux, Adm. Sotheby.

10th April

Duke & Duchess of Leeds, Countess Nelson, Sir Joseph & Lady Scott, Gen. Sir Wm. Meadows, Maj.Gen. Dickson.

17th April

Earl of Malmesbury, Lady Smith, Sir Wm. Oglander

24th April

Duke of Gordon, Duke of Leeds, Bishop of Killalla, Lord Dundas, Lord Landaff, Vicountess Newark, Lady Call, Lady Matthers, Lady Forbes, Hon. Mrs. Lysight, Sir H. Rivers, Sir William Montgomery, Sir F. Shuckburgh, The Algerine Ambassador, Gen. Tarleton, Gen. Clarke.

1st **May**

Lord & Lady Kilmorey, Lady Gordon, Lady Bridport, Lady Cotton, Sir J. Lethbridge, Sir C. Ross, Sir M., Lady & Miss Biddulph, Gen. Leith

8th May

Lady Allen, Sir John & Lady Aubrey, Sir H. & Lady Wilkinson, Sir G. Pigott, Maj.Gen. & Mrs. Broadhurst, Dean of Wells.

15th May

Lady Smith, Sir James & Lady Crawford, Dean of St Asaph, Maj.Gen. & Mrs. Crosbie, Maj. Gen. & Mrs. Trent, Col. Gregory

22nd May

Lord St Asaph, Marquis de Sombray & family.

6th **June**

Lord Kirkudbright, Lord O'Bryen, Lady Clarke, Sir T. Baring, Sir E. Lyttleton, Vice-Adm. Sotheby, Rear Adm. Crawley.

12th June

Lady Baring, Sir Henry, Lady & Miss Cosby.

19th June

The Marquis of Bute & Family, Marquis of Salisbury, Lady Clarke, Lady Forbes, Rt. Hon. Sir James Beesley, Hon. Lieut. Barnard, Hon. Miss Massey, Sir J. Aubrey, Sir J. Kennaway, Sir W. James, Sir E. O'Brien, Sir

J. Fellowes, Sir W. Day, Sir E. Orson, Adm. Hargood.
27th June
Lady Fleming, Lady J. King, Hon.Col. & Mrs. Hallybarton

3rd **July**
Earl Spencer, Lady Shuckburgh, Lady Travers, Lady M. Ponsonby, Hon.Rev. F. Knollis, Sir James Stuart.
10th July
Dowager Countess of Spencer, Lady Bath, Hon. Mr. Bailey, Hon. Mrs. Brown, Sir H. Lippincott, Gen. Coulten, Maj.Gen. Winter, Dean of Wells.
17th July
Marques of Huntley, Lord Donerealle, Lady Ann Murray, Lady Clarke, Sir Wm. Wynn, Count Turnerelli.
31st July
Lady E. Drummond, Gen. Nightingall.

14th **August**
Lord & Lady Elliott, Lady Bedingfield, Sir John & Lady Smith, Sir Wm. & Lady Cockburn
21st August
Lady Clarke, Sir James Fellowes, Gen. Dickson, Lieut-Gen. & Mrs. Leighton.
28th August
Lord & Lady Coventry, Lady J. James, Lady Deerhurst, Hon. Wm. Lygon, Sir J. Shuckburgh.

4th **September**
Earl of Westmoreland, Lord Craig, Lady Button, Lady Rivers, Hon. Mr. Berkeley, Sir J. Graham, Gen. & Mrs. Darby, Adm. Phillips.
11th September
Duchess of Dorset, Countess Craven, Hon. S. Bathurst, Hon. Evan Baillie, Sir F.Buller, Sir R. & Lady Bedingfield, Judge Hardinge, Adm. Lumsden.
25th September
Marquis of Bute & family, Lord Dudley, Lord Newark, Lady J. James, Sir Joshua Meredith, Sir John & Lady Aubrey, Sir Lucas Pepys, Sir J. Gillman.

2nd **October**
Lord Hood, Dowager Lady Dering, Sir B. Chinnery, Sir R. & Lady

Wilmott, Gen. De Watville, Maj.Gen. & Mrs. Dunn.

9th October

Lord Newark, Lady Gore, Lady Amalt, Chief Justice Mansfield & Family, Rt. Hon. Sir Wm. Scott, Sir James & Lady Fitzgerald, Gen. & Mrs. Cliffe, Adm. Montague & family, Vice-Adm. Lumsden.

16th October

Earl of Scarborough & family, Marchioness of Thomond, Lady Rolland, Sir J.C. & Lady Hippisley, Sir Wm. & Lady Barker, Sir S. Falkener, Lieut.Gen. & Mrs. Champagny, Maj. Gen. M'Neill, Hon. Col. & Miss Knollis.

23rd October

Marquis of Bath, Marquis of Bute, Earl of Cork, Lord J. Thynne, M.P. Lieut-Col. Palmer, M.P. Lord Gwydir, Lady Dorchester, Lady Clarke, Lady Styles, Hon. Dudley Cheston, Hon. Mrs. Bennett, Count Le Pulletier, Sir Sam. ...... Adm. Bowyer

30th October

Bishop of Bath & Wells & family, Lord Ebrington, Baroness Robeck, Dowager Lady Dering, Lady Acton. Lady Sydney, Lady Waller, Lady Clerke, Sir Wm. & Lady Paxton, Sir J.C. & Lady Hippisley, Sir Henry Wilkinson.

6th November

Duke & Duchess of Somerset, Duchess of Montrose, Lady Desart, Lady C. Drummond, Lady O'Bryen, Lady De Clifford, Baron de Puyll, Hon. Mrs. Day, Sir John Trevelyan, Sir T. & Lady Baring, Sir A. Bayntun, Sir J. Hanham, Gen. & Mrs. Powell, Gen. Stuart, Adm. Mann, Lieut.Gen. Campbell, Maj.Gen. & Mrs. Disney & family.

20th November

Countess of Normanton, Lady Addington, Lady Thornton, Lady & Miss Russell, Lady Jane & 2 Miss Loftus, Hon. Edw. Massey, Hon. J.B. Rodney, Sir Hugh & Lady Bateman, Sir Wm. & Lady Watson, Sir J. Gillham, Adm. Aylmer.

27th November

Countess Belmore, Lady Dorchester, Hon. D. Carleton, Hon. R. Carleton, Sir Thomas & Lady Burke, Sir Chas. Pole, Sir George Thomas, Gen. Champagny, Lieut.Gen. Waller, Maj.Gen. Goldie.

11th December

Dowager Lady & the Misses Rumbold, Baron & Baroness DeTuyll, Baron Hompesch, Hon. Col & Mrs. Hallyburton, Sir Edward & Lady

Leslie, Sir John Colpoys, Lieut.Gen & Mrs. Drummond, Maj. Gen. Deare

18th December

Countess of Lucan, Lord Glastonbury, Lord Somerville, Lady Jane James, Lady Lewis, Lady Tuit, Sir J. W. C. Smith, Sir Evan Baillie, Sir W. Richardson, Sir J. Gore, Sir R. Baker, Sir C. Hippisley, Rev.Sir J. Hanham, Adm. Sir I. Coffin.

1812

8th January

Countess Fortescue, Lord H. Austen, Lady Pearson, Lady Galloway, Sir M. Wood, Sir John Anstruther, Sir Henry, Lady & Miss Cosby, Gen. Hope & family, Gen. Montague, Gen. Tarleton & family

15th January

Earl of Leven and Melville, Lord Bradford, Lady Dorchester, Lady M. L. Melville, Hon. A. I. Melville, Sir H. Lippincott, Sir Wm. A'Court & family, Sir Wm. Vyner, Sir R. Phillipson, Gen. & Mrs. Powell.

22nd January

Lady & the Misses Elford, Lady C. Gould, Lady Staines, Sir S. & Lady Walthen, Sir J.C. Hippisley, Sir J. Nisbet, Vice-Adm. M'Dougall.

5th February

Earl of Mount-Edgecombe & family, Viscount Hawarden, Lord & Lady Vernon, Lord Newbttle, Lord Vallentort, Lady C.L. Long, Dowager Lady & Miss Craven, Hon. D. M'Donald, Hon. Mr. Villiers, Sir F. Vane, Sir Wm. Richardson, Sir H. & Lady Carew, Gen. Browne & family, Adm. Sutton & family.

19th February

Lady Gardiner & family, Lady E. Pratt, Lady C. Durham, Lady Buxton, Lady Forbes & family, Lady Dering, Hon. Alex. Melville, Sir T. Acland, Adm., Mrs. & Miss Bury.

26th February

Duke of Alva, Lady Lester, Sir John Blunden, Sir F. Vane, Count Le Pelletier, Gen. & Mrs. Vowles, Rear-Adm. & Lady Charlotte Durham

11th March

Earl of Clonearty, Lady Clarins, Lady Willes, Sir C. & Lady Blunt, Sir C. & Lady Berry, Sir J.H. Williams & family, Sir A. Cathcart, Gen Layard

18th March

Earl & Countess of Lindsey, Viscountess Newark, Lord Arundel, Dowager Lady Bolton, Lady Seton, Lady Ann Deering, Lady Hawarden, Lady Rivers, Hon. Mr. & Mrs. Hyde, Hon. Rev. Mr. Knollis, Sir James Ridell, Sir H. Rivers, Sir J. Blunden, Vice-Adm. & Mrs. Gould

25th March

The Earl and Countess of Rothes, Earl of Aberdeen, Lady Gleneairn, Lady M. Hamilton, Lady Horton, Lady J. Hale, Lady Mary Leslie, Dowager Lady Smith, Sir John & Lady Aubrey, Sir W. Smith, Sir J.

Meredith, Sir W. Mansell, Sir Wm. Scott, Gen. Sir B. Spencer.

8th April
Lord Harrowby, Lady Glynn, Lady O'Brien, Hon. Lady Turner, Adm. Sir J & Lady Duckworth, Sir S. Romilly, Sir Edward, Lady & the Misses Lacon.
22nd April
Earl of Charlemont, Lady E. Cadogan, Lady Mackintosh & family, Sir W. Cunningham, Adm. Sir J. C. & Lady Greenly, Gen. Lumley.
29th April
Lord Aston, Lady Somerville, Hon. Mr. & Mrs. Pierrepoint, Gen. Morshead, Gen. French & family, Gen. Gawler.

13th May
Earl Camden, Lady S. Stuart, Hon. Mr. & Mrs. Barnewall, Sir R. Hoare, Maj.Gen Broderick, Adm. Tyler
20th May
Earl & Countess of Wilton, Bishop of Bath & Wells, Viscount Newark, Gen. & Mrs. Powell, Gen. Philippon, Adm. Kempe
27th May
Earl & Countes of Manvers, Dowager Countess D'Alton, Lady Colville, Lady Amith, Sir S. Athen

3rd June
Lady Elphinstone, Hon. P. Pierrepont, Sir J. Caldwell, Adm. Sir R., Lady & Miss Onslow, Adm. Aylmer, Adm. Graves, Adm. Tyley, Adm. Crawley, Gen. Harvey, Gen. & Mrs. Powell, Hon. Col. Carleton.
24th June
Earl & Countess of Cork, Lord Bishop of Bath & Wells, Lord & Lady G. Thynne, Hon. Mr. Bridgeman, Sir J. Burgess, Sir W. Call & family, Sir W & Lady Vachell, Maj.Gen. Raymond, Adm. Graves.

1st July
Lady Walker, Sir J. & Lady Smith, Sir R. Woodford, Hon. Capt. Murray.
8th July
Sir J. & Lady H. Williams & family, Sir J. & Lady Langham & family, Sir F. Maxwell, Lieut.Gen. & Mrs. Bright, Maj. Gen., Mrs. & 2 Misses Stovin.
15th July
Earl & Countess of Shannon & family, Countess of Caryafort, Comte de

Sommery, Lady Probyn, Lady Ann Fortescue, Lady Ford, Hon. Miss Massey, Sir James and Lady Fitzgerald, Sir H. Rivers, Sir W. Dunbar, Gen. Raymond.

22nd July

Lord & Lady Berwick & family, Lord Sahden, Sir R. Hoare, Gen. Ogilby.

5th August

Bishop of Norwhic, Sir T. & Lady Stanley, Sir J. Caldwell, Gen. Kempt.

26th August

Duke of Dorset, Duchess of Dorset, Earl & Countess of Cavan, Countess of Malmsbury, Countess Dowager of Galway, Lord Whitworth, Lady Clarina, Lady A. Lambert, Lady Colthorpe & family, Lady Sackville, Sir M. & Lady Rivers, Gen. & Mrs. Powell & family.

2nd September

Earl & Countess of Besborough & family, Earl & Countess of Coventry & family, Countess of Desart, Lord & Lady Elliot & family, Lord & Lady Glenbervie & family, Lord & Lady Osborne, Loord Killeen, Lady Wilson, 3 Hon. Messers Strangeway, Sir C. Bampfylde, Gen. Morrison, Gen. J & Mrs. Reynolds & family, Adm. & Mrs. Moorson & Family, Adm. & Miss Bury, Adm. Phillips, Dean of Wells.

9th September

Earl of Westmoreland, Ciscount Southwell, Viscount Carlton, Hon. Mr. Shute, Sir J. Ribton, Sir J. & Lady Murray, Sir J. Fitzgerald, Lieut.Gen. & Mrs. Leighton, Maj.Gen. Charleon

16th September

Earl of Harrowby, Chief Justice Mansfield & family, Lady Carr, Hon. Capt. Murray & family, Maj.Gen M'Leod.

23rd September

Lord St Asaph, Lady Bouverie, Hon. Mr. Tuchett, Hon. Miss Curzon, Maj.Gen. Conyngham & family, Adm. Graves

30th September

Marquis & Marchioness of Lansdowne, Sir James, Lady & Miss Fitzgerald, Sir F. Bohun, Sir G. Salmon, Lieut.Gen. Sir Eyre Coote, Adm. & Mrs. Bertie, Adm. & Mrs. Christie & family.

14th October

Lord Sandon, Lady Rivers, Lady Smith, Hon. Mr. Barnewell, Hon. Mr. Bridgeman, Hon. Mrs. Agnew, Sir A. Agnew, Sir J. Nicholls, Sir F. Burdette, Gen. Gordon, Adm. & Miss Graves

21st October

Earl & Countess of Wilton, Lady Harewood, Lady & 2 Misses Brabozo, Lady C. Stuart, Hon. Mr. Beresford, Hon. Colonel Brown, Hon. Miss De Courcy, Sir R. Romilly, Rear Adm. Barton.

28th October

Lord St Asaph, Lady Clonbrock, Sir W. A'Court, Sir R. Wallond, Sir R. Milnes, Gen. & Mrs. Dickson, Gen. Delpratt, Gen. Rigby, Consul-Gen Blanckly.

4th **November**

Duke of Argyle, Marquis of Buckingham, Bishop of Bath & Wells & Lady, Bishop of Cloyne, Lord Headley, Lord G. Seymour, Dowager Lady Carew, Lady Pilkington, Rt. Hon. Charles Abbot, Hon. J. Grenville, Hon. A. Onslow, Hon. Capt. & Mrs. De Courcey, Sir W & Lady Parker, Sir H. Carew, Gen. Burton, Gen. & Mrs. Farmer, Rear Adm. Linzie

11th November

Earl of Malmesbury, Bishop of Limerick, Lord De Clifford, Lord Somerville, Lady Sidwell, Lady Talbot, Hon. C. Gordon, Hon. Mrs. Agnew, Sir Rupert & Lady George, Sir W. Bruce, Sir C. Rivers, Gen. & Mrs. Powell & family.

18th November

Earl & Countess of Caernarvon, Lord Gwydir, Lady & Miss Rycroft, Lady W. Ackland, Hon. Mr. & Mrs. Villiers, Hon. Mr. Quin, Hon Mrs. & Miss Rowden, Sir James Handy, Sir J. H. Williams, Sir Hugh & Lady Bateman.

25th November

Earl of Pembroke, Viscount & Viscountess Ranelagh, Countess of Lonsdale, Lord H. Somerset, Lord Lismore, Lady Rivers, Lady M. Lowther, Lady E. Lowther, Dowager Lady & Miss Louis, Hon. Mr. O'Callaghan, Sir R. Perle, Sir R. Bedingfield, Sir Edw. & Lady Laslie, Rear Adm. Sir R.G. Keats, Gen. & Mrs. Champagne, Gen. Ambrose, Rear-Adm. & Mrs. Wolley.

2nd **December**

Lord & Lady O'Bryan, Lord Southwell, Lord Lismore, Lady Clanbrassil, Sir H. Strachey, Sir J. & Lady Scott, Sir S. Hayes.

9th December

Earl & Countess of Cavan, Marchioness Dowager of Thomond, Lady Bateman, Lady Sitwell, Lady Meadowes, Hon. Mrs. Blackwood, Sir W. & Lady James, Sir James Mackintosh, Adm. Sir J.C. Greenly, Gen. De

Courcey, Gen. Grenfille, Lieut.Gen. Baron Dreschel, Maj.Gen. Pietre, Russian Adm. Grieg.

16th December

Countess Augusta Baker, Lady Paxton, Lady H. Harvey, Lady Rowden, Hon. Mrs. Rowden, Sir B. Hobhouse, Sir G. Collyer, Sir W. Mansfield, Sir J. & Lady Nesbitt, Sir Chas. Rich, Sir J. C. Hippisley, Lieut.Gen. & Mrs. Drummond, Maj.Gen. M'Neill.

23rd December

Earl & Countess of Caernarvon, Lady C. Drummond, Hon. G. Neville, Sir George Sitwell, Sir A. Agnew, Sir E. Baillie, Sir R. Harding, Gen. & Mrs. O'Loghlan, Maj.Gen. Lightburne.

30th December

Earl & Countess of Craven, Countess of Lucan, Lord E. O'Brien, Hon. Mrs. Dundas, Hon. Mrs. Portman, Sir J. H. Luxton, Sir H. Hill, Sir J. Graham, Sir G. Collyer, Vice-Adm. & Mrs. Purvis.

1813

6th **January**
Hon. R. B. Bernard, Sir J. Purcell, Sir M. Ximenes, Sir W. Taylor, Sir S. Whitcombe, Sir J. Brenford, Sir W. Paxton, Sir J. H. Caxton, Adm. Philips.
13th January
The Russian Prince Koslovsky, Earl of Powis, Earl & Countess of Northesk, Lord Somerville, Lord Forbes, Lady Ann Carnegie, Lady Wynn, Sir W. Brabazon, Sir S. Noyes, Sir Alexander & the Misses Grant, Gen. Johnston, Adm. Domet.
20th January
Lord J. Thynne, Lord W. Stuart, Lady Gresley, Sir J. C. Greenly, Sir Mark Wood, Sir J. & Lady Hippisley, Gen. & Mrs. Powell & family, Adm. Robinson.
27th January
Earl & Countess Fortescue, Earl & Countess of Cork, Lord Bradford, Lord Lismore, Lady Jerningham, Hon.Capt. & Mrs. Boyle & family, Hon. Mrs. Dashwood, Hon. Mrs. Day, Sir W. Meadows, Sir R. Milnes, Sir T. White, Gen. & Mrs. Mead, Adm. Holloway.

3rd **February**
Lord W. Somerset, Lord Colville, Lady Willes, Lady M'Intosh, Hon. W. Mowbray, Sir J. Yorke, Count Wyer, Gen. Popham.
10th February
Earl & Countess of Cavan, Lord & Lady Neville, Lord & Lady Buringdon, Lord Colville, Baroness Spencer, Lady E. Spencer, Lady Munro, Lady & Miss Burton, Hon. Gen. St Leger, Sir R. Buxton, Sir W. Dunbar, Maj.Gen. Gordon, Adm. Berry & Family.
24th February
Earl & Countess of Cork, Viscount & Viscountess Galway, Lord Vernon, Lady Paxton, Sir P. & Lady Hale, Sir R. Miller, Le Comte Minchiani, Gen. Hokins

3rd **March**
Viscount Bolingbroke, Lady Talbot, Lady Rumbold, Lady Elphinstone, Hon. Mr. St. John, Sir W. Elford, Sir G. Pownall, Sir R. Blosse, Sir J.R. & Lady Miller, Gen. Grigg.
17th March
Lady Smith, Hon. R. Plunkett, Sir C. Crawley, Sir W. Brabazon, Sir M.

Foulkes, Sir H. Protheroe, Sir S.C. Boevey, Adm., Mrs. & Miss Holloway, Adm. Bury.

<u>24th March</u>

Lady ?Rodsey, Lady E. Duncombe, Lady Harland, Lady D. Browne, Hon. Miss Blackall, Sir S. & Lady Hayes, Sir R. Crawford, Sir T. Wheate, Gen. H. Cumming, Adm. Sotheby, Adm, Loghmere, Adm. & Mrs. M'Dougall.

<u>31st March</u>

Lady A. Gordon, Lady Burton, Sir J.R. Miller, Sir S. & Lady Falkener, Sir W. Dunbar, Sir S. Wathen.

<u>14th **April**</u>

Viscount Sandon, Lady Cotton & family, Lady Russel, Lady Ephinstone, Rt. Hon. Rear Adm. & Mrs. Gardner, Hon. Mr. Yelverton, Sir Hugh & Lady Smith, Sir V. Gibbs, Sir B. Chinnery, Sir J. Scott, Sir T & Lady Biddulph, Sir G. Paul, Gen. Gordon, Adm. Sawyer.

<u>21st April</u>

Viscount Kilcoursie, Lord & Lady J. Murray, Count & Countess de Salis, Sir J. & Lady Aubrey, Sir J.W. & Lady Jervis, Sir C. Paxton, Adm. & Mrs. Hargood, Adm. & Mrs. Holloway.

<u>28th April</u>

Viscountess Bridport, Lord & Lady Grantham, Lord Southwell, Lady De Spencer, Hon. Mr. Yelverton, Hon. Mr. & Mrs. Fitzwilliam, Hon. Mr. Maule, Hon. Capt. De Courcy, Sir A. Agnew

<u>5th **May**</u>

Lord & Lady J. Murray, Lord Nelson[3], Lady Biddulph, Lady M. Wood, Sir J. & Lady Kennaway, Gen. Stuart, Gen. Gordon.

<u>26th May</u>

Duke of Buccleugh, Lord Dunsany, Lady Smith, Hon. Mrs. Rooke, Sir J. & Lady Aubrey, Sir R. Hoare, Sir J. Collard, *Generals* Campbell, Gordon.

<u>9th **June**</u>

Lord Adair, Lady Elphinstone, Lady Saxton, Hon. Mr. Bridgman, Sir J.R. Miller, Sir W. Dunbar, Sir P., Lady & Miess Hales, Sir J. Chichester, Sir J. Hawkesley.

<u>30th June</u>

[3] The older brother of Admiral Lord Nelson; he was a clergyman.

Marquis of Salisbury, Earl of Pembroke, Lady A. Murray, Lady Smith, Lady & Miss Paxton, Hon. Mr. Lumley, Sir R. Hoare, Sir E. Synge, Sir A. Bertie & family, *Generals* Gordon, Kerr, M'Kenale & wife.

7th **July**
Lord & Lady Wentworth, Lord Fortescue, Lady Collier, Lady Lloyd, Sir C. & Lady Mordaunt, Sir J. Pinhern, Sir A. Grand, Sir R. Brownlow, Baron de Schmuden.
14th July
Earl of Cork, Countess De Rohan, Lady Wallscourt, Hon. Mr. Scott, Gen. Lightburne.
21st July
Lady J. Hay, Sir J. Dumaresq
28rd July
Archbishop of Tuam, Lord Goge, Lady Beauchamp, Maj.Gen. Vandeleur.

18th **August**
Lord Braybrook
25th August
His R.H. the Duke of Cambridge, Earl of Kenmare, Lord Wentworth, Lord Harburton, Lady Goold, Lady Browne, Gen. & Lady Hamilton, Gen. Johnson.

8th **September**
Earl & Countess of Cork, Lord Clonmell, Lady Bridges, Hon. E.S. Cooper, Gen. Sir J. Hamilton, Sir W. James, Sir F. Falkner, Adm. Graves
29th September
Marquis & Marchioness Camden, Earl Carleton, Lady Hamilton, Hon. Mr. & Mrs. Moore, Lord Chief Justice Mansfield, Sir Wm. & Lady Backer, Sir P. Paget, Sir E. & Lady May, Judge Hardinge.

6th **October**
Marquis of Bath & family, Viscount Hood, Lady Burton, Hon. Mr. & Mrs. Howe, Hon. Mr. & Mrs. Lason, Sir R. Nagle, Lieut.Gen. & Mrs. Dickson, Adm. & Mrs. Gardner.
13th October
Marquis & Marchioness of Lansdown, Lady Saxton, Rt. Hon. Gen. Canning, Hon. Mrs. Strange, Sir J. Smith, Sir G. Paul, Sir E. May, Count Putusoû, Maj. Gen. Lee, Adm. Wolesly, Adm. Sawyer, Adm. & Mrs. Graves.

20th October

Duke of Somerset, Rt. Hon. G. Saxton, Hon. & Rev. Mr. & Mrs. St Leger, Sir James & Lady Fitzgerald, Sir W. Farquhar, Sir G. Worrall, Judge & Mrs. Daly, Gen. De Castres, *Admirals* Aylmer, Christie, Nichols, Morris & wife, Reeve & wife

27th October

Earl of Charleville, Countess of Ely, Lord Andover, Lord Gwydir, Lady Sidney, Lady Clarked, Lady Stepney, Sir A. Hood, Sir J. Scott, Gen. Sir J. Stuart, Gen. & Mrs. Cliffe, Lieut.Gen., Mrs. & Miss Benton.

2nd November

Countess Delawson, Lady Clonbrock, Lady Call, Hon. G. Toler, Gen. Sir Eyre Coote, Sir S. Northcote, Sir R. Baker, Sir W. & Lady Wynne, Sir G. & Lady Temple, Sir C. Saxton, Sir T. Picton, Sir E. Horne, Sir W. Richardson, Sir W. & Lady Watson, Dean of Wells, Gen. Ambrose

10th November

Her Royal Highness the Duchess D'Angouleme, Margravine of Anstpach, Countess Delaware, Lord Somerset, Lord Malpas, Lady Saxton, Sir W. & Lady Meadows, Sir J. & Lady Hamlyn & family, Sir W. Chichester, Gen. Molyneaux, Gen. Hopkins, Adm. & Mrs. Pender.

17th November

His Royal Highness le Duc D'Angoulême, Marquis of Huntley, Countess de Choissey, Dowager Countess De Lawarn, Lord & Lady G. Thynne, Dowager Lady Drake, Hon. Mr. & Mrs. Villiers, Hon. Mr. & Mrs. Hope, Sir J. Leicester, Governor Penn.

1st December

Earl Manvers, Lord Bective, Lady Parker, Lady Smith, Lady Elphinstone, Lady S. De'Crespigny

15th December

Lord Clifton, Lady Keith, Hon. Mrs. Cockayne, Hon. Miss Elphinstone, Sir Hugh & Lady Bateman, Sir T.C. Boevey, Sir J.C. Hippisley, Sir B. Hobhouse, Sir J. & Lady Smith, Adm. & Mrs. Halkett, Adm. Clements

22nd December

Viscount Weymouth, Count & Countess Laval, Countess Belmore, Lord Somerville, Lord, Lady & Miss Henniker, Lady Saxton, Lady J. Douglas, Lady Flamborough, Lady Sheukburgh, Lady C. Rawdon, Hon. Mrs. Kennedy, Gen. Dunne, *Admirals* Manworthy, Aymer, Graves & wife

29th December

Countess of Cork, Lord Folkstone, Lord Southwell, Lady F. Fane, Lady

C. Drummond, Lady L. Boyle, Hon. Sir. G. Berkeley, Sir O. & Lady Gordon, Maj.Gen. & Mrs. Bradshaw

Circus, photo S. Waldock

1814

5th **January**
Earl Pomfret, Lady C. Worresley, Lady G. Pownall, Lady Renscomb, Capt. & Lady T. Hale, Sir W. Macartney, Sir H. & Lady Carew, Sir G. Powell, Gen. Jones.
12th January
Count & Countess Orloff, Lord Say and Sele, Dowager Lady & Miss Carew, Lady Elton, Hon. Mrs. Bertie, Adm. Sir R. Keates, Sir J & Lady Scott, Gen. Drummond, *Admirals* Robinson, Fleming
19th January
Lord Southwell, Count Swedenbourg, Sir J. Nesbitt, Sir P. & Lady Musgrave, Lieut.Gen. Monro, Maj. Gen. De Castro, Adm. Graves & family.
26th January
Hon. R. Plunkett, Sir J. Gifford, Sir J. & Lady Mawby, Sir M. Blackiston, Gen. Bethune, Maj.Gen. Ponsonby.

2nd **February**
Viscount Bury, Lord & Lady Templeton, Viscountess Galway, Lady Dalrymple, Hon. Miss Agar, Sir C. Sinclair, Sir J. C. Greenly.
9th February
Marquis & Marchioness of Bath, Earl Dalhousie, Viscount Weymouth, Lord Walisewort?, Lord John Russell, Lord Southwell, Hon. Adm. Fleming, Hon. Miss Arundell, Sir J. Lethbridge, Sir W. Richardson, Sir W. & Lady Ball, Lieut.Gen. Berkley, Adm. Thornborough.
16th February
Earl of Pembroke, Dowager Countess of Pembroke, Lord Kensington, Lord Banden, Lord Bolton, Hon. Mr. & Mrs. Fortescue, Hon. E. Byng, Sir C. Blount, Sir M. Foulkes & family, Sir R.C. Hoare, Sir R. Blossie, Sir A. Hood, Adm. Spry.
23rd February
Lord Landaff, Lady Herbert, Sir W. B. Guise, Sir B. Wrey, Sir J. Hanham, Sir R. Bydingfield, Sir S. Wathen, Sir J. C. Greenly, Sir W. Aylett, Sir J. C. Hippisley, Gen. Stuart, Adm. & Mrs. Matiley.

2nd **March**
Earl of Kenmare, Marquise de Tourville, Lord Kingsmill, Lord Clarina, Hon. Mrs. Cawthorn, Sir J. Hamlyn, Sir P. & Lady Hall, Gen. Bradshaw, Gen. Grace.

9th March

Earl of Macclesfield, Lord & Lady Elliott, Lord & Lady Bolton, Lord Kilsale, Lord J. Russel, Lady de Spaen, Lady Owen, Hon.&Rev. Mr. Windsor, Sir W. & Lady Patton, Sir O. & Lady Gordon, Sir T. & Lady Whitchcote, Gen. & Mrs. Hopkins, Gen. & Mrs. Carleton, Gen. Batemen, Gen. & Mrs. Cameron, Maj.Gen. Peachey, Adm. Fisk.

16th March

Lord Lifford, Hon. Mr. Byng, Sir W. Elford, Gen. & Mrs. Vandeleur, Gen. Butler, Gen Brown.

23rd March

Bishop of Waterford, Lady Bedingfield, Lady Gresley & family, Sir A. Hood, Sir J. Dashwood.

30th March

Countess of Pembrokd, Lady Isabella King, Sir B. Gibbs, Sir W. Johnstone, Sir E. Bynge, Sir J. D. King, Gen. Kidd, Commodore & Mrs. Borlase.

6th **April**

Lord & Lady Dufferys, Lord Kensington, Lord Newbottle, Lord Rosehill, Lady Whetman, Hon. Col. Knollie, Adm. Sir J.L. & Lady Ducksworth, Sir W. Cunningham, Sir W. Brabazon, Sir G. Giffurd, Sir A. Cathcart, Sir ? Denny, Chancellor Douglas.

13th April

Countess Dysart, Dowager Lady Rivers, Dowager Lady Pembroke, Lieut.Gen. Sir J. Affleck, Sir J. Morris, Sir H. Hamilton, Sir J. Mansfield, Sir J.R. Miller, Maj.Gen. Bradshaw, Maj.Gen Dunlop.

20th April

Lieut.Gen. Sir J. Wilson, Gen. M'Lean, Gen. Bateman, Adm. Fisk

27th April

Lord Somerville, Hon. Mr. Leeson, Sir Henry Rivers, Adm. Fleming.

4th **May**

Lord Glenbervie, Countess Bellamont, Lady Gordon, Lady Carangie, Lady H. Bagot, Lady K. Hunloke, Hon. Col. Burron, Gen. Sir W. Avlette, Sir H. & Lady Lawson, Sir J. Gifford, Gen. Cliffe, Gen. Halkett.

11th May

Viscountess Richmond, Lady B. H. Verr, Hon. R & Lady Bagot, Sir D. Mackworth, Sir J. Meredith, Sir J. Baker, Sir G. Barlow, Gen. Blount.

18th May

Lady Denny, Lady Meath, Hon. Mr. Barlow, Sir R.C. Hoare, Sir J. &

Lady Aubrey, Sir W. Bateman, Sir E. Hartop, Sir J. Lethbridge, Gen. Winter, Maj.Gen. M'Lean.

25th May

Lady Bruton, Sir W. Elford, Sir W. Cooper, Baron Von Hoskell.

1st **June**

Lord Kenmare, Sir F. & Lady Millman & family, Sit W. Conyngham, Lieut.Gen. Monro.

8th June

Hon. Capt. Curzon, Hon. Mrs. Holland, Sir J. Nasmyth, Sir J. R. Miller, Sir G. Paul, Gen. Oakes.

15th June

Viscountess de Richemont, Lady Thompson, Sir Philip & Lady Hale, Sir R. & Lady Blosse, Sir F. Ford, Rear Adm. Clements.

22nd June

Earl Kenmare, Rev. Sir C. Wheeler, Sir W. Wynne, Sir H. Lawson, Adm. & Mrs. Aylmer

29th June

His Royal Highness the reigning Duke of Saxe-Weimar, with Colonel de Zurschwitz & Mr. Mellish; Earl & Countess of Cork, Lady Leslie, Hon. Mr. & Mrs. Yelverton, Sir S. Wathen, Sir R.C. Hoare, Gen. Amherst, Gen & Mrs. Hopkins, Adm. & Mrs. Linzee.

6th **July**

Lord Southwell, Viscount de Richemont, Lady Kingston, Sir H. Russell, Sir J. Hawkins, Gen. Lightburne, Gen. Buller.

13th July

Lady Wilson, Lady Middleton, Hon. Mrs. Kennedy & family, Gen. Sir John Stuart, Vice Adm. & Mrs. Hargood.

20th July

Lord Cathcart, Count De Lomenie, Countess de Bashi & daughter, Lady Ford.

28th July

Earl Fortescue, Lord Kenmare, Lord Teignmouth, Lady Knatchbull, Lady Le Despencer, Lady Shipworth, Lady Elsmore, Lady Wilson, Hon. R. Moore, Hon. Mr. Clifford, Hon. Mr. C. Clifford, Sir W. & Lady Bush, Sir P. Wilson.

On the 25th, the Marquis of Worcester was married to Miss Georgiana Frederica Fitzroy at the house of Mr. Culling Smith in Upper Brook Street, by Hon. Rev. G.V. Wellesley attended by her RH the Duchess of

York, Dukes of Beaufort, Grafton & Wellington, Marquis of Wellesley and other branches of the respective families.

3rd August

Count Jennison, Sir T.D. Acland, Sir E. Knatchbull, Sir P. Hawkes, Sir F. Dennis, Sir J. Hoare, Sir A. & Lady Dickson, Gen. Kidd, Adm. Bowen & family, Adm. Rolls, Rear-Adm. Monkson.

10th August

Duke of Leinster, Lord & Lady Dillon & family, Lady Le Despencer, Sir C. Bunbury, Sir R. I. Blosse, Sir D. Mackworth, Gen. & Mrs. Popham & family, Gen. Huller.

17th August

Earl of Oxford, Lady Middleton, Lady Wilson, Lady Sampson, Sir J. Colpoys, Lieut.Gen. & Mrs. Bowles.

24th August

Countess Talbot, Lord Sidmouth, Lady Ibbetson, Lady Acland & family, Sir V. Gibbs, Gen. & Mrs. Nicholson, Lieut.Gen. & Mrs. Leighton.

31st August

Duke of Berwick and Alba, Chief Baron of Scotland & family, Hon. Mrs. Vane, Sir R.C. & Lady Glynn, Sir J. Hoare, Sir W. Bush, Gen. Moone, Vice Adm. Orway & family.

7th September

Earl of Ossory, Lord & Lady Grenville, Lord Templeton, Rt. Hon. T. Grenville, Hon. Miss Massey, Judge & Mrs. Dair.

14th September

Lord Stewart, Count de Laval, Lady Clarina, Mr. & Lady? Henrietta James, Hon. B. Blackwood, Hon. Mrs. Yorke, Sir R & Lady Hales, Sir R. Hoare, Gen. Ryall, Lieut.Gen Monro, Adm. Christin.

21st September

Earl of Carnarvon, Lord Munson, Lady H. Herbert, Lady E. Herbert, Lady E. Montague, Sir W. James, Sir C. Styles, Gen. Byng, Gen. Moore, Gen Donkin, Gen. Butter.

5th October

Countess D'Alton, Lorrd Hood, Lady Keith, Sir H. Strachey, Sir W. Roberts, Gen. Butler, Adm. & Mrs. Hargood, Adm. & Mrs. Thornborough, Adm. & Mrs. Wolseley.

12th October

Lord & Lady Elliot, Lord & Lady Thynne, Countess De Front, Lady

Dering, Lady A. Digby, Sir W. & Lady Cockburn, Sir W. & Lady Barker, Sir W. Murray, Sir A. Gledstape, Gen. Bolton, Lieut.Gen. & Mrs. Dickson, Maj.Gen. Eden, Maj.Gen. Goldie, Adm. & Mrs. Murray & family, Adm. Macnamara.

19th October

Lord & Lady melvile, Lord Rochfort, Count Orloff, Hon. Mr. & Mrs. Moore, Hon. Mr. & Mrs. St Leger, Chief Justice & Lady Mansfield & family, Sir J. Hoare, Sir J. Throgmorton, Gen. Dundas.

26th October

Lady A'Court, Maj.Gen. Sir Wm. & Lady Cockburn, Sir James Fitzgerald, Gen. Gore, Adm. & Mrs. Hargood.

2nd November

Earl & Countess of Cork, Dowager Countess of Caernarvon, Lord & Lady Keith, Lord Ellenborough, Lord Enniskillen, Lady Myers, Lady Ann Talbot, Rt. Hon. W. & Mrs. Dundas, Hon. Mr Herbert, Sir J., Lady & Miss Fitzgerald, Sir R. Wilmot, Sir Hugh Bateman, Sir W. Richardson, Gen. Eyre, Gen. Kyd, Adm. Hackett.

9th November

Lord Boringdon, Lord H. Paulett, Lord Barrington, Lady Darring, Lady E. Talbot, Sir C.W. & Lady Mallett, Sir & the Misses M'Lean.

16th November

Lord C. Lennox, Lady C. Long, Hon. Mrs. Mackay, Sir J. C. Hippisley, Sir J. Hoare, Lieut. Gen. Sir B., Lady & Miss Henderson.

23rd November

Lady L. Lennox, Lady H. Vere, Hon. Miss Elphinstone, Sir F. Moresby, Sir J.C. Sinclair, Gen. Brown, Gen. M. Ni-l

30th November

Hon. Lady Smith, Lady O'Brien, Lady S. Lennox, Sir E. & Lady Leslie, Sir D. Smith, Gen. M'Lean, Maj.Gen. Pawlett, Adm. & Mrs. Bowen, Rear Adm. Monkton.

7th December

Earl & Countess of Cork, Earl of Caernarvon, Lord Gwydir, Lady Willoughby, 2 Ladies Herbert, Dowager Lady Clonbrock, Hon. Miss Ryder, Sir ? Palmer, Gen. Ambrose, Gen. Stewart, Gen. Vicary, Gen. Hughs, Rear Adm. Otway.

14th December

Earl of Shrewsbury, Marquis de Sommery, Countess of Lucan, Dowager

Lady Carrick, Hon. R. B. Bernard, Hon. Mr. Arundell, Hon. Mr. Plunkett, Sir W. Manset, Rev. Sir C. Rich, Sir J.C. Hippisley, Sir B. Hobhouse, Sir J.W. Smith, Adm. & Mrs. Sarsay & family, Rear Adm. & Mrs. Surridge.

21st December

Lord Bishop of Meath, Lord & Lady Selsey, Lord Kirkudbright, Lord F???? Lady Call, Hon. Capt. Peachy, Sir W. Bruce, Gen. Sir J. Stewart, Gen. M'Neil.

28th December

Lord Wallscourt, Lord E. O'Bryen, Lord Kinton, Hon. Miss Peachy, Sir W. Sharidan, Sir J. & Lady Scott, Sir W. Hartley, Gen. Rafe, Gen. Bradshaw, Gen. & Mrs. Peachy, Maj.Gen. Kyd, Adm. Halkern.

1815

5th **January**
Earl & Countess of Jersey, Earl of Liverpool, Earl & Countess Fortescue, Count Paplin, Lord Bruce, Dowager Lady Galway, Sir W. & Lady Wynn, Gen. Hamett, Maj.Gen. & Mrs. L'Estrange, Adm., Mrs. & Miss Holloway, Adm. & Mrs. Morris.
12th January
Lord & Lady Ormond, Dowager Lady Dering, Lady E. Fane, Lady Sidwell, 2 Ladies Herbert, Lady Talbot, Lady Digby, Sir A. Hood, Aid A. Blennerhassett, Lieut.Gen., Mrs. & Miss Wemys.
19th January
Countess of Carysfort & family, Countess of Lucan, Lord & Lady Colville, Rt. Hon. Dowager Lady Amherst, Lady C. West, Lady Waller, Lady T. Frere, Hon. J. Coventry, Adm. Sir T. Bertie.
26th January
Lord H. Thynne, Lord Weymouth, Lady & Miss Burton, Lady Waller, Lady S. Frere, Lady Bayley, Hon. Rev. Mr. Peachey, Hon Mr. & Mrs. Fortescue, Adm. Sir Isaac Coffin, Sir C. Coke, Sir W. Paxton, Sir W. Brayon, Gen. Montgomery, Gen. R. Stuart, Gen. Lightburne, Gen. Elley, Adm. Barry, Rear Adm. Ballard, Rear Adm. Levesan.

1st **February**
Lady Despencer, Sir W. & Lady Hargood, Sir J. & Lady Morris, Sir W. Brabazon.
8th February
Earl & Countess of Cork, Earl of Yarmouth, Lord & Lady Anson, Lady Clinton, Lady Rivers, Lady G. Proby, Lady Kingston, Hon. Mr. & Mrs. Bridgman, 2 Hon. Messrs Boyle, Hon. Capt Carleton, Sir J. & Lady Hippisley, Sir C. Wheeler, Sir J. & Lady Arundell, Sir L. & Lady Blunden, Sir H.W. Ellis, Adm. Monckton, Gen. Stuart, Lieut.Gen. Gore.
15th February
Earl & Countess of Northesk, Lord & Lady Elliott, Lord & Lady Say and Serle, Lord & Lady Exmouth, Lady Anne Carnegie, Hon. Mrs. Pelham, Hon. Capt. Carleton, Adm. Sir R. Keaton, Sir J. Lethbridge, Sir W. Wynn, Sir A. Hood, Gen. Milner, Adm. Spry.
22nd February
Earl Carysfort, Lord & Lady Ashdown, Lord & Lady Colwell, Lady Amherst, Lady C. Long, Sir J. Smith, Sir V. Vyvyan, Gen. Eden, Gen. Michell, Gen. & Mrs. Cameron.

1st March

Earl & Countess of Northesk, Lord Petre, Lord Hinton, Lady C. Dormsy, Lady & Miss Elford, Sir R. & Lady Bedingfield & family, Sir P. & Lady Halve, Maj.Gen. Sir C. Colville, Adm. Sir I. Coffin, Adm. Sir W. & Lady Effington, Gen. Bateman, Gen. & Mrs. Cameron, Gen. Mackenzie, Gen. Riall.

8th March

Lord & Lady Henniker, Countess de Front, Lady Drummond, Hon. G. Campbell, Hon. Miss Jones, Sir T. Clifford, Sir R. J. Blosse, Sir W. Mansell, Adm. Bury.

15th March

Countess of Suffolk, Lady Exemouth, Lady Tuite, Lady Blarney & family, Hon. Mrs. Turner, Adm. Sir J. Gore, Sir J.H. Williams, Sir T. Bertie, Sir J. Arundell, Sir P. & Lady Baghott, Sir T. Burton, Gen. Riall, Gen. Bateman, Gen. Popham, Gen. Blachford.

22nd March

Earl & Countess of Ormond, Lord Rosehill, Lady Clarke, Lady Thompson, Lady Nepean, Hon. Miss A.M. Roach, Sir R.C. Hoare, Sir J. Framlington, Sir W. Robarts, Sir J. Dumaresq, Gen. Jones, Adm. Bowen.

30th March

Hon. Mrs. Tuson, Hon. Mrs. Bartley, Sir W. Trunton, Sir W. Dunbar, Sir J. Sone, Sir J. Gilpin, Gen. Riall, Rear Adm. Linzee.

5th April

Viscountess Anson, Lady Thompson, Lady Tannton, Marquis de St. Gery, Hon. Mrs. Frankland, Sir O. & Lady Gordon, Sir J. & Lady L. Wren, Adm. Otway.

12th April

Viscount & Viscountess Hawarden & family, Lady Bertie, Lady Colebrooke, Lady Seton, Col. Sir H. Pynn, Sir J. Edgerton, Sir H. Strutchey, Gen. Mutshead.

19th April

Lord Colville, Dowager Lady Abdy, Hon. Mrs. Villiers, Hon. Mrs. Roche, Sir A. Cathcart, Sir H. Pine.

26th April

Sir J. & Lady Smith, Sir S. Smith, Sir A. Hood, Sir F. Vane, Gen. St. Leger, Gen. Riall.

3rd May
Hon. Mrs. Frankland, Hon. Mrs. Fellowes, Sir R. Hankey, Sir W. Stretchey, Sir G. & Lady Jenningham, Sir W. Paxton, Maj.Gen. Sir C. Wale, Baron D'Anheim.
10th May
Lady Hunloke, Hon. Col. & Miss Knollis, Sir R. Crawford, Gen. Riall, Adm. Holloway, Vice Adm, Wolsely.
17th May
Marchioness of Exeter, Lord Colville, Lady Ferguson & family, Hon. Mrs. Yorke, Sir J. Radcliffe, Sir H. Smith.
24th May
Lord Cranston, Lady Drummond, Hon. Mr. & Mrs. Leeson, Hon. Mrs. Sewell, Sir J. Lethbridge, Sir J. Seaton, Sir J. & Lady Aubrey, Gen. Jones, Gen. T.M. Hopkins, Adm. Young.
31st May
Lady E. Keith, Hon. J.C. Maude, Hon. Mr. Howard, Gen. Sir Thomas Picton, Sir H. Pine, Sir P. Baghot, Chevalier de Tinseau, Maj.Gen. & Mrs. Lethbridge.

7th June
Countess de Caviliac, Vice Adm. Sir W. & Lady Hargood, Sir H. Smyth, Gen. & Mrs. Hopkins, Adm. Clement.
14th June
Dowager Duchess of Beaufort, Lord de Clifford, Lady Smythe, Lady C. West, Hon. R. Plunkett, Sir A. Elton, Sir W. A'Court, Sir R. C. Hoare, Gen. Grant, Maj.Gen. Richardson, Adm. Murray.
21st June
Lady Thompson, Lady Brabazon, Hon. Col., Mrs. & Miss Warneford, Sir F. Ford, Sir J. Bayly, Sir W. Ousley, Sir S. & Lady Northcote, Sir P. Baghott, Gen. & Mrs. Mitchell & family, Gen. Wyndham, Maj.Gen. & Mrs. Richardson, Adm. Domett.

28th June
Lord Clare, Lady Gordon, Hon. Mrs. Tuson, Sir C. Wale, Sir J. Stewart, Sir J. Heard, Sir J. Hawkins, Gen. Potts, Gen. Whittingham.

5th July
Marquis Cornwallis, Earl & Countess of Cork & family, Countess Dalton, Lord & Lady Strangeford, Lord Poyning, Hon. Mrs. Roch & family, Sir C. Cole, Sir J. & Lady Gray & family, Gen. Monro, Gen. Grenville.

12th July
Dowager Lady Strangford, Lady Somers, Lady C. Lemon, Sir R. & Lady Baker, Sir T. Stile, Sir W. & Lady Drummond, Vice Adm. Sir W. Domett.
19th July
Lady Petre, Hon. Rev. Mr. Turnour, Hon. Mrs. Tuson, Sir W. Cole, Sir V. Vyvyan, Gen. Murray.
26th July
Countess of Kingston, Lady E. Smith, Sir W. Cole, Sir J. C. & Lady Hippisley, Lieut.Gen. E. Barnes

2nd **August**
Lord & Lady Sunderland, Sir R. & Lady Blosse, Adm. Holloway.
9th August
Marquis of Salisbury, Count St. Autenin, Sir R. & Lady Price & family, Sir J. Aubrey, Sir F. Falkiner, Sir S. Baghott, Sir J.C. & Lady Hippisley, Sir S. Wathen, Lieut.Gen. & Mrs. Leighton, Maj.Gen. Baynes.
16th August
Hon. Col, M'Mahon, Hon. Mr. Brock, Hon. S. Wathen, Hon. J. Preston, Sir W. Acland, Maj.Gen. & Mrs. Goldie, Adm. Aylmer.
23rd August
Bishop of Hereford & family, Lord S.G. Osborne, Lady Trimleston, Lady O'Brien, Count de Funchall, Hon. Mrs. Allen, Hon. Mrs. York, Hon. Miss Douglas, Sir A. Flinn, Sir R. Wilmott, Sir J. Fuller, Gen. Morris, Gen. S. King.
30th August
Hon. J. Browne, Sir Hugh & Lady Bateman, Sir P. Baghott, Sir C. Morgan & Family.

6th **September**
Earl of Pembroke, Viscount & Viscountess DuDrisnay, Lord Elliot, Count Woronzow, Countess of Galloway, Countess Ballien, Lady Wilson, Lady Bingham, Sir F. Millman, Sir J. Sewell, Sir W.H. Cowes, Sir S. Whitcombe???, Gen. Sir C.Green, Gen. Long.
13th September
Earl Cowper, Sir J. Fitzgerald, Sir T. Dallas, Sir W. A'Court, Sir W. Browne, Sir R. Baster.
20th September
Duke of Devonshire, Marquis & Marchioness of Worcester, Earl & Countess of Jersey, Earl & Countess Cowper, Earl of Rochford, Viscount

Carleton, Viscount Granville, Lord & Lady Granville Somerset, Lady Stanley, Lady Coote, Sir J. & Lady Gordon, Sir E. Synge, Gen. Morrison

27th September

Lady Horton, Lady Hodson, Hon. Mrs. Grimstone, Sir R. A. Hodson, Gen. Garnstin, Gen. Cunningham, Maj.Gen de Rottenburgh, Adm. Murray.

4th **October**

Earl & Countess of Darnley, Sir W. & Lady Wolseley, Sir W. & Lady Watson, Sir C. Bampfylde, Sir H. Smith, Gen. & Mrs. Browne, Gen. Moore, Gen Brook.

11th October

Viscount Hood, LadyWilson, Sir P. Baghott, Sir A. & Lady Hood, Adm. Sir H. & Lady Trollope, Adm. Aylmer, Gen. Dunkin, Gen. & Mrs. Dickson.

18th October

Marquis of Bath, Earl of Cork, Viscount Weymouth, Lord & Lady J. Thynne, Lord Henry Thynne, Lady Isabella Thynne, Hon. G. Pellew, Hon. F. Pellew, Sir R & Lady Salisbury, Sir J. Mansfield & family, Sir S. & Lady Shepherd, Adm. Sir W. Young, Adm. Bowen & family, Gen. Bell.

25th October

Lord R. Spencer, Lady Hawarden, Lady T. Hale, Lady Stanley, Lady Stewart, Hon. Mr. Strange, Judge Osborne, Maj.Gen. & Mrs. Horsford, Rear Adm. & Mrs. Bedford, Rear Adm. Monckton.

1st **November**

Viscount Chetwynd, Hon. Miss Chetwynd, Sir W. Barker, Sir R. Crawford, Sir W. & Lady Wynne, Sir W. Struth, Sir T. & Lady Clifford, Sir W., Lady & Miss Richardson, Sir J. & Lady Fitzgerald, Maj.Gen. Sir W. Inglis, Count de Funchall, Gen. Lightburne, Lieut.Gen. Dunn, Lieut.Gen. Daubeny, Rear Adm. & Mrs. Clemens.

8th November

Lord & Lady Henniker, Lady R. Spencer, Lady C. Herbert, Countess De Camiliac, Hon. Col. Knollis, Gen. Sir William, Lady & Miss Cockburn, Sir A. Elton, Sir C. & Lady Chalmers, Sir C. Wheeler, Sir R. Hankey, Sir W. Stewart, Sir T. Stepney, Sir G. Martin, Gen., Mrs. & Miss Pure.

15th November

Lord Bolingbroke, Lord James O'Brien, Lady Bingham, lady C. Well, Hon. Maj. Digby, Lieut.Gen. Sir J. Abercrombie, Adm. Sir G. Collier, Sir

H. Strachey, Sir H. M'Leon, Sir T. & Lady Agar, Gen. Lee, Gen. Bradshaw.

23rd November

Lord Gwydir, Lord Adare, Count & Countess Darmio, Lady C. Hoare, Lady T. Hale, Lady Williamson, Dowager Lady Haywarden, Adm. Sir W. Young, Sir G. Williams, Sir H. Fletcher, Sir S. Hood, Sir S. Wathen, Lieut.Gen. Campbell, Maj.Gen. Marriott & family.

29th November

Lord Henniker, Lord R. Spencer, Count D'Escars, Hon. W. Lumley, Sir J. Cotterell, Sir R. & Lady Milnes, Sir E. Baillie, Sir W. Young, Gen. J. Lee. Gen. Layard, Lieut.Gen. & Mrs. Drummond, Adm. Bowen.

6th **December**

Earl of Caernarvon, Lord Bishop of Clogher, Lord & Lady Aylmer, Lord Hawarden, 2 Ladies Herbert, Lady Call, Princess Tallyrand, Sir J & Lady Cradock, Sir P. Baghott, Gen. Ambrose, Maj.Gen. Macauley

13th December

Countess of Shaftsbury & family, Lady Clunbrock, Lady Glade, Sir R.C. Hoare, Sir S. Craddock, Sir G. Martin, Capt. Sir E. Stanhope, Gen. Bateman, Maj.Gen & mrs Brooke.

20th December

Duke & Duchess of Somerset, Earl Bathurst, Earl & Countess of Cork, Lord Seymour, Lady M.A. Sturt, Hon. Mrs. Cockayne, Hon. Miss Elphinstone, Sir B. Hobhouse.

27th December

Lady E. Fane, Lady T. Hales, Lady Johnstone, Sir G.O. Paul, Sir A. Agnew, Sir J. Scott, Sir H. Lippincott, Sir J. & Lady Morris, Maj.Gen. & Mrs. Peachy, Maj.Gen. Ambrose.

1816

3rd **January**

Lord S. Chichester, Hon. Col. Lillie, Hon. Mrs. Hall, Sir W. Brabazon, Sir H. Maclean, Sir P. Baghott, Sir G.A. Stephen?.

11th January

Earl & Countess of Cork, Countess of Buckinghamshire, Bishop of Norwich, Lord Tara, Lady Pollen, Lady M. Trotter, Hon, Mrs. Bourne, Sir W. Cunningham, Sir F. Ford, Sir M. Williamson, Gen. Doveton, Maj.Gen. Skinner, Adm. Nicholls.

17th January

Bishop of Salisbury, Countess of Galloway, Lord & Lady Audley, Lady Carnegie, Maj.Gen. Sir W. Peacock, Sir A. Agnew, Sir T & Lady Shelley & family, Adm. Monckton.

24th January

Viscountess Galway, Sir W. Roberts, Maj.Gen. Sir W. Dunbar, Maj.Gen. Sir Manley Power, Gen, McLean, Gen. Grant.

31st January

Lord & Lady Tara, Lady & Miss Tyler, Sir H. Lambert, Sir S. Whitcombe, Sir J. Ramsey, Sir E. & Lady O'Connor, Sir A. Agnew, Sir M. Blackstone, Sir W. Wynne.

7th **February**

Earl & Countess of Cork, Baroness Howe, Lady Anstruther, Lady Curvine, Hon. Mr. Barnewell, Sir J. C. Hippisley, Sir I. Polk, Sir W. Waller, Sir W. Wilmot & family, Sir T. Brisbane.

14th February

Lady Gardiner, Lady Drummond, Sir W. Cunningham, Sir H. & Lady Carew, Sir J.C. Hippisley, Sir P. Baghott, Adm. Sir W. Domett, Gen. & Mrs. Johnson, Gen. Pathers, Adm. Spry.

21st February

Lord Ousley, Lady Ford, Lady Tyler, Sir J. D., Lady & Miss D. Hay, Sir W. Roberts, Sir W. Brahighm, Gen. Molyneux, Gen. Mitchell.

28th February

Duke of Richmond, Earl & Countess of Cork, Lord Hawarden, Lady & Miss Place, Sir W. Macartney, Sir G. & Lady Wellbrook, Sir T. Gifford, Sir P. Baghott, Sir J. C., Lady & Miss Hippisley, Adm. Spry.

6th **March**

Earl Manvers, Lady Shelly, Sir J., Lady & 3 Misses Hamlyn Williams,

Sir W. Brabazon, Sir W. & Lady Gordon, Gen. Blackford.

13th March

Earl & Countes of Northesk, Earl Poulett, Lady A. Carnegie, Lady E. Carnegie, Lady Tyler, Lady Smith, Hon. Mrs. Puson, Sir W. Roberts, Sir P. Baghott, Sir J. Ferguson, Sir ? & lady & Miss Saumerez, Gen. Scott, Gen. Fuller.

20th March

Lady P. Lindsay, Lady Delancey, Hon. Mr. & 3 Misses Coventry, Sir R.C. Hoare, Sir T. Arthbutnot, Sir H. Smyth, Gen. Orr, Gen., Mrs. & Miss Despard, Gen., Mrs. & Miss Dalrymple, Rear Adm. & Mrs. Wilkinson.

27th March

Lady M. Trotter & family, Lady C. West, Sir R. Blosse, Sir G.O. Paul, Sir W. Bruce, Sir W. & Lady Struth, Sir P. Baghott, Adm. Kempe.

3rd **April**

Lady Pearson, Hon. Mr. Gunter, Sir A. Catheart.

10th April

Lord Chief Justice Gibbs, Lord Kensington, Lord Kingsborough, Lady Pollen, Lady Wynn, Hon. Mr. Montague, Sir J. Maclean, Sir R & Lady Waller, Sir J. Hay, Sir H. Massey, Sir P. Baghott, Gen. Ryall.

17th April

Lord Hill, Lady F. Bentinck, Lady Mount Sandford, Lady Harland, Hon. B. Cochrane, Hon. Col. De Courcy, Sir J. Fisher, Sir W. Hamilton.

24th April

Lady Hamilton, Sir J. Gore, Sir J. Wilson, Sir J. Forbes, Lieut.Gen. & Mrs. Hopkins.

1st **May**

Lady Somerville, Lady O'Brien, Lady Kingsmill, Sir J. & Lady Fellowes, Gen. O'Meara.

8th May

Lady Clancarty, Lady Smith, Lady H. Drummond, Lady Welch, Hon. Mr. Fitzwilliam, Hon. Mr. Pellew, Sir J. Farquharson, Sir W. Ouseley, Adm. & Mrs. Linzee.

15th May

Lord Bishop of Bath and Wells, Hon. Mr. Chichester, Sir G. Williams, Sir R. Crawford, Sir W. Elford, Sir W. Cunningham, Gen. Cliffe, Adm. Kempe, Governor, Mrs. & Miss Craven.

22nd May
Countess of Fingal, Countess Dalton, Lord Killeen, Lady Carr, Lady H. Plunkett, Lady A. Trenchard, Hon. Mrs. Pelham, Hon. Mrs. Eld, Hon. Mrs. Trevelyan, Hon. Miss E. Smythe, Sir A. Elton, Sir P. Baghott, Adm. Sir Charles, Lady & Miss Tyler, Adm. & Mrs. Linsey, Gen. Morrison, Gen. Lightburn.
29th May
Lord Bishop of Cashel, Lady Oakeley, Sir C.& Lady Blois, Sir G. Tapps, Sir J. C. Hippisley, Adm. Sir W. Domett, Adm. & Mrs. Young, Maj.Gen. G. Brown.

5th **June**
Lady Smith, Rt. Hon. G. Canning, Hon. Mrs. Yorke, Sir J.H. Williams, Sir R & Lady Vaughan, Adjutant-General Maillard.
12th June
Hon. Mr. J. Coventry, Sir M. & Lady Bilbury & family, Sir P. Baghott, Sir H. Smith, Sir C. Mordaunt.
19th June
Duke of Buccleugh, Lady C. Fitzgerald, Hon. R. Plunkett, Sir Henry, Lady & Miss Cosby, Sir C. Murnaun? Gen. Dickson.
26th June
Lord G. Stuart, Lady E. Burnett, Sir W. A'Court, Sir W. Payne, Sir S. Watkins, Sir H. Smith, Adm. Luke.

3rd **July**
Duke of Gordon, Duke of Buccleugh, Marquis of Salisbury, Marquis Cornwallis, Countess of Shaftsbury, Lord Bravbrook, Lord Glastonbury, Lady Baring & family, Hon. Mrs. Tuson, Sir W. Maclin, Gen. Grenville.
10th July
Lord Bishop of Bath and Wells, Lady E. Trenchard, Hon. W. Dundas, Sir R. Crawford, Sir P. Baghott, Sir W. Roberts, Lieut.Gen. Elliott, Rear Adm, Clemens.
17th July
Countess of Cork, Lady Sherborne, Sir W. & Lady Drummond, Sir G. Pownall, Gen. Kerr
24th July
Countess of Loudon and Moira, Lord & Lady Lisle & family, Lady Hood, Lady Searldale, Lady Carr, Gen. Farrington.
31st July
Earl & Countess of Waldegrave & family, Marquis de Corberon, Marquis

de Sommery. La Viscomtesse de Sourches, Lady Somerville, Lady K. Stewart, Hon. Mr. Fitzwilliam, Sir J. Dumaresq, Sir R. Vaughan, Adm. Holloway & family, Adm. Wolseley

7th **August**

Lord & Lady Leslie, Lady Carnegie, Sir Hugh Smith, Sir J. Gore, Sir P. Baghott, Gen. Bingham, Gen. Cook, Liut.Gen. & Mrs. Leighton.

14th August

Countess Waldergrave, Sir A. Gladstanes, Sir S. Wathen, Sir H. Smith, Sir H. Russell & family, Maj.Gen. & Lady C. Moore.

21st August

Lord & Lady Thornton, Lady Saxton, Lady Hunter, Sir J.D. & Lady Fowler, Sir F. Naysmith, Sir W. Herchell[4], General Farringdon, Adm. Vashon.

28th August

Countess of Shaftsbury, Lady Bolton, Sir H. Smith

4th **September**

Lord Vernon, Lord Bishop of Lichfield, Lady B. Ponsonby, Lady Mary Ann Sturt, Sir R. Hoare.

11th September

Sir Jas. & Lady Fitzgerald, Lady O'Brien, Hon. Mr. & Mrs. Fitzwilliam, Count Christian Wyman, Sir C. Baynes, Sir Benj. & Lady Hobhouse & family.

18th September

Duc & Duchess of Orleans, Earl of Clare, Lord Calthorpe, Lord Colville, Hon. Mrs. Yorke, Sir R. Wilmot, Sir W. Herschell, Gen. Richardson, Gen. Rooke.

25th September

Earl & Countess Waldegrave, Lord & Lady Scarsdale, Lady Elizabeth Cavanac, Hon. Miss Wood, Sir G. Paul, Sir P. Baghott, Sir Albert & Lady Gladstanes, Maj.Gen. & Mrs. Coming, Don J. Piedra, Baron Varasell.

2nd **October**

Countess of Kilkenny, Lord Rochford, Lady B. Ponsonby, Sir G. Collier, Lieut.Gen. & Mrs. M'Farlane.

9th October

[4] Properly Herschell, the famous astronomer who lived at 19 New King St, Bath where he discovered Uranus. He also wrote music.

Lord Newport, Lady A. Boyce, Lady Keith, Adm. Sir T. Bertie, Adm. Sir W. & Lady Hargood, Sir J. Gore, Sir T. Lethbridge, Sir J. Poole, Sir H & Lady Davy[5], Gen. & Mrs. Dickson, Lieut.Gen. & Mrs. Dunn, Dean of Ely, Dean of Raphoe.

16th October

Marquis of Bath, Earl & Countess of Cork, Lord & Lady J. Thynne, Lady L. Boyle, Lady & Miss Thompson, Lady Sullivan, Count C. Wymon, Gen. Sir W. & Lady Cockburn, Sir A. Elton, Sir F. Ford, Sir J.C. Hippisley, Rear Adm. & Mrs. Ballard.

23rd October

Earl Waldegrave & family, Lady Glode, Count d'Erlach de Hindelbank, Baron d'Escher Berg, Hon. Mr. Bruce & family, Hon. Mrs. Mortimer Tucker, Gen. Sir Wm. Aylett, Gen. Bolton, Gen. & Mrs. Hopkins.

30th October

Lady Staines & family, Hon. Rev. J.E. Turnour, Hon. Mr. Noel, Sir E. Antrobus, Sir H. Bruce, Sir J. Mansfield & family, Maj.Gen. Molyneux

6th **November**

Marquis Camden, Countess de Nolle, Lady Riddell, Lady O'Brien, Hon. Mr. & Mrs. Cochrane, Sir E. Tucker, Sir A. Chichester, Sir M & Lady Lopes, Maj.Gen. & Mrs. Goldie, Adm. Young.

13th November

Countess Spencer, Lord Audley, Viscountess Mount Earl, Lady Rivers, Lady Horton, Baron Often, Sir Wm. Barker, Sir J. Gifford, Sir G. Williams, Sir S. Humphries, Gen. Morgan.

20th November

Earl of Portsmouth, Lord Bishop of Bath And Wells & lady, Lord Sidmouth, Lord O'Brien, Lady Lethbridge, Sir G. Paul, Sir S, Wathen, Sir Thomas & Lady Baring & family.

27th November

Hon Mrs. E. Turnour, Sir N. Peacock, Gen. Popham, Gen. Buchan, Gen. Chowde, Gen. Morshead, Gen. Ambrose, Adm. Gordon.

4th **December**

Lord Gwydir, Dowager Lady Lethbridge, Sir E. Stanhope, Sir P. Baghott, Sir J. Clifford, Sir Jas. Fitzgerald.

11th December

[5] Sir Humphrey Davy disputed inventor of the Davy Lamp which made mining safer and who lived under the odium of having discovered sodium.

Lady Jervis, Hon. Mr. Grey, Hon. Mrs. Cockayne, Sir W. A'Court, Sir F. Ford, Sir A. Chichester, Sir W., Lady & Miss Wolseley, Col. Sir N. Campbell, Gen. & Mrs. Drummond.

18th December

Earl of Cork, Lord O'Brien, Lady Tuite, Lady Flamborough, Hon. Capt. Agar, Sir G. Powell, Sir J.C. Hippisley, Rev. Sir C. Rich, Gen. Gascoigne & family, Lieut.Gen. & Mrs. M'Neale, Maj.Gen. Rudyard.

25th December

Lord Chief Justice Gibbs, Lord Wodehouse, Lord, Lady & Miss Henniker, Countess Lucan, Lady L. Lennox, Lady Ford & family, Vice Adm. Sir Edw., Lady & Miss Bulter, Sir B. Wrey, Sir W. & Lady Struth, Sir E. Stanhope, Sir J. Gifford, Sir G. Drummond, Sir C. Blunt.

1817

1st **January**
Earl Grey, Lady E. Fane, Lady Wodehouse, Lady Charlotte & Mr. Ram & family, Hon. W. Dundas, Hon. Mr. Seymour, Sir W. & Lady Leighton, Sir R.A, Alleyne, Baron Witilper, Gen Walker & family.
8th January
Marquis of Exeter, Lord & Lady Bacon, Lord Cecil, Lady Butler, Lady Pollen, Hon. W. Cuit, Hon. Mr. Caulfield, Sir G. Williams, Sir E. Stanhope, Sir C. Blunt, Gen. J. Buchan, Maj.Gen. & Mrs. Kerstman & family.
15th January
Lady Glode, Dowager Lady Hearne, Hon. Mr. Moor, Hon. Capt. Carleton, Sir J. Gore, Sir R. & Lady Liston, Gen. Boswell & family, Lieut.Gen. Dalrymple.
22nd January
Baron de Arabotm Lady Elford, Hon. S. Curzon, Hon. Miss Broderick, Adm. Sir G. Montague, Rear Adfm Sir J. Gore, Vice Adm. Sir W, Domiett, Vice Adm. Sir J & Lady Morris, Capt. Sir J. R. Eustace, Sir J. Carmichael, Sir C. Dalrymple, Sir W. Cunningham, Gen. Poyntz, Lieut.Gen. Croible.
29th January
Marquis & Marchioness of Bath, Countess of Germaine, Count Zenobie, Lady Elton, Lady Wodehouse, Lady A'Court, Hon. B. & Mrs. Cochrane, Maj.Gen. Sir G. Calcraft, Vice Adm. Sir W. Hotham, Sir W. Carroll, Gen. Munro, Gen. Vincent, Lieut.Gen. Broderick, Maj.Gen. Elliot, Adm. Young & family.

5th **February**
Maj.Gen. Hon. James Ramsay, Hon. W. Noel, Hon. D. Carleton, Hon. Mrs. Browne, Sir W. Elford, Sir P. Baghot, Gen. Robinson, Gen. Barry, Lieut.Gen. & Mrs. Cameron, Lieut.Gen. Michel, Maj. Gen. & Miss Dyer.
12th February
Countess of Cork, Sir E. Stanhope, Sir G. Eyre, Sir D. Hill, Maj.Gen. Sir W. Inglis.
19th February
Earl & Countess of Northesk, Lady Anne Carnegie, Lady E. Carnefie, Sir P. Blount, Sir J.C. Hippisley, Sir L. Williams, Gen. Sir Chas. Hastings.

5th March

Baron Nicolai, Lord Chief Baron, Lord Colville, Lord Hinton, Bishop of Quebec, Lady Smith, Lady Own, Sir C. Colville, Sir W. Congreve, Sir L. Otway, Sir O. Gordon, Vice Adm. Manley, Rear Adm. Spranger.

12th March

Countess of Ely, Sir C. & Lady Chadd & family, Sir P.,Lady & Miss Hales, Sir J. Gifford, Sir R. Grierion, Sir D. De Burgh, Gen. Ord, Maj.Gen. & Mrs. Peachy.

19th March

Earl & Countess of Cork, Lord Bishop of Gloucester, Lady Horton, Sir W. Williams, Sir H. Smith, Sir P. Baghott, Sir G. Collier, Sir T,& Lady Blosse, Maj.Gen. Buchan.

26th March

Countess Caledon, Hon. Mrs. Bearde, Maj.Gen. Sir W. Peacocke

2nd April

Earl of Hardwicke, Earl & Countess of Waldegrave, Archbishop of Tuam, Lord Chief Justice Gibbes, Lord Clifton, Sir W. & Lady Lennon & family, Sir J. Buchan.

9th April

Marquis of Bath, Earl of Liverpool, Earl of Galloway, Viscount Weymouth, Lord J. Thynne, Lady C. West, Lord Mayor of London, Sir G. Paul, Sir J. Montgomery.

16th April

Earl of Digby, Lord & Lady Castlecoote, Sir J. Shaw, Sir A. Elton, Sir E. Singer, Gen. Dalrymple, Gen. & Mrs. Popham, Gen. M'Creach, Maj.Gen. Adams, Adm. Holloway, Adm. Young, Rear Adm. & Mrs. Wilkinson.

23rd April

Earl Powis, Lord Chief Justice Gibbs, Lady T. Hales, Sir H. Smith, Sir R. & Lady Kemys, Sir E. Stanhope, Sir W. Domett.

30th April

Countess St Martin de Trout, Sir T. Cochrane, Sir W. Elford.

7th May

Duke of Dorset, Bishop of Hereford, Hon. & Rev. M. Mahon & family, Sir J. Thomas, Sir A. Cathcart, Sir J. & Lady Radcliffe, Sir. G. Paul.

14th May

Countess of Shaftsbury, Sir A., Lady & Miss Wood, Sir E. & Lady Hartopp.

21st May

Lord Hill, Lady Scott, Hon. Mr. Coventry & family, Hon. R. Eyre, Hon. Capt. Noel, Hon. Mrs. G. Noel, Sir W. Bruce, Sir T. Clifford, Sir G. Noel, Adm. & Mrs. Dilkes.

4th **June**

Earl & Countess of Cork, Sir G.E. Leeds, Sir H. Smith, General Reid, Adm. Kempe, Dean of Gloucester & family.

11th June

Countess of Bellamont, Lord Rivers, Lady Hanmer, Lady Dashwood, Hon. Mr. & Mrs. Quin, Sir A. Elton, Lieut.Gen. Blackman, Adm. Spry.

18th June

Marquis of Salisbury, Earl of Cork, Lady Scott, Lady Holmes, Sir D. Baird, Sir G. Noel, Adm. Caldwell

25th June

Earl of De Lawar, Hon. Mr. Percival, Hon. Mr. Coventry, Sir H. Bateman, Sir W. Elliott.

2nd **July**

Earl of Manvers, Lady & the Misses A'Court, Hon. D. Massy, Hon. Miss Edgar, Sir R. C. Hoare, Sir T. Frankland, Gen. Sir W. Aylett, Gen. Dunn, Gen. Campbell.

9th July

Viscount Beauchamp, Lady Turner, Hon.Capt. Agar, Sir G. Noel, *Sirs* J. Carnegie, R. Williams, J. Cope, P. & Lady Hull, H. Stracey, Adm. Spry, Adm. & 3 Misses Otway, Gen. Walker.

16th July

Viscount Molesworth, Lord & Lady Robert Seymour, Hon. Mr. Arundel, Hon. J. Coventry, Hon. Mrs. Everard, Sir H. Smith.

23rd July

Viscount & Viscountess Exmouth, Lady Blount, Lady L. Cadogan, Sir J.C. & Lady Hippisley, Sir J. Dalrymple, Sir Edw. Baker & family, Adm Young.

30th July

Gen. Marriott

6th **August**

Earl of Hardwick, Viscountess Pollington, Sir G. Pocock, Sir J. Pollen, Sir R. George, Adm. Sir J. Beresford, Maj.Gen. & Mrs. Rudyard.

13th August

The Portuguese Ambassador & Suite, Sir A. Campbell, Adm. Ballard.

20th August
Lady A. Forbes, Sir W. & Lady Herschell
27th August
Marquis & Marchioness of Ely, Earl of Hardwick, Lord Sherbourne, Lord Rivers, Lord Aylmer, Lady Pollington, Lady J. Hair, Hon. Mr. Dutton, Hon. Mrs. Yorke, Sir G. Graham.

3rd **September**
Hon. Mrs. Brooks, Sir. H. Strachey
10th September
Marquis & Marchioness of Bath, Marquis & Marchioness of Ely, Lord Rivers, Bishop of Clonsort with Lady, Sir A. Bertie, Sir E. Wingate, Sir H. Dashwood, Sir W. Bruce, Sir G. & Lady Nugent & family, Sir A. Gladstanes, Rev. Sir A. Elton, Gen. Popham, Gen. Charlton, Lieut.Gen. & Mrs. Leighton, Adm. Christie.
17th September
Marquis of Lansdown, Lord Bruce, Lord Weymouth, Lord & Lady Egerton, Lady Raffles, Ladies J. & E. Thynne.
24th September
Lord & Lady Ebrington, Lord & Lady Ducie, Lord & Lady Arden, Hon. Mr. Carleton, Hon. Misses Perceval, Sir W. Bruce, Adm. Mrs. Christie & family.

1st **October**
Earl & Countess of Waldegrave, Lord Clare, Lord Lawton, Lady Reade, Lady Cottolt?, Sir J. Murray, Sir J. Reade, Sir S. Homfrey, Gen. Read.
8th October
Sir H. Carew, Sir Jas. & Lady Ratclyffe, Rev. Sir A. Elton.
15th October
Marquis of Bath, Lord J. Thynne, Lord Somerville, Lord Apsley, Lady A'Court, Sir F. Shuckburgh, Maj.Gen. Raymond.
22nd October
Earl & Countess of Waldegrave, Lord Chief Justice & Lady Gibbes, Lady C. & Miss Long, Lady Prevost & family, Lady Graham, Gen. Sir W. & Lady Cockburn, Gen. Sir T.W. Stubbs, Sir C. Bampfylde, Sir B. De Burgh, Sir L. & Lady Palk.
29th October
Earl & Countess of Cork, Earl of Carnarvon, Countess Nugent, Lady L. Boyle, Lady Williams, Lady Jervis, Hon. Maj. Cochrane, Adm. Sir W. & Lady Hargood, Adm. Sir W. Younge, Sir H. & Lady Carew, Sir G,

Ousely, Sir T. Shirley, Sir Chas. Hastings, Gen. Holdham, Maj.Gen. Travers.

5th **November**

Her Most Gracious Majesty the Queen, His RH the Duke of Clarence, Her RH the Princess Elizabeth.

Marquis Camden, Earl & Lady Poulett, Lord J. Thynne, Lord G. Thynne, Lord Colville, Lady Staines & family, Hon. Col. & Miss Knollis, Hon. B. Plunkett, Hon. Mrs. Brown, Hon. Miss Broderick, Gen. Sir H. & Lady Dalrymple, Maj.Gen. Sir W. Inglis, Sir H. & Lady Bateman, Sir W, & Lady Watson, Sir J. Perring, Sir C. Greville, Sir J. Fitzgerald, Sir G, Drummond, Sir W. Wynn, Sir T. Crawley, Sir W, Richardson, Sir W. & Lady Struth, Sir J. Trevelyan, Adm. Macnamara.

12th November

Marquis of Bath, Viscount & Viscountess Anson, Viscount Weymouth, Viscount Molesworth, Rt.Hon. Lady Trimleaton, Lady Ford & family, Hon.Capt. & Mrs. Poulett, Sir A. Elton, Sir H. Strachey, Sir P, Baghott, Sir J.W. & Lady Smith, Maj.Gen. & Mrs. Goldie, Maj.Gen. Bateman, Adm. Otway & family, Vice Adm. Robinson, Rear Adm. Taylor, Rear Adm. Ballard.

19th November

Lady J. Turnour, Lady C, Thynne, the Ladies Stanhope, Dowager Lady Selsey, Sir W. & Lady Barker, Sir C. & Lady Chadel & family, Hon.Col. Brown, Hon.W. & Lady E. Campbell, Hon.Maj. Murray.

26th November

Her Most Gracious Majesty the Queen, His RH the Duke of Clarence, Her RH the Princess Elizabeth.

Countess of? Elchester, Countess of Melville, Lord & Lady De Clifford, Lady A. Forbes, Lady T. Hale, Lady Morrison, Hon. Mrs. Strange, Maj.Gen. Sir W. Inglis, Sir Alex. Wilson, Sir James Graham.

3rd **December**

Dowager Marchioness of Bath, Earl & Countess of Cork, Earl & Countess of Ely, Earl of Winchelsea, Bishop of Gloucester, Lord & *Ladies* G. Tayane, C. Thynne, L. Boyle, J. Hall, Elton; Hon.Capt. & Mrs. Poulett, Hon. Mrs. Cockayne, Hon. Mrs. Holland, Hon. Mrs. Forbes, Hon. Miss Maddey, Sir Henry, Lady & Miss Halford, *Sirs* C. & Lady ?Codcington, H. Strachey, A. O. & Lady Molesworth, R. & Lady Vaughan, R. & Lady Joddrell, H. Choton, H. Carew, Gen. Dickson, Gen.

Merrick, Lieut.Gen. M'Neill, Maj.Gen. Hutchinson, Adm. Otway, Adm. Holloway.

10th December

Earl of Shaftsbury, Earl & Countess of Waldegrave, Lord & Lady J. Thynne, Lord Weymouth, Lady A'Court, 3 Ladies Cooper, Lady Sullivan & family, Lady ???, Rt. Hon. The Chancellor of the Exchequer, Sir W. Richardson, Sir H. Malpas, Sir R. Peel, Sir E. & Lady Elmsall, Sir H. Matthews, Sir F. Baker, Sir J. Boyd.

17th December

Earl of Caernarvon, Earl & Countess of Cork, Lord Arundel, Lady Wynn, Hon.&Rev. Mr. Peachey, Hon.Capt. Pellew, Sir F. & Lady Hardett, *Sirs* W. Kemp, J. Evans, C. Rich, T.& Lady Lethbridge, J. & Lady Scott, Rev. Sir C. Rich, Gen. Ambrose, Gen. Milner, Lieut.Gen Meyrick, Lieut.Gen & Mrs. N. Hopkins, Commissioner Boyle.

24th December

Duchess of Marlborough, Lord Gwydir, Dowager Lady Smith, Sir T., Lady & Miss Shelley, Sir C. B. Godrington & family, Sir W. Richardson, Sir W. Kempt, Sir R., Lady & Miss Gresley, Sir G. Sitwell, Adm. Otway.

31st December

Earl Rivers, Lord Hill, Lady Sydney, Lady E. Fane, Hon. Mrs. P. Fraser, *Sirs* C. Hastings, Alex. & Lady Hood, W. Brabazon, C. Blunt, Gen. Eden, Lieut.Gen. Michell.

1818

7th **January**
Earl & Countess of Cork, Lord Weymouth, Lord J. Thynne, Hon. Mr. & Mrs. Bridgeman & family, Sir G. C???, Sir J. Pollen, Sir J. Boyd
14th January
Marquis of Ormond, Lady Jones, Lady Willoughby, Lady De Clifford, Hon.Capt. Noel, Rev. Sir T.C. Miller.
21st January
Bishop of Bath And Wells, Bishop of Bangor, Earl & Countess of Cork & family, Lady Pollen, Lieut.Gen. Sir H. Cosby, Adm. Sir J. Galpass. Sir F. Shuckburgh, Sir W. Ball, Adm. Bowen, Gen. Orr, Lieut.Gen. Milner, Maj.Gen. Walker.
28th January
Lord De Clifford, Dowager Lady Brownlow, Lady Forbes, Lady A. Place, Hon.Capt. & Miss Castle, Lady A, Sir J. Evans, Sir J. & Lady Radcliffe, Sir H. & Lady Davie.

4th **February**
Lord Bishop of Bath And Wells, Lord & Lady Arundel, Lord Clare, Lady Backley, Lady Le Despencer, Sir J.R. Eustace, Sir W. Brabazon, Sir J.R. Ximenes, Gen. Garston.
11th February
Countess Molyneux & family, Lord & Lady Henniker, Dowager Lady Cope, Hon.Rev. E. Rice, Sir J. Kemp, Sir A. Brice, Sir B. Codrington & family, Sir A. Birch, Sir W. Methuen, Sir J.F. & Lady Smith, Dean of Tuam.
18th February
Marquis Thomond, Countess of Cork, Lord Hay, Lady ???? ????, Lady L. Cadogan, Lady L. Morrison, Lady J. King, Hon. Mrs. Bridgeman, Sir G. & Lady Nugent, Sir J. Boyd, Sir J. Scott, Sir W. R???, Sir J. Tompkins, Gen.Nichols, Rear Adm, ???, Rear Adm. Spranger.
25th February
Baroness Le Despencer, Dowager Lady Rivers, Lady Gardiner & family, Hon. Rev. E. Rice, Hon. Mrs. Frankland, Sir F. Baker, Sir J. Pollen, Gen. Sir H. White, Gen. & Mrs. Morelay.

4th **March**
Lord Dynevor, Lady Lee, Hon.& Rev. R. Cust, Sir F. Henniker, Sir J. Boyd, Sir G. Paul.

11th March

Earl of Northesk, Lady Otway, Dowager Lady Smith, Hon. Mrs. Magenis, Hon. Mrs. Bridgeman, Sir P., Lady & Miss Hales

18th March

Duchess of Leeds, Earl & Countess of Cork, Earl of Harrowby, Lord & Lady Clinton, Lady Vaughan, Ladies M. & G. Ryder, Hon. Mrs. H. Fane, Hon. Mr. Eliott, Sir L. & Lady Otway, Sir R. Crawford, Vice Adm.Sir E Buller, Adm. & Miss Spry.

25th March

Lady Rodney, Lady Hamilton, Lady Jones, Lady & Miss Buller, Hon. & Rev. C. Glyn, Adm. Sir I. Coffin, Sir H. N. Lumsden, Sir W. Gomm, Adm., Mrs. & Miss Holloway, Adm. Woolley, Gen. Orr, Gen. Maitland, Gen. Merrick.

1st **April**

Marquis de Sommery & family, Sir T.B. Lethbridge, Sir W. Brabazon, Sir J. Majoribanks, Sir J. Simeon, Sir T. Ramsay, Rear Adm. &Mrs. Wilkinson.

8th April

Lady T. Hale, Sir R. & Lady Gifford, Lieut.Gen. Sir Charles & Lady Colville, Lieut.Gen. & Mrs. Nelson, Lieut.Gen Orr, Maj.Gen. Head.

15th April

Admiral I. Coffin, Sir A. Cathcart, Sir F. Sykes, Sir C. Blunt

22nd April

Marquis of Huntley, Earl & Countess of Cork, Countess of Portsmouth, Viscount & Viscountess Falmouth, Lord Clinton, Lord Colville, Hon. C. Boyle, Sir H. & Lady Mathias, Sir E. Stanhope, Governor Penn, Gen. Bateman, Rear Adm. Linzee.

29th April

Lord & Lady Cawdor, Lady A. Wallope, Lady Falmouth, Hon. V. Gardener, Sir J. Power, Sir G. Paul, Sir. R.C. Hoare, Gen. & Mrs. Archdale.

6th **May**

Earl of Kingston, Earl of Mayo, Lord Sidmouth, Lord Exmouth, Lord Liford, Lady C. Dormer, Lady Stourton, Lady Tynte, Sir J. Power, Sir W. Call, Sir J. Craddock, Sir W. & Lady James, Sir W. Wyan, Adm. Johnson

20th May

Lord & Lady Rodes, Lady Lloyd, Lady Le Despencer, Lady M. Long, Lady Stourton, Hon. Mr. Lumley, Sir G. Frankland, Sir G. Colyer, Sir F.

Hill, Sir T. Dyke, Sir W, & Lady Wake.

27th May

Marquis of Salisbury, Earl & Countess of Waldegrave, Lord Lidford, Lord Sidmouth, Lord Stourton, Lady Dundas, Hon. Mr. Verney, Adm. Sir I. Coffin, Sir W., Lady & Miss Watson, Sir A. Bertie, Sir W. Brabazon, Sir W. Elford, Gen. Archdail.

3rd **June**

Earl of Kingston, Viscount Kingsborough, Lady Scott, Lady Wilkinson, Sir R. Crawford, Sir P. Baghott, General Bowyer.

10th June

Lord Vallefort, Lady Howard, Hon. Miss Roderick, Sir E. Stanhope, Sir O. Gordon, Lieut.Gen. Sir J. Athwaythe.

17th June

Lord Sidmouth, Lord R??lan, Lord & Lady John Thynne, Lady Jervis, Sir W. Struth, Sir E. Batley, Sir E. & Lady Thornborough, Lieut.Gen. Sir Affleck, Gen. Balford.

1st **July**

Lord Strewart, Lord Elgin, Lady Carter, Lady Charterton, Sir R.C. Hoare, Sir J. Cradock, Sir G. Paul, Sir W. Congreve, Rear.Adm. Sir W & Lady Hotham, *Generals* Grenville, Harper, Popham.

8th July

Earl St. Vincent, Margravine of Anspach, Lord J. Russell, Lord Million, Lady Honyman, Count Wyman, Hon.Col. & Mrs. Knollis, Sir E. & Lady Baker, Sir F. Bullet, Sir E. Hartop, Sir F. Stovin, Sir T. Preston, Gen. Mitchell.

15th July

Earl & Countess Waldegrave & family, Lord Beresford, Lord Bruton, Rt. Hon. G. Canning, Sir R. Vaughan, Sir C. Padmore, Sir G. Calcraft.

22nd July

Earl & Countess of Cork, Sir W. Hotham, *Generals* Orde, Farrington & family.

29th July

Earl Granville, Count Leiven, Hon. Mr. Eardly, Gen. & Mrs. Wilson.

5th **August**

Earl & Countess Waldegrave, Lord & Lady Roden, Sir W. Brabazon, Sir D. Mackworth, Sir H. Strachey, Maj.Gen. Sir T. Brisbane.

12th August

Lord Weymouth, Lord J. Thynne, Count Schellenberg & family, Sir G. Collier.

19th August

Lord Porchester, Lady Jocelyn, Lady Baynes, Hon. Mr. Leeson, Hon. Mr. Barnewall, Hon. Miss Burton, Sir W. H. Robinson, Sir T. Heskyth & family, Gen. Slade.

26th August

Lord & Lady??? Lady Rodney, Hon. &Rev Mr. St. Leger, Hon. Mr. & Mrs. Jones, Hon. Mrs. Yorke, Sir W. Honeyman, Sir L. Holmes, Sir J. Keane, *Admirals* Sir A. Bertie, Holloway, Rear-Adm & Mrs. Ballard, Judge Daly

2nd **September**

Earl & Countess Waldegrave, Lady Audley, Lady Booth, Sir C. Wheeler, Judge Ogden, *Generals* Grenville, Skinner, Dean of Winchester

9th September

His Imperial Highness the Grand Duke Michael & Suite, Viscount Weymouth, Lord Audley, Lord J. Thynne, Lord Northesk, *Ladies* Robinson, Castle Stuart, Rodney; Hon. Mrs. Hewitt, Hon. Spencer Cowper, Sir T. & Lady Ramsay, Sir H. Strachey, Sir T. Stepney, Sir T. Jones.

16th September

Marquis of Lansdowne, Earl of Cork, Earl & Countess of Waldegrave & family, Bishop of Herefod, Lord Chief Justice Downs, Lord Carrington, Lady Staines, Hon. Mr. Vernon, Sir W. Congreve, Sir W. & Lady Robinson, Sir W. Owen.

23rd September

Marchioness of Bath, Lord & Lady Powerscourt, Lord Rivers, Lord H. Thynne, Lady Glode, Sir J. Carr, Sir T. Plastow, Gen. Sir W. Aylett.

30th September

Lord Bruce, Lady Butler, Adm. Sir A. Bertie, Sir W. James, Sir M. Murphy, Sir J. Carr, Sir T. & Lady Stepney, Sir R. Grierson.

7th **October**

Duke & Duchess of Somerset, Lord Macdonald, Lady Hughes, Lady Morgan, Hon. Mrs. Newcomen, Admiral Sir W. & Lady Hargood, Sir H. Chester, Sir D North, Sir S. Cumming, Sir J. Day, Sir E. Stanhope, Gen. Boyd, Lieut.Gen. & Mrs. Leighton.

14th October

Earl of Coventry, Lord & Lady Holland, Countess de F???, Dowager Lady Smith, Lady Lloyd, Hon. Mr. Fox, Sir J.C. & Lady Hippisley & family, Sir J. Trevelyan, Sir R. Williams, Sir P. Hill, Gen. Ryal, Gen & Mrs. Dickson, Adm. Douglas.

21st October

Marquis & Marchioness of Bath, Marquis Camden, Earl & Countess of Cork, Earl St Germain, Viscount Weymouth, Lord & Lady J. Thynne, Lord H. Thynne, Lord E. O'Brien, Baronesse de Rolle, Lady de Clifford, Lady Morgan, Hon. Mr. & Lady E. Campbell, Sir J. Davy, Sir S. Hayes, Sir A. & Lady Willson, Sir E. Knatchbull, Sir G. Williams, Maj.Gen & Mrs. Browne.

28th October

Countess S????, Lady Lethbridge, Lady Molesworth, Hon. Miss Massey, Sir H. Stepney, Sir W. Jones, Adm. Sir W. Young, Adm. Sir C & Lady Pole, Gen. ?????, Lieut.Gen. Dickson.

4th **November**

Earl of Coventry & family, Earl of Rodes, Countess of Cork & family, Lady Collins, Hon. Mrs. Browne, Sir J. & Lady Gardiner, Sir J. Palk, Sir J. & Lady Gordon.

11th November

Lord Bishop of Meath, Countess of Roseberry, Lady M. Keith, Lady Dunbar, Lady Elton, Lady De Clifford, Hon. Mrs. Ryder, Sir A. Hood, Sir H. Crawford, The Knight of Glynn, Sir S. Worthing, Sir P. Hill, Gen. Hart, Adm. Blackwood, Vice Adm. & Mrs. Linzee, Rear Adm. Carpenter.

18th November

Countess of Ilchester, Lady Barker & family, *Ladies* Burdett, Sheffield, Tremliston, Hughes; Hon.Col. Browne, Hon. Mrs. Strange, Sir G. Paul, Sir S. & Lady Hayes, Rev.Sir C. Wh???, Gen. M'Lean.

25th November

Lady Peacocke, Gen. Goldie, Lieut.Gen M'Neill.

2nd **December**

Earl & Countess of Cork, Earl Stanhope, Countess Nugent, Lady Penham & family, Lady Montgomery, Hon. Miss Oakley, Sir H. & Lady Blair, Sir J. & Lady Sherbrooke, Sir F. Baker, Sir H. Dalrymple, Sir W. Young, Sir J. Gifford, Sir H. Strachey, Sir W. Paxton, Gen., Mrs. & Miss Burton, Lieut.Gen. Layard.

9th December

Viscount Weymouth, Lord Tara, Lord Kinlock & family, Lady Northcote,

Lady P. Turner, Lady Burgoir, Sir W. Inglis, Sir S. Wathen, Sir T.B. & Lady Lethbridge, Sir G. Paul, Sir H. Rayse, Sir W. Struth, Sir F. & Lady Baker, Maj.Gen. Ambrose.

16th December

Duke & Duchess of Somerset, Marquis of Lansdowne, Marquis of Bath, Earl of Douglas, Lord ???land, Lord Arundel, Lady Hyde, Lady Burgoyne, Lady E.???

23rd December

Count N???, Lord & Lady Tara, Lord Gwydir, Lord Colville, Lady Willoughby, Lady Staines, lady Sheppard, Mr. & Lady C. Ram, Hon.Capt. Pellew, Sir S. & Lady Northcote, Sir J.C. & Lady Sharbrooke, Sir W. & Lady Wyen, Sir T., Lady & Miss Shelle, Sir P. Baghott, Sir J. Morris, Sir H. Strachey, *Generals* Mitchell, Peachy, VonHoward.

30th December

Lord Bishop of St David's, Lady E. Fane, Hon. J. Coventry, Hon. Miss Barnett, Sir F. Ford, Sir S. Sheppard, Sir W. Dasher, Sir G. Paul, Sir C. Clockart, Sir F. Burdett, Gen. Sir J. Hamilton, Maj.Gen. Mahon.

1819

6th **January**
Marchioness de Somery, Lord Bishop of Bangor, Lady M. Sheppard, Hon. Mr. Langley, Hon. Mrs. Bertie, Sir J. Stewart, Sir W. Richardson, Sir P. Baghott, Sir h. Carew, Sir J. & Lady Talbot & Family, Gen. Hopkins, Gen. Keraterman.
13th January
Earl St Germain, Lord Bruce, Lord Kirkcudbright, Lord Colville, Hon. Mrs. Tuson, Sir R. Williams, Sir M. Power, Sir J. & Lady Dunlae?, Gen. Sir H. Dalrymple, Maj.Gen. Sir J. Lyon, Gen. Cameron, Adm. & Mrs. Monckton.
20th January
Earl Clare, Lord Aplsey, Count de Chapelles, Lady Glode, Lady D'Arey, Lady Scott, Hon. Mr. Fitzgibbons, Hon. Mrs. Tuson, Sir C. Wheeler, Sir J & Lady Gordon, Rear Adm. Sir J. & Lady Morris.
27th January
Earl & Countess of Cork, Lady Clifton & family, Lady Ford, Hon. D. Massey, Hon. Miss Ongley, Sir D. Prutt, Sir J. R. Eustace, Sir J. Etty, Sir W. Struth, Sir W. Davey, Gen. Poulett

3rd **February**
Lord Neville, Lady Bayntun, Hon. Miss Devereux, Sir L. Otway, Sir W. Watson, Sir J. Davy, Sir J. M'Lean, Sir S. Wathen, Adm. Sir W. Domett, Lieut.Gen. Parkinson.
10th February
Lord Colville, Lady Sheffield, Lady Bolton, Lady M. Vaughan, Sir J. & Lady Williams, Sir A. & Lady Hood, Sir E. & Lady Synge, Sir J. R. Eustace, Sir J. Kempt, Sir J. Lillie, Sir W. Peacock, Adm., Mrs. & Miss Bury, Gen. Kyd.
17th February
Earl & Countess of Cork, Lord & Lady Clinton, Baron Longuille, Sir W. Williams, Sir W. Elford, Sir E. & Lady Strange, Sir J. Pollen, Gen. Poulett, Lieut.Gen. Michell, Maj. Gen Moore.
24th February
Countess of Ely, Lady & Miss Gresley, Lady Bordett, Hon. Col. ???ellis, Hon.&Rev Mr. Windsor, Hon. Mrs. Newcomen, Hon. Miss Boscawen, Sir L. Holmes, Sir F. Hartwell, Sir J. & Lady ??erbrooke, Sir P. & Lady Blake, Sir A. Chichester, Sir R. Gresley, Adm. Hooloway, Gen. Orr.

3rd March

Earl of Thanet, Lady Gardiner, Sir J. Gordon, Lieut.Gen. Sir J. & Lady Hamilton.

10th March

Ladies Holmes, Park, Place & family, C. D'Acy; Sir P. Baker, Sir H. Vivian, Sir J. & Lady Hale, Sir W. Roberts, Sir H., Lady & Miss Sawyer, Gen.Popham.

17th March

Lord Bishop of Clogher, Lady Somerville, Sir E. Hartopp, Vice.Adm Sir D & Lady Gould, Adm. Hodgson

24th March

Lady Dorchester, Hon.Capt. Pellew, Hon & Rev. Mr. Knollis, Sir Kingsmill, Sir G. Druett, Sir R.C. Hoare, Sir T. Ramsay, Gen. & Mrs. Popham.

31st March

Lady H. Poulett, Lady S. O'Brien, Sir J. Stewart, Sir W. Richardon, Sir J. Fellowes, Adm. Macnamara, Rear Adm. Springer.

7th April

Countess Allosand, Baron Villobra, Hon. Mrs. Frankland, Lieut. Gen. Sir B. & Lady Leighton

14th April

Marchioness Thomond, Lord Bishop of Sodor And Man, Lord Colville, Lady S. Murray, Lady Anstruther, Hon. Mr. H. Fane, Hon. Mr. W. Manie?, Sir A. Wilson, Sir A. Cathcart, General Powlett, General Morshead.

21st April

Viscountess Boyne, Lord Blaney, Lady Hearn, Sir C. Colville, Sir S. Sheppard.

28th April

Hon. Miss Devereux, Sir E & Lady Berry, Sir G. Paul, Sir W. Roberts, Sir W. Struth, Sir H. & Lady Lawson, Sir H. & Lady Mathias.

5th May

Lord E. O'Brien, Lady Dorchester, Lady Thornberry, Rev. Sir A. Elton, Sir J. Dunn, Sir R.C. Hoare.

12th May

Lady Keith, Hon. Mr. Eardley, Sir H. Palliser, Sir W. Richardson, Sir W. Robinson, Sir H. Lawson, Rev.Sir C. Wheeler, Gen. Sir H. Vane.

19th May
Earl & Countess of Buckinghamshire, Lord Bentinck, Lady Middleton, Hon. Capt. Watson, Sir T. Digby, Adm. Bertie
26th May
Bishop of Sodor And Man, Lady Muncaster, Sir C. Smith

2nd **June**
Dowager Lady Rivers, Lady le Despencer, Lady S. Murray, Hon. Mr. Carleton, Sir N. Bond, Sir F. Armitage, Sir G. Paul, Gen. Dickson
9th June
Earl of Elgin, Sir B. Wrey, Sir R. Crawford, Sir E. Dolben, Gen. Molineux
16th June
Marquis of Salisbury, His Excellence the Spanish Minister to the United States Don Onis, *Ladies* Hardest, R. O'Brien, Bertin, R. Crawford, C. D'Arcy, R. Dolben, Brook; Sir R. C. Hoare, Sir J. Davy, Rev. Sir C. Wheeler, General Powlett.
23rd June
Count & Countess Deconey, *Ladies* Wynne, Somerville, S. Clarke; Sir E. Lacon, Sir P & Lady Hall, Sir E. Hartopp, Sir W.L. Peacocke.
30th June
Lord & Lady Arundell, Sir J. Cradock, Sir? Preston

7th **July**
Marquis d'Herrecourt, Hon. Mr. Blayney, Sir R. Crawford, Sir J. James, Sir R. & Lady Williams, Gen. Morrison, Gen. Gore
14th July
Baron Theroe, Lady Lethbridge, Sir G. & Lady Noel. Adm. & Mrs. Linzee
21st July
Lord Aubrey, Sir E. Winnington, Sir J. Broughton, Sir S. Warren, Sir J. Falkener, Gen. Morrison, Gen. Dickson.
28th July
Lord & Lady Holland & family, Count de Ribauwart, Count de Quarry, Sir E. Synge, Sir J. Brisbane, Sir W. Coulson, Chevalier G. De Thuiay. Chevalier A. De Thuiay, Adm. Wolseley, Adm. Macnamara

4th **August**
Marquis of Bath, Earl of Cork, Hon. Mr. Boyle, Hon Miss Broderick, Lady Pinhorn, Lady E. Thone, Sir G. Paul.

11th August
Earl & Countess of Waldegrave, Lord Glenbervie, Lady Roycroft, Lady Anderson, Baron Wulf, Hon. Sir J. W. & Lady Smith.
18th August
Lord Bradford, Lady Anderson, Baron & Baroness de Reuben, Sir J. Whitbread, Sir W. Struth.
25th August
Lord Carnegie, Lady Audley, Lady C. Howard, Hon. Mrs. Herbert, Hon. Mrs. Montgomery, Sir C. Holloway, Sir J.C. Hippisley, Sir D. Mackworth.

1st **September**
Lord Westmoreland, Baron Graham, Count Dudioff, Lady M. Hope, Hon. Mrs. Murray, Sir C.M. Pole, Sir J. Yorke.
8th September
Marchioness of Clanricarde, Lord Amherst, Baron Stewart, Lady Treat, Hon. Mr. Talbot, Sir. J. Cox, Gen. Morrison.
15th September
Duke & Duchess of Somerset, Lord Webb Seymour, Sir A. & Lady Chichester, Sir H. Strachey, Sir. J. Cradock, Sir J. & Lady Grant, Sir J. Watkins, Adm. & Mrs. Dilkes.
22nd September
HRH the Duke of Sussex, Duke of Leinster, Earl & Countess of Waldegrave, Countess Mangedon, Lord Grenville, Dowager Lady Reed & family, Lady Davis, Lady Hughes, Hon. Mr. Villiers, Hon. W. Shirley, Sir W. South, Sir G. Smart, Sir W. Owen, Sir H. & Lady Hawley & family, Sir E. Blount, Sir W. Eland, Sir J. Mansfield, Maj.Gen. Sir T. Brisbane, Adm. Christie & family, Gen. Morrison.
29th September
Duke of Wellington, Marquis of Bath, Baron Auston? Lord Blaney, Lord J. Thynne, Lady Bedingfield, Lady Somerville, Lady & Miss Best, Sir W. Blunt, Sir W. De Crespigny, Justice Best, Adm. Bullard, Gen. Pitt, Gen. & Mrs. Bradshaw, Gen. & Mrs. Goldie.

6th **October**
Lord & Lady Teignmouth & family, Hon. Mrs. Cadogan, Judge Ogden & Family, Sir N. Peacock, Sir W. Cooper, Sir T. Ramsay, Maj.Gen. & Mrs. Jackson.

13th October
Duke & Duchess of Somerset, Duke de San Carlos, Lord & Lady Bayning, Dowager Lady de Clifford, Lady Hyde Parker, Sir J. Trevelyan, Sir W. Adam, Sir J. May, Sir R. & Lady Bedingfield, Sir H., Lady & Miss Hawley, Rev. Sir C. Wheeler, Gen. Poulett.
27th October
Countess de Front, Hon. Mrs. Hewitt, Hon. Mrs. Fortescue, Sir A. & Lady Chichester, *Admirals* Sir W. Hotham & family. Bullen & wife, Dacres; Gen. Donkin, Gen. Grant.

3rd **November**
Prince Sapieta, Lady B. Bourke, Hon. J. Coventry, Hon. Mrs. Brown, Sir H. & Lady Baynton, Sir W. & Lady Watson, Maj.Gen. Sir W. Inglis, Gen. Kebou, Gen. Powell & family, Adm. Holloway & family.
10th November
Lord Gwydir, *Ladies* Willoughby, Gladstanes, Leslie, Walker, C. Fitzgerald; Hon. Col. Browne, Hon. Mrs. Murray, Sir M. Somerville, Sir H. W. Wilson, Sir J.C. Hippisley, Gen. Sir W. & Lady Cockburne, Adm. Fahie.
17th November
Earl of Caulchaven, Lady Gray & family, Lady Randell, Lady F. Campbell, Hon. Mr. Bantley, Sir P. Paget, Sir I. Palk, Sir R. Baker.
24th November
Earl of Arundell, Lord & Lady Teignmouth & family, Lord Danssney, Lady S. Kent, Lady Sullivan, Sir J. Cotterel, Sir T. & Lady Acland & family, Adm. Sir W. Young, Maj.Gen. Adams.

1st **December**
Lord Dacres, *Ladies* Tuite, Carr, Glade; Hon. Miss Ryder.
8th December
Lady T. Hales, Lady Baynton, Lady Milhurst, Hon. Mr. & Mrs. Bushbridge, Sir O. & Lady Gordon, Sir E. Synge, Gen. & Mrs. Gore.
15th December
Earl of Cork, Lord Bishop of Down, Lord Arundell, Sir E. & Lady Baker, Sir T.B. Lethbridge, Sir J.C. Hippisley, Sir J. W. Smith, Sir J. Owen, Sir J. Gifford, Adm. Wolseley, Gen. Pigott, Maj.Gen. Ambrose. s
22nd December
Lord Bishop of Gloucester, Hon. & Rev. Mr. & Mrs. Douglas, Hon. Mr. & Mrs. Taylor, Hon. Miss St. Leger, Sir H. Strachay, Gen. Michell, Lieut.Gen. Winter.

29th December

Marquis of Lansdown, Marquis Camden, Lord Bishop of ???n, Lord Howden, Lady Waller, Hon. Mr. Eardley, Hon. Mr. Devereux.

1820

5th **January**
Lady B. Bonverie, Lady M. Keith, Sir T. & Lady Shelley & family, Sir J.C. Hippesley, Sir W. Wynne, Sir R. & Lady Jebson, Sir G. Prevost, Adm. Sir J. & Lady Saurnarez & family, Gen. Dixon & family, Gen. Holcombe, *Maj. Gen.s* Bowness, Kemmis, Browne.
12th January
Lady Wolsely, Lady E. Fane, Lady Waller, Hon. & Rev. Mr. Windsor, Gen. Sir H. White, Sir R. Williams, Sir C. Pratt.
19th January
Lord & Lady Prescott, Baron Osten, Sir W. Clinton, Sir A., Lady & Miss Hood, Gen. Hill, Lieut.Gen. A. Campbell.
26th January
Earl Elgin, Viscountess Galway, Lord Ashtown, Lord & Lady Bolingbroke, Sir L. Otway, Sir R., Lady & the Misses ?????, Sir J. & Lady Salusbury, Sir E. Sands, Sir R. Price.

2nd **February**
Lord Bishop of Norwich, Lord & Lady Arundel, Lord & Lady Ashton, Viscomte de Ambroise, Lord J. Stuart, Lord E. O'Brien, Lady C. Ram, Hon. A. Thelluson, Adm. Sir E. & Lady Thornborough, Sir T.B. Lethbridge.
9th February
Countess of Galloway, Lady Hankey, Sir H. Pyne, Sir W. Robinson, Sir J. Gifford, Adm. Liugue, Gen. Burton, Gen. Alexander, Maj.Gen & Mrs. Brooke.
23rd February
Lord Bishop of Bath And Wells, Lord J. Thynne, Lady Bayntun, Hon. & Rev. Mr. Windsor, Sir R.C. Hoare, Sir W. Watson, Lieut.Gen. Michell.

1st **March**
Lord Biship of Bangor, Countess of Cork, Lady Carr & Family, Lady C. Kerr, Lady Gardiner, Hon. Mr. Eardly, Hon. Capt. Pellew, Sir O. Gordon, Sir T.B. Lethbridge, Adm. Holloway & family, Adm. Wolseleey, Lieut.Gen., Mrs. & Miss Cameron.
8th March
Earl & Countess of Northesk, Lord Bolingbroke, Hon. H. Arundell, Hon. Mrs. Freemantle, Sir H. Pinn, Sir J. Gifford, Sir J. Cockburn, Adm. Sir J. Saumarez.

15th March
Marquis of Drogheda, Lord & Lady Bolton, Lord Sandos, Lady B. Henniker, Sir I. P. Coffin, Sir W. Smith, Sir S.C. Hartop, Sir W. Struth, Gen. Pawlett, Gen. Wemyss.
22nd March
Duke of Marlborough, Lord & Lady Bolingbroke, Lord Ingesbrie, Rt. Hon. C. Bagot, Rt. Hon. M. Bathurst, Sir J.C. Hipplsley, Sir W. Bagshaw, Sir D. & Lady Baird, Sir S. Wathen, Sir C. Robinson, Sir C. Robert, Gen. & Mrs. Coffin.
29th March
Lord J. Churchill, Sir F. Blos, Sir W. Bagshawe, Sir J. & Lady Lilley, Adm., Mrs. & Miss Bury.

5th **April**
Lord Bolton, Admiral Sir E. & Lady Bullen, Adm. Sir H. & Lady Sawyer, Adm. Monkton, Lieut.Gen. Orr.
12th April
Dowager Lady Clifford, Rt.Hon. G. Canning, Hon. Mr. Eardley, Hon. Miss? Fane, Gen. Sir W. Peacocke, Sir E. B. Baker, Sir E. & Lady Stanhope, Sir J. & Miss Mansfield, Ad. Tate, *Generals* Lightburne, O'Donovan, Hopkins.
19th April
Lady Carr, Hon. Mr. Talbot, Hon. Mrs. Tuson, Sir J. Clark, Sir R. Jephson, Sir T.B. Lethbridge, Sir J. Gifford, Gen. Hopkins.
26th April
Count Urbna, Lady Clonbrock, Hon. W. Burrell, Hon. C. Moore, Sir A. & Lady Chichester, Sir S Wathen, Sir W. Campbell, Sir W. Roberts, Sir J. Davy, Sir H. & Lady Mathias.

3rd **May**
Duke of Montrose, Lord Harecourt, Hon. Mr. Blaney, Lieut.Gen. Sir J. Affleck, Sir Edw. & Lady Berry, Rear Adm., Mrs. & Miss Monckton.
10th May
Earl Paulett, Earl Waldegrave, Earl & Countess of Mayo & family, Lady Scott, Lady Johnson, Hon. & Rev. Mr. Strangeways, Hon. N. Fellowes, Dean of Bristol.
17th May
Marquis of Salisbury, Baron & Baroness Dimsdale, Lord Fitzroy, Lady M. Vaughan, Lady Percival, Hon. & Rev. F. Knollis, Hon. Mrs. Bertie, Sir D. & Lady Forrest, Sir J. Davey, Sir W. Wynn, Sir W. De Montmorency, Rear Adm. & Mrs. Bullen, Gen. Dickson.

<u>24th May</u>
Marquis de Tourville, Vicomtesse de Buffevent, Lord & Lady Cawdor, Dowager Lady Louis, Lady Johnson, Hon. Mr. Boyle, Sir E. Buller, Sir H. Trollope.
<u>31st May</u>
Earl of Brecknock, Lady E. Gover, Lady E. Johnson, Sir E. Hartopp, Sir J. Thomson, Sir W. Elton, Gen. Hardy.

<u>7th **June**</u>
Lord Bishop of Hereford, Countess Tagoahy, Lady Radcliffe, Hon. Mrs. Bertie, Sir H. Trollope, Sir E. Hartopp, Sir A. Campbell, Rev. Sir A. Elton.
<u>14th June</u>
Lord & Lady Cawdor, Marquis Riccardi, Lady Holmes, Lady Anstruther
<u>21st June</u>
Lord Powerscourt, Lord Josceline, Sir R & Lady Bickerton, Sir R.C. Hoare, Adm. Monckton.
<u>28th June</u>
Prince de Broglio, Lord Miltown, Hon. Miss Byng, Sir J. & Lady Buchan, Sir J. Davie, Sir B. & Lady Chinnery, Sir G. Herbert, Sir E. Denny.

<u>5th **July**</u>
Lord & Lady Aylmer, Baron Osten, Baron Dunsdale, Lady Johnson, Lady C. D'Arcy, Sir W. Wyun, Sir R. Vaughan, Sir P. Hales, Sir E. Denny, Sir C. Hawkins.
<u>12th July</u>
Hon. Mr. Barnwell, Hon. Mrs. Murray, Sir E.B. Baker, Sir W. & Lady Bagshawe, Sir E. & Lady Hartopp, Gen. Grenville.
<u>19th July</u>
Sir R.C. Hoare, Sir J. Davie, Sir F. Hartwell, Gen. Travers.
<u>26th July</u>
Marquis of Salisbury, Lady Somerville, Gen. Sir J. Affleck, Sir G. Leeds, Gen. Powers, Adm. Spry.

<u>2nd **August**</u>
Marquis of Bath, Lord & Lady Arundell, Lord & Lady Rous & family, Lord & Lady Muncaster, Baron Steir, Lady E. Campbell, Sir J. Stewart, Sir H. Strachey, Sir F. Findyer & family, Adm. Monckton.
<u>9th August</u>
Hon. J.J. Percivall, Hon. Mrs. Bennett & family, Sir E. Synge, Sir H. Trollope, Rev. Sir A. Elton, Gen. Hughes.

16th August
His Highness Prince Louis of Lichtenstein, Lord & Lady Rous & family, Dowager Lady Amherst, Hon. J.C. Villiers, Hon. Mr. Melville, Sir T. & Lady Preston.
23rd August
Ladies Darley, Smith, Mortimer, Louis; Hon. Miss St Leger, Hon. Miss E. Smith, Sir W. Mortimer, Sir L. Otway, Sir G. Pownall, Sir J. Steward, Sir P. De Haviland.
30th August
Count Itterburgh, Count Zamoyski, Baron Pallear, Lady Perceval, Sir H. Strachey.

6th **September**
Lord Henniker, Lady Ford, Lady Gardiner, Sir E. & Lady Baker, Sir G. Pownell, Sir E. Synge.
13th September
Earl of Ilchester, Lady Johnson, Lady Walsh, Sir S, Wathen, Adm. Halkett.
20th September
Lord Bishop of Cork, Lord Erskine, Lord Colville, Lady Perceval, Sir T. Tyrrwhit, Gen. & Mrs. Dickson.
27th September
Earl of Kingston, Lord E. O'Brien, Lord Rivers, Lady E. Campbell & family, Hon. Mrs. Vernon, Hon. Miss Broderick, Rev. Sir A. Elton, Sir W. Campbell, Sir T.B. Lethbridge, Sir P. Baghott, Gen. Powlett.

4th **October**
Baron Hamilton, Lord Audley, Sir L. Otway, Rear Adm., Mrs. & Miss Monckton, Commodore Hardy, Gen. & Mrs. Jackson, Gen. & Lady Wynyard, Gen. Lethbridge.
11th October
Dowager Countess of Ilchester, Lord Lilford, *Ladies* Bateman, De Clifford, Gage, Muncaster; Hon. Mr. Strangeways, Hon. Mrs. R. Pasmore, Sir B. & Lady Chinnery & family, Sir J. Trevelyan, Sir H. Sawyer, Adm. Sir W. & Lady Hargood, Rear Adm. Brooking.
18th October
Count & Countess Byland, *Ladies* Cape, Buchanan, Butler, De La Zouche; Hon. H. Talbot, Hon. Mrs. Holland, Sir A. & Lady Hood; Sir Hugh & Lady Bateman, Rev. Sir C. Wheeler, Sir B. Codrington & Family, Sir R. Crawford, Gen. & Mrs. Goldie, Gen. Skinner & family.

25th October
Lord Glenbervie, Dowager Lady de Clifford, Lady Mount Earl, Sir R. Blair, Sir H. Peyton.

1st November
Lord Bishop of Bath And Wells, Lord & Lady Arundel, Lord O'Brien, Lord Somerville, *Ladies* Belmore, Baynton, Ford, Sullivan, Trent; Hon. Col. Browne & family, Sir J. & Lady Coxe Hippisley, Sir W. & Lady Pole, Sir E. Synge, Sir G. Collier, Lieut.Gen. Sir F & Lady de Rottenburgh, Gen. Benson, Adm. & Miss Nugent.
8th November
Lady Wynne, Sir T. & Lady Ramsay, Sir W. Stewart, Sir H. Strachey, Sir H. Robinson, Sir W. & Lady Watson, Sir T. Browne, Sir J. & Lady Campbell, Sir J. & Miss Mansfield, Gen. Sir W. Cockburn, Maj.Gen. Kerr, Maj.Gen. Traver, Rear Adm. Ballard, Rear Adm. & Mrs. Bullen.
15th November
Lady Glode, Ladies C & E Bourke, Hon. Mrs. Strange, Sir W. & Lady Holtham, Sir J. & Lady Ramsay, Sir J. & Lady Campbell, Gen. Dickson.
22nd November
Earl & Countess Waldegrave, Lord J. O'Brien, Lady Belhaven, Lady Trimleston, Lady Bernard, Hon Mr. Boyle, Sir R. Blair, Sir C. & Lady Hastings, Adm. & Mrs. Monkton.
29th November
Archbishop of Cashell, Lady Perceval, Lady Scott, Hon. Miss Grimstone, Sir W. James, Sir S. Wathen, Sir E. Stanhope, Lieut.Gen ?Risart.

6th December
Lord Calthorpe, Lord Fitzroy, Sir C. Price, Vice Adm. Robinson, Lieut.Gen. Winter.
13th December
Duke & Duchess of Somerset, Marquis Camden, Baron Fagel, Le Marquis de Thuisy, Le Chevalier A. De Thuisy, *Ladies* Fitzgerald, Gage, Selsey, Hankey; Hon. Mr. Herbert, Hon. Miss Mackay, Sir W. & Lady Bagshawe, Sir C. Mordaunt, Sir F. Vane, Sir J. & Lady Graham, Sir W. Inglis, Gen. Ambrose.
20th December
Marquis of Lansdown, Marquis of Bath, Earl & Countess of Waldegrave, Earl of Ormond, Viscount & Viscountess Falmouth, Lord Bishop of Chester, Lord Henniker, Lord E. Chichester, Lady Smith, Lady S. Bathurst, Mr. Justice & Lady Best, Sir H. & Lady Martin, Sir L. & Lady Palk & family, Sir E. Pore, Sir J. C. & Lady Hippisley, Sir H. Strachey,

Sir I. Coffin, Rev. Sir C. Rich, Adm. Hamilton, Gen. Bateman, Gen. Groot.

27th December

Prince Sapieta, Earl Poulett, Dowager Lady Rumbold, Lady Castlestuart, Lady Steward, Hon. Mr. Talbot, Sir C. Wheeler, Sir F. Baker, Sir P. Baghott, Sir R. & Lady Bickeston, Sir T. & Lady Shelley & Family, General Ryd, Gen. Bell.

Chapter 13: Places to visit around Bath

Assuming a desire to ride out or drive out, a horse is necessary. Fortunately, horses are often offered for sale at the various livery stable, where owners wishing to sell take them.

The livery stables are also there for the stabling your horse if you do not live in a place with convenient mews, or if you do not have your own stable staff. Remember that keeping a horse and groom yourself will cost upwards of £120 a year. Keeping a horse at a livery stables would cost a little over half of that.

There are many pretty rides about the city, and remaining in the valley may be more agreeable in inclement weather than braving the windy towns; there is much shelter to be had riding to the village of Kelston, along the lower road to Bristol, the London road or the newer road from Lambridge to and beyond Swainswick. Such rides afford a great variety of picturesque views of wooded hills, fruitful valleys and the serpentine path of the River Avon.

Listed below, however, are a selection of excursions which might be attractive in fine weather for picnicking, or for a day's visit, not neglecting the fine stately houses of the vicinity.

Visiting stately homes is a genteel occupation, and from the middle of the 18th century, guide books were published regarding the fifteen or twenty most famous properties. Other houses were mentioned in local guide books like 'The New Bath Guide, or useful Pocket Companion'. Some houses were open only on designated open days; others one might tour by tipping the housekeeper well when the owner was away, and thus safe from tourists. Such a tour was given to Elizabeth Bennett in 'Pride and Prejudice' when she visited Pemberley. Some opened to the public on designated days on a regular basis, like Corsham House [qv below.]. Generally, one sent a servant to enquire whether it was convenient to view a particular house, and if it was, the housekeeper would do the honours, expecting a good vail of between 1/- and half-a-crown [2/6d]. Naturally the quality of the tour will vary between the knowledgeable and enthusiastic to the ignorant and slatternly, as described by various visitors to various houses. Some were not above selling off souvenirs! Naturally one looks for the elegance of neo-classical or Palladian houses, but the picturesque, fashionable enough from the 1790s to be lampooned in plays and novels, might lead to a desire for the gothic ruin amidst the vistas of nature, carefully arranged to greater beauty by the likes of 'Capability' Brown. Antiquities too are fashionable, as an alternative to the experience of the Grand Tour, since the wars with France preclude continental travel.

I have borrowed if not always the precise words of the earlier guides then, I hope, their spirit.

<u>Popular places to visit</u>

Lansdown	4 miles from Bath
Claverton Down	under 1 mile
Midford Castle	2 ½ miles [on road to Longleat]
Farley [Farleigh] Castle	6 miles
Norton St Philip	7 miles
Stanton Drew	8 miles
Bow-wood	18 miles
Badminton	13 miles
Corsham House	10 miles
Longleat	17 miles
Stourhead Ho., Stourton	24 miles from Bath, 7 from Longleat
Maiden Bradley	20 miles from Bath, 4 from Stourton.
Wardour Castle	10 miles from Stourhead
Wells	19 miles from Bath
Glastonbury Abbey	6 miles from Wells
Stonehenge	
Cheddar Cliffs	3 miles from Wells
Wookey Hole	2 miles from Wells
Bristol	13 miles from Bath

One might conveniently make several leisurely outings, covering several days, in visiting a number of these places, for example, going first to Midford Castle, a slight detour to Farley Castle, on the way to Longleat, and thence to Stourhead. Or, a trip to Wells might then see visits to Glastonbury Abbey, the Cheddar Cliffs and Wookey Hole.

Claverton Down

This down is to the east of Bath and is a good outing for an invalid. There are a number of agreeable landscapes. To the right in ascending the hill is Prior Park, initially the residence of Lord Hawarden, then of Ralph Allen, a friend of Pope. It commands some excellent views including one of the City of Bath. On the road leading to Claverton Down is a Cold Bath supplied by a spring.

Lansdown

From a drawing by Samuel Grimm, 1738

Lansdown has already been mentioned in connection with the race course.

The land belonged to the Blathwayte family, and the Eastern end of the track is close to the 'Blathwayte Arms' on the Lansdown road. Opposite it may be found a site to delight those who would rather sketch picturesque views than watch horse-racing. This is Chapel Farm and its annexe of a former hospital for pilgrims on their way to or from Glastonbury. The chapel has scanty remains, but the east end remains, partially hidden in ivy, with the tracery of old windows. A mile and a half further along the Lansdown road may be found a monument erected

to Sir Bevil Grenville in 1720, by his grandson, Lord Lansdown.
It is a conspicuous object at the extreme end of the down, and marks where he fell during the civil war, in 1643. Sir Bevil was a Parliamentarian under Sir William Waller. His monument is of ashlar stone, 25 feet high and surmounted by the family griffin and with the escutcheon of the Grenville family. [aka Granville or Greville]. His eldest son assisted with the Restoration of the Monarchy and was enobled as the 1st Earl of Bath.
Landsdown is one of the most elevated hills in the west of England. It is covered with sheep, and there is a view over the Bristol Channel, parts of Wales and Gloucestershire.
As well as the monument there are the ruins of a fort said to be Saxon.

Midford Castle

Two and a half miles from Bath, this is an elegant embattled gothic structure situate on a rocky projection, surrounded by a handsome terrace, with gardens and woods, commanding picturesque views over the vale and opposite hills. Built around 1775 by the late Henry Disney Roebuck esq, combining the grandeur of the gothic with modern conveniences. It is on the road to Longleat. It was built on a floorplan echoing the shape of the club used in playing cards. Though folklore suggests this was due to having won the money to build it in a card game, this is unlikely as the 'stem' was added later as a porch. The layout appears to have been taken from an article published in Builder's Magazine, in 1774. In 1810 it was purchased by one of the Conollys of Castletown House in County Kildare, who added the porch and added the nearby stables and chapel.
Stone quarrying is a local industry. Stone is carried on a horse drawn rail-way to the canal and transported via the Somerset Coal Canal and the Kennet and Avon Canal to Bath and London.
Rev. Richard Warner disapproved of this edifice: "*How we may lament that when art attempted anything in a scene for which nature had done so much, she did not work with the tools of taste!*"

Farley Castle

Farley Castle from The New Bath Guide, etc, 1807, PD.

The castle is a ruin but with walls and towers and gatehouse are a reminder of its days of glory. The Hungerfords lived here from 1369 to 1681, a wealthy family who prided themselves on being able to ride from their home to Salisbury all on their own land.
The land and a manor house appears to have belonged before them to Lord Berghersh, and is first mentioned in the reign of Edward III, in 1343, whose granddaughter sold it to the Hungerfords. Sir Thomas Hungerford raised this incarnation of the castle; he was steward to John of Gaunt. The family wealth was increased during the Hundred Years War during which time the castle was extended.
In the Regency its proprietor is Joseph Houlton esq. whose family acquired it when Sir Edward Hungerford gambled away his family's fortunes. The gatehouse has the crest of the Hungerfords, the wheatsheaf and two sickles. The Hungerfords were Parliamentarian.
The castle chapel has a single aisle, and the ceiling has what was once a fine painting of the resurrection. It is the burial place of the Hungerfords and many other prominent persons. In a recess is s a handsome monument of Sir Edward Hungerford and his wife lying on a black marble slab. In the vault, which is approached from without, there are six leaden coffins after the Egyptian fashion, being anthropomorphic. Two of them are the infant offspring of two of the wives of Sir Edward Hungerford. Though the church is not early, there is a semi-circular stone over the south door

having letters from the Saxon alphabet, which was used up to the close of the 14th century. It may indicate sanctuary.

Norton St Philip

Not far from Farley Castle, this village has little of note but its great antiquity, though it has some wealth in consequence of the woollen manufactory. The church affords some remnants of tales which may be fanciful, the most remarkable of these being the representations of two female figures cut in stone on the floor of the nave close to each other. Martinus Scriblerus tells us they are the effigies of a double female born in a neighbouring village, two complete bodies attached to each other at the side. They achieved maturity but one sickened and died, and the other could not be separated from the putrefying body of her sister. No date or other evidence is afforded. Another legend is that the officially known Chevers Lane, referred to as Bloody Lane, flowed with blood after a battle of the Monmouth Rebellion in 1685. The George Inn claims to be Britain's oldest tavern, and is in the centre of the village. It was built in the 14th or 15th century as a wool store for the priory and to accommodate travellers to the annual wool fairs held from the late 13th century. [*which ceased only in 1902]*. The Fleur-de-lis is the other ancient inn here.

Stanton Drew

Here in this small village in the Chew Valley is an antiquity said to be the remains of a druid's temple, much in the same form as at Stonehenge, being a circle of large pillars. They are about 6 feet high. The diameter is 90 paces, though there is no apparent ditch. Among the common folk, the monument bears the name of a Wedding, from a folk tale that as the bride was going to be married, she and her company were changed into pillars of stone. There are three great stones over the churchyard wall, known as the Cove, and another at some slight distance called the Hauteville Quoit. It is the local legend that Sir John Hauteville [whose monument, reclining with his foot on a lion is in a niche in Chew Magna church indicating he was a crusader] flung this 30 ton stone from the top of nearby Maes Knoll. This may be conflating the tale of the gigantic crusader, Bohemund, whose stepfather was Richard of Hauteville, and whose reputation of strength was considerable.
The church is 15th century with a 13th century doorway and tower and a

medieval tithe barn and vicarage. The vicarage has two monsters at the corner of a window. Fragments of the 13th century windows may be found in the churchyard wall. The bridge over the River Chew is also 13th or 14th century, with two pointed arches and a central cutwater.
The toll gate is called the Round House but is more nearly hexagonal, two storied and thatched with gothic windows.
There are coal mines in the vicinity.

Bow-wood [Bowood] *[Wiltshire]*

This is the seat of the Marquis of Lansdown. It may be found off the London road to Calne, ie via Chippenham. Recent enlargements include a fine piece of water and a mausoleum in the memory of the late Earl of Shelburne. The first house was build c. 1725 on the site of a hunting lodge. The second Earl of Shelburne was created Marquis of Lansdowne for negotiating peace with America after the War of Independence, and he commissioned Robert Adam to enlarge the house and decorate the rooms. The orangery and menagerie were designed by Adam, who also designed the mausoleum. In the 1770s the 'big house' and the 'little house' were joined by a large drawing room. Capability Brown was responsible for the grounds comprising over 2000 acres, his work carried out in the 1760s. The sinuous lake, gently sloping lawns and arboretum with a Doric temple folly then in the Pleasure Grounds [now beside the lake] are considered one of his finest parks. There is a fine Italianate terrace with fountains and clipped yews. [Note to modern readers; the newer, 'big house' was demolished in 1955, but the joining drawing room was bought by Lloyd's of London and forms their Committee Room.]
Below the lake is the village called Manning's Hill, which was sacrificed for this feature. The villagers' opinion of Mr. Brown's design are not recorded.

Badminton *[Gloucestershire]*

Seat of the Duke of Beaufort.
The mansion house is very noble and is furnished with a number of fine family and other paintings. The park is very extensive, the walks extremely pleasant and the gardens elegant. William III visited and is said to have told the duke of the time that it was no wonder he ever came to court as his own place was so stately. The existing house was held by the Somersets, and was modernised in the 1620s; the 3rd Duke of Beaufort

adapted this by raising a Jonesian centrepiece in the north front, reducing two-bay flanking elevations from 5 storeys to 3. The 4th duke renovated and extended the house in the Palladian style after 1745. He brought Canaletto to England, and his two paintings of the house remain there. The house is strongly associated with fox hunting.
In the grounds may be found The Ragged Castle, a folly built c. 1751 [yes, the sport of Badminton has arisen from the popularity of the game amongst the children of the 8th duke in the 1860s, being known before this time as Battledore and Shuttlecock and a game suitable for young ladies as well as gentlemen. The Badminton Horse Trials are 20th century]
A mile or so from this house is a large square camp said to be made in the civil wars, double ditched, at Little Sodbury. In the parish of Horton is a lesser camp of 8 acres. Both of these camps give fine prospects over the vale of Berkley and the River Severn.
The parish church of St Michael and All Angels in Great Badminton is attached to the Duke's residence and was built in 1785 serving as the principal burial place of the Somerset family.

Corsham House *[Wiltshire]*

Corsham lies off the road to Bath via Chippenham. The house is the seat of Paul Methuen, esq. The palace of Ethelred the Unready lay near the present house, and after the Conquest it was the retiring place of the Earls of Cornwall. The present house was built in the year 1582 by Thomas Smythe. Before coming into the hands of Mr. Methuen it was one of the seats of Sir Edward Hungerford. The Hungerfords were prominent Parliamentarians during the Civil War; the wife of the commander of the New Model Army, Lady Margaret Hungerford, had built the almshouses in the centre of the town. She is buried amongst the ruins of Farley Castle where her effigy is carved in white marble. Sir Paul Methuen purchased the house for his cousin, also Paul Methuen in 1745. Its present proprietor has improved it, adding an apartment 70'x24' and 24' high to house his pictures, which are reckoned the finest collection in the west of England.
The park and gardens afford a variety of picturesque and beautiful prospects; Lancelot 'Capability' Brown was commissioned to redesign and enlarge the house and landscape the park 1761-64. He retained the gabled front and state rooms, also the Elizabethan stables and riding house. The picture gallery is a triple cube, and has a coffered plasterwork ceiling over a high cove stuccoed in scrolls.

The garden has a park separated from the pleasure grounds using a ha-ha so the view from the house would not be obstructed. Brown intended to enlarge the fish ponds, which was not completed for another 40 years; and constructed an orangery and built a Gothic bath house. [the bath house is the only one of these surviving to the 21st century]. He also created a 'Great Walk' stretching a mile through clumps as trees. An ornamental arch was build so that the family and their guests could walk underneath the public right of way without having to cross it. Screens of trees also obscure roads and fields around. As Brown died before it could be completed, Paul Cobb Methuen commissioned Humphrey Repton to complete it, in 1795.
There is also a folly ruin, built in 1797.
Genteel company have permission to view the house and pictures on Tuesdays and Fridays.

Longleat *[Wiltshire]*

The seat of the Marquis of Bath.
This noble seat is found at Horningsham on the road to Stourton. It is an ancient and magnificent structure, and for size and number of apartments is equal perhaps to any house in England. There are said to be 170 rooms! The paintings in general are tolerably good, especially a head of the unfortunate Jane Shore. [*one of the mistresses of Edward IV, accused of conspiracy under Richard III and subject of the 1714 play by Nicholas Rowe, shown regularly in theatres during this period as well as appearing in Shakespeare's 'Richard III' and Heywood's 'Edward IV'.]* This picture indeed is worthy of admiration, not so much for its execution or design as for the beauty, humility and resignation which are divinely worked in the countenance.

This seat has been greatly improved by the celebrated Mr. Brown; the park is very extensive and well planted, the water pleasingly disposed, and the whole forms a scene of great beauty and magnificence.

Originally an Augustinian priory, the present building was constructed for Sir John Thynne in 1566, using Scottish artisans, and occasioned the building of the first non-conformist chapel in England for these Scottish Presbyterians to worship.
Longleat House stands at the end of a straight walk of ¾ mile between two splendid avenues of trees. The house itself is perhaps the most

magnificent example of 16th century architecture in England. It is 800' round, crowned in domes and cupolas and with sculpted figures on the parapets. In 1803 it was said that 'far from being locked up to exclude mankind, [Longleat] is always open, and visitors are allowed to freely amuse themselves.' Casual callers are made welcome, and shown everything; a most generous Marquis cannot be imagined. The great hall has a magnificent oak screen and oak ceiling, with a gallery at one end, adorned with hunting pieces. The staircase leading to the saloon is of the finest. The whole building is unsurpassed in beauty. Walls are rich with tapestry, and all the ceilings are different, carved and painted. The collection of paintings rival any gallery, and the portraits cover those people who made an impact on history. Queen Elizabeth came to see this house whilst it was being built, and Charles II delighted in staying here.
Longleat does not lack the romantic disposition of a ghost, as it is said to be haunted by 'The Green Lady; this was the wife of Thomas Thynne, 2nd Viscount Weymouth, Louisa Carteret. She is said to grieve over the death of her lover, discovered and killed by her husband, though there is no historic foundation to this story. She died in childbed in 1736 in the London house in Grosvenor Square. Her second son succeeded to her family estates when her brother died in 1776. Her portrait may be seen.
The gardens were remodelled by Brown under the patronage of Thomas Thynne, 1st Marquis of Bath, 1734-1796. The second Marquis made some modernisations including replacing the original staircase, and had outbuildings, including the orangery, built.
The Thynne family were Royalist during the civil war, but supported Monmouth during the Upsrising.

Stourhead House Stourton *[Wiltshire]*

The seat of Sir Richard Colt Hoare, bart.
This seat is not large, but has an air of grandeur, and is well designed for pleasure and convenience. In the drawing room is a very curious cabinet, which formerly belonged to the famous Pope Sextus Quintus. On it are paintings of the Pope and others of the Peretti family, the last of which family became a nun, and gave the cabinet to a convent in Rome, whence Mr. Hoare purchased it.
In this room and in the other apartments are a great number of fine paintings.
Opposite the west front of the house is a lawn of considerable extent, on

each side of which are planted rows of Scotch firs, and at the end is an obelisk, 100' high, encircled by a range of elms. From the obelisk, looking through an avenue is an enchanting prospect of a pavilion, at the foot of which is a fine piece of water. Here a ferry boat may convey one to the opposite side of the lake, where one might enter a shrubbery, which leads along the river to a romantic grotto. In one room of the grotto are the lines,

"Nymph of the Grot, these sacred Springs I keep,
And to the murmur of these waters sleep;
Oh! Spare my slumbers, gently tread the cave,
And drink in silence, or in silence lave."

The figure of the nymph herself is elegantly formed, and the waters tinkling around her, with the gloom and stillness of the place have an effect of pleasant melancholy. The grotto is in the truest style of rural simplicity.

On leaving the grotto one next ascends a flight of steps into the shrubbery, which leading along the borders of the river brings one to the Pantheon, where there are a choice assemblage of beautiful views. In front is an elegantly formed piece of water, with the cavern of Neptune and a temple dedicated to Flora; on the right, an ancient cross in imitation of Egyptian granite, a handsome stone bridge, the temple of Apollo and a profusion of groves, properly diversified and adapted to their situations.

From the pleasure ground one enters a gloomy wood which leads by a gentle ascent to a rustic pile called the Convent, in which is a good painting dug from the ruins of Glastonbury Abbey, and an ancient drawing of Jesus. From the Convent one descends into an extensive Wilderness, which leads to the summit of the hill on which Alfred's Tower is placed. The building is triangular, of modern [*late Georgian, pre 1807 but probably 19th century*] date and built of brick; the height is 155' and the number of steps 321. The views are most striking from every side, round one turret which has a railed gallery in the securest manner. Over the portal of this is the inscription:

"Alfred the Great, AD 879, on this summit erected his standard against Danish invaders; to him we owe the origin of juries and a creation of a naval force. Alfred, the light of a benighted age, was a philosopher and a Christian, the father of his people and the founder of English monarchy and liberties."

The rest of the gardens are interspersed with temples, statues and other buildings of exquisite taste. Six springs which feed the river Stour arise in the grounds. At the eastern end of the lake is a fine 5-arched Palladian

bridge. Also in the grounds is the Bristol cross, with figures of the original medieval kings carved on it and additional 17th century ones, which was removed from Bristol's streets in 1733 after having stood there since 1373. Henry Hoare had it restored and set up here in 1763.
Stourton's 14th century church is also worth a visit, and some windows have fragments of ancient glass and there are some fine monuments. *[in 1902 the house was gutted by fire, but many heirlooms were saved and the house rebuilt in near identical style; it was given to the National Trust in 1946]*

<u>Maiden Bradley *[Wiltshire]*</u>

This is the seat of the Duke of Somerset, and came into the family at the end of the 16th century. It is a plain, substantial stone mansion with two large wings projecting at right angles from the body of the structure. The countryside spreads bare and unadorned before the house, and nothing affords any traces of the one-time magnificence of the family. The church adjoins it to the left. Beating the bounds still takes place here. There are three coaching inns, one of them the 'Somerset Arms' and three turnpike roads run through Bradley, to Frome, Wincanton and Bruton.
The Maiden part of the village name refers to an early leper house for women. After dissolution it passed into the hands of the Seymour family where it remains. A small silk manufactory is established here, associated with Bruton. Children in Bradley, who begin work at 6 years of age, spin the silk to be woven in Bruton. The youngest make three ha'pence to tuppence a day, the most experienced can make half-a-crown to three shillings a week, but they work from 5am to 6pm.

<u>Wardour Castle *[Wiltshire]*</u>

The seat of Lord Arundel. This mansion is truly magnificent. The grounds around it are disposed to great advantage. The ruins of the old castle, some mile from the new house, still has the appearance of ancient grandeur. This castle was defended, during the Civil War, by the 61-year-old Lady Blanche Arundel, daughter of Edward, Earl of Worcester, and she held the castle with only 25 men against a parliamentary army of 1300. She surrendered it at last on honourable terms. The house contains a great number of fine pictures, including one of the Civil War heroine.
The pleasure grounds, shrubbery, groves and woods are elegantly formed;

the beauties of the terrace walk have met with general admiration and convey pleasing picturesque ideas. Rev. Richard Warner considers the views inferior to those from the old castle, and the belt of trees sweeping round a little lawn in front to be detrimental to the prospect. To the south, a wider range is given to the eye, to take in the plains and fields of Wiltshire and the distant hills of Dorset. The walk to the old castle has plantations to break up the landscape, admired by Brown himself. It is a serpentine ascent to the terrace along the side of the sweeping hill on which the castle stands, shaded by noble hanging woods, with well contrived openings to permit views of the countryside of Somerset and Wiltshire, Glastonbury Tor, Stourhead etc.

The old castle was build in the 1390s, and was partially destroyed 1643/44. It is the only hexagonal castle in Britain.

The new house is Palladian in style, designed by James Paine. The building of the house began in 1769 and was completed in 1776. It is constructed of limestone ashlar blocks with hipped Welsh slate roofs. It has a square main block with flanking pavilions. The north front has a rusticated basement below a *piano nobile* or main floor, with mezzanine and attic floor over. It has a rare rotunda staircase, 144' circumference. It is lit from above from a dome at its summit. Two flights of stairs take a semi-circular sweep to right and left and conduct to a gallery of which 8 Corinthian pillars support the top, and 6 uniform recesses contain the doors opening to different bed chambers. A grand organ occupies one segment of the circular gallery and a figured iron railing with gilded ornaments surrounds the whole. The first apartment is the saloon which has some excellent paintings including two Vandykes, one of Henrietta Maria and one of one of the Cliffords of Chudleigh. There are further fine paintings in the drawing room including more Vandykes, the children of Charles I and the daughters of Savage Earl of Rivers. Also here are a head of a woman by Rubens, and Sir Thomas More by Holbein and three portraits by Lely. The other rooms also have fine paintings by masters.

There is a Roman Catholic chapel as part of the house which has excellent acoustics and is magnificent in crimson and gold. The Arundel family have a gallery at the western end and the ground floor is for servants and villagers of the Catholic faith, for there is a Catholic seminary here.

The state bed-chamber is named for the bed fitted up for Charles I when he visited the original castle.

The village affords a neat inn near the gate of the mansion, which may be viewed every day after 12 noon.

The City of Wells

This city has one of the finest cathedrals in England. The west front is very magnificent, and has ever been admired for its ancient imagery, being an entire pile of statues, tier upon tier on a front almost square, and 150' across. It is strictly Gothic, without either the elegance or simplicity to strike the eye of any from the Georgian age. The exterior is awe-inspiring and venerable, the interior attended to with respect to neatness and convenience.

The city is named from three wells dedicated to St. Andrew, one in the market place and two within the grounds of the Bishop's Palace and the Cathedral. There has been a cathedral here since the time of Ina, and the Saxon edifice was replaced by the Normans, but only a few Norman stones remain, the majority of the cathedral being begun in the 12 century and finished in the 13th. The bishop's palace is a moated edifice and the vicar's close worth a visit. The northern wall has one of the finest porches in England, lofty, with a vaulted roof. The stringcourse is finished with dragons swallowing their strings, their tails twisting in the mouldings. The capitals of the columns show King Edmund crowned and full of arrows.

One of the wonders of Wells is the clock. In the north transept, it is one of the group of famous 14th to 16th century astronomical clocks in the west of England. The surviving mechanism dates from the last fifteen years of the 14th century. The dial shows the universe, in the antique pre-Copernican notion in which the earth is at the centre, and the sun and moon revolving around the central earth. Another dial is mounted on the outside wall driven by the same mechanism, which was installed later.

The inner circle shows the moon, demonstrating its phase. Above the clock to the right is a figure known as Jack Blandifers, who hits the bell with a hammer held in his right hand, kicks his heels every quarter to ring the two bells hung beneath him. A set of jousting knights chase each other every 15 minutes running round to strike the bells with their battle axes outside the walls.

The dial outside has two figures above a plainer clock face, which appear to be striking two bells.

The mechanism was converted to pendulum and anchor escapement in the 17th century.

[the original mechanism is in the Science Museum in London, where it

was placed in 1884]
The interior of the cathedral is also magnificent, and filled with carvings. It can scarcely be covered in so brief a guide, and deserves its own guide book.

Cheddar cliffs

About three miles from Wells are the stupendous cliffs of Cheddar, well worthy of observation.

Wookey Hole

Two miles from the City of Wells in one of the Mendip hills is found this famous cavern, one of the greatest natural curiosities of England. In this subterranean cavern are a number of encrustations, representing different figures, particularly the tomb, as they call it, of the Old Witch of Wookey, who is said to have resided here.

Glastonbury Abbey

Six miles from Wells are the ruins of Glastonbury Abbey, formerly the richest and most magnificent in the world. The time of its foundation is not known for certain, but it was most liberally endowed by King Ina, who had the great church built, and it benefitted by Edward the Elder, Eldred, Edgar and other Saxon kings and nobles. At the Conquest, King William stripped it of several of its possessions and bestowed them on his followers. In 1083 he made one Tustin, a Norman, abbot thereof.

Stonehenge

This wonderful curiosity is near the Duke of Queensbury's seat. The distant effect of this Druidic Temple is not so striking as the description of its magnitude might lead us to imagine, since being an isolated object situated in the heart of the plain with nothing as a standard of comparison, every impression of its greatness is swallowed up and overwhelmed in that idea of immensity which the prospect on every side presents to the mind. As we approach it however the mind finds all distractions vanish.
The monument consists of four concentric arrangements of stones, the two outward circular, the two inner, elliptical. The whole is surrounded

by a ditch at the distance of 105' from the external circle of stones. Of the outermost circle, the general dimensions of each stone are: height, about 14', thickness 3-4'; breadth 6-7'. They consisted originally of 30 rude upright pillars, standing 3 1' apart from each other, crowned or connected by as many imposts or transverse stones, each about 10' in length, and 3' in thickness. The whole forms a large circular enclosure 97' in diameter. The interval or space between the two stones which point exactly North-East is greater than between the others and seem to afford an entrance to the interior of the circle. Only 17 of these upright stones and 6 of the connecting stones are now in their original situation.
The second circular structure occurs at 9' distant from the inner side of the outer ring, consisting of smaller upright stones, none of them connected at the top save that which fronted the entrance as a second portal to the more sacred parts of the edifice. There appear to have been 29 of these upright, but only 9 retain their original position. 13' inside this is an oval of about 60' in its longer diameter, 52' in its shorter, formed by 7 huge Trilithons, or combinations of stones of two uprights and an incumbent impost, separate and distinct from each other. The largest pair are 28' high, the breadth each 7' and the thickness 3', gradually tapering from base to summit. The Imposts are 16' in length, 4'6" in breadth and 2'6" in thickness. Each Trilithon is supposed to weigh 70 tons. Only 2 of these are standing, a third having fallen after the thaw in January 1797. They seem to raise in size away from the entrance. The inner most elliptical range decrease in height away from the entrance. They were 19 in number, 8' high by 2'6" broad and 1'6" thick. The altar stone stands towards the upper end of this, 4'x16', broken into 3 fragments, all deeply embedded. *On this, the carcases of the victims, or at least such parts of them as the priests devoted to the gods, were consumed by fire.* [sic; as written in 1807] The encircling ditch is 30' wide.
[the monument is now much restored but less accessible to the public for reason of conservation. And predates the druids by more time than the antiquaries of the Regency even knew existed.]

<u>Bristol</u>

The city of Bristol is of course a port, second city in England for trade, wealth and number of inhabitants.
It has a cathedral in College Green, formerly the collegiate church of the St. Augustine's monastery until dissolved by Henry VIII. There are 18 churches in the city, most magnificent being St. Mary Redcliffe, outside

the walls, built in the reign of Henry VI. The altar has three fine paintings by Hogarth and over them a painting by Fresham representing Jesus raising Jairus' daughter from the dead.

Queen Square, a large square, has an equestrian statue of William III in copper on a base and pediment of Portland stone. On the north side of the square is the custom house, and in the centre, many pleasing walks shaded with trees.

The Quay is more than half a mile in length, and is thought to be the most commodious in England.

Bristol also has wells, the Hotwells, thought to be especially efficacious for dysentery, spitting of blood, consumptions, coughs, and diabetes and also is excellent in inflammations and scorbutic [relating to scurvy] cases and is impregnated with lime. The season for drinking the water is March to September, when the place is much frequented by the nobility and gentry. There are two assembly rooms next to the wells, where they have balls, concerts, public breakfasts etc during the season. There are many lodging houses in the city as well as in the village of Clifton on the hill above.

Beyond the wells are tremendous rocks known as St. Vincent's Rocks extending a considerable distance on each side of the river Avon, where is found in great abundance that beautiful fossil called Bristol Stone.

About 5 miles from Bristol is Lord Clifford's elegant house and gardens at King's Weston, in the neighbourhood of which is one of the richest and most picturesque and varied set of prospects, commanding at one view the Bristol Channel, and the mouth of the rivers the Severn and the Avon, looking into the counties of Gloucester, Somerset, Wiltshire and a long line of the Welsh coast and counties.

In the vicinity of Salisbury one might also visit Wilton House, the seat of the Earl of Pembroke, in which are a number of busts, statues and paintings. Also the ancient seat of Lord Radnor.

At Hestercomb, the seat of Mr. Bampfylde, at Halsewell, Lady Tynte, at Egmore Castle the Earl of Egmont. The gardens of Hestercombe are a striking object. A hermitage in them, with the figure of an old witch painted in the centre panel occasioned the genteel compliment from the late Dr. Langhorne:

"O'er Bampfylde's woods, by various nature graced
A witch presides! But then, that witch is TASTE."

Enmore Castle is remarkable for the peculiarity of its building – a quadrangle of dark-coloured stone round a court; it is surrounded by a dry fosse 40' wide and 16' deep from which are openings to the offices, stables, etc under the lawn.
Haleswell House is beautifully situated, in the middle of an ornamented park, about two miles from Enmore. The rides in this park are very extensive and command a great variety of beautiful prospects and rich landscapes.

Bibliography

Mike Chapman 2010, Kensington Meadows local nature reserve, *Bath, a desk-based historical assessment*
David Gadd, *Georgian Summer*
R.S. Neale, 1981, *Bath, a social history 1680-1850*
Arthur Mee, 1940, *The King's England: Somerset*
" " 1939, *The King's England: Wiltshire*
Margaret Baker, 1968, *Discovering the Bath Road*
J. W. Morris, 1888, *Handbook to Bath*
Adrian Tinniswood, 1998, National Trust enterprises, *The Polite Tourist*
W. Everitt, 1840, *Views of Bath and its vicinity*

Contemporary Period:
R Cruttwell, printer, for A. Taylor, 1799, *Bath*
Richard Phillips, 1810, *A Guide to all the Watering and Sea Bathing Places etc*
John Cary 1812 *A New and Accurate Itinerary to the Great Roads etc*
John Feltham, 1810, *A Guide to all the Watering Places and Sea Bathing Places etc*
J. Savage, 1807, *A New Bath Guide*
W. Taylor, 17??, *The New Bath Guide or Useful Pocket Companion.*
Rev. Richard Warner, 1801, *Excursions from Bath*
W.C. Oulton, 1805, *The Traveller's Guide, or English Itinerary*

Online resources

Greg Roberts, blog: Wicked William's Story
Jane Austen's World blog
The Bath Magazine
Kathryn Kane's Regency Redingote
Regency History, Rachel Knowles
Bath Chronicle and Weekly Gazette, British Newspapers Online.
The Online Archive

46140547R00197

Printed in Poland
by Amazon Fulfillment
Poland Sp. z o.o., Wrocław